# DISEASES OF THE LUNGS: THEIR PATHOLOGY, SYMPTOMATOLOGY, DIAGNOSIS, AND TREATMENT

Published @ 2017 Trieste Publishing Pty Ltd

ISBN 9780649563180

Diseases of the Lungs: Their Pathology, Symptomatology, Diagnosis, and Treatment by Ch. Gatchell

Edited by Trieste Publishing Pty Ltd.
Cover @ 2017

www.triestepublishing.com

# CH. GATCHELL

# DISEASES OF THE LUNGS: THEIR PATHOLOGY, SYMPTOMATOLOGY, DIAGNOSIS, AND TREATMENT

Trieste

# DISEASES OF THE LUNGS

GATCHELL

# DISEASES OF THE LUNGS

THEIR

## PATHOLOGY

## SYMPTOMATOLOGY, DIAGNOSIS

## AND TREATMENT

BY

### Chas. Gatchell, M. D.

PROFESSOR OF DISEASES OF THE CHEST AND PHYSICAL DIAGNOSIS IN THE
CHICAGO HOMŒOPATHIC MEDICAL COLLEGE; ATTENDING PHYSICIAN TO
COOK COUNTY HOSPITAL, CHICAGO; FORMERLY PROFESSOR OF
THE PRINCIPLES AND PRACTICE OF MEDICINE IN THE
UNIVERSITY OF MICHIGAN; AUTHOR OF "POCKET-
BOOK OF MEDICAL PRACTICE"; EDITOR OF
THE "MEDICAL ERA"; SECRETARY
OF THE AMERICAN INSTITUTE
OF HOMŒOPATHY

CHICAGO
ERA PUBLISHING COMPANY
1902

AS EXPRESSIVE OF
MY ESTEEM
FOR ONE WHO HAS DONE
SO MUCH
TO GIVE CHARACTER AND VALUE TO
MEDICAL LITERATURE
THIS BOOK IS DEDICATED
TO

# Wm. C. Goodno, M. D.

# PREFACE

The purpose in preparing this work has been to present to the profession the subject of diseases of the lungs in a form which, while not too much condensed, yet partakes of the character of an epitome. The effort has been to give every topic belonging to each diseased condition in a form readily accessible, and at the same time in such shape as to be of practical value. In the matter of the treatment of the various diseases no attempt at condensation has been made; it is given as fully as would be done in a larger work. Especial care has been taken, also, to present the important subject of pathology in a manner to be of value to the student as well as to, the studious physician. Departure from usual methods of classification of some diseases will be found. Thus, broncho-pneumonia, because in its pathology, its clinical history and its therapeutics it is related to bronchitis rather than to pneumonic fever, is considered in connection with the former disease. As a matter of convenience for the student a glossary of terms has been added.

CH. G.

CHICAGO, APRIL, 1902
100 STATE STREET

# CONTENTS

## SECTION I.

Bronchitis of the Larger Tubes............................ 9
Bronchitis of the Smaller Tubes.......................... 18
Plastic Bronchitis ........................................ 24
Chronic Bronchitis ........................................ 27
Broncho-Pneumonia ...................................... 33
Asthma ................................................... 41
Pulmonary Emphysema .................................. 53
Bronchiectasis ............................................ 59

## SECTION II.

Pneumonic Fever .......................................... 67
Pulmonary Fibrosis ...................................... 102
Brown Induration of the Lungs........................... 108
Collapse of the Lungs.................................... 110
Pneumonoconiosis ........................................ 113
Pulmonary Syphilis ...................................... 116
Tumors of the Lungs..................................... 118

## SECTION III.

Acute Pneumonic Tuberculosis............................ 121
Chronic Pulmonary Tuberculosis......................... 127
Fibroid Phthisis ......................................... 163
Diseases of the Bronchial Glands........................ 167
Hemoptysis .............................................. 169

## SECTION IV.

Pleurisy ................................................. 177
Plastic Pleurisy ......................................... 178
Sero-Fibrinous Pleurisy .................................. 186
Purulent Pleurisy ........................................ 197
Chronic Pleurisy ........................................ 205
Tuberculous Pleurisy .................................... 206
Pneumothorax ........................................... 207
Hydrothorax ............................................. 212
Hemothorax ............................................. 214
Chylothorax ............................................. 214

# CONTENTS

## SECTION V.

Embolism of the Pulmonary Artery........................217
Thrombosis of the Pulmonary Artery.....................220

## SECTION VI.

Active Hyperemia of the Lungs...........................223
Passive Hyperemia of the Lungs..........................226
Edema of the Lungs......................................227
Abscess of the Lungs....................................231
Gangrene of the Lungs...................................233

## SECTION VII.

Hydatids of the Lungs...................................237
Hydatids of the Pleura..................................240
Actinomycosis ..........................................240
Pulmonary Mycosis ......................................242
Clubbing of the Fingers.................................243
Pulmonary Osteo-Arthropathy ............................244

Glossary................................................245

# DISEASES OF THE LUNGS

## SECTION I.

### BRONCHITIS.

**Synonym.**—Bronchial catarrh.

**Definition.**—Catarrhal inflammation of the mucous membrane of the bronchial tubes; the chief symptoms are cough, expectoration and difficult breathing.

**Varieties.**

    I.   **Acute Bronchitis:** (a) of the larger tubes; (b) of the smaller tubes.

    II.  **Chronic Bronchitis.**

    III. **Plastic Bronchitis.**

### I.—BRONCHITIS OF THE LARGER TUBES.

#### ETIOLOGY.

**Predisposing Causes.**

**Heredity.**—In some instances there is an inherited tendency to inflammation of the respiratory mucous membrane.

**Age.**—Those of all ages are subject to bronchitis, though it is most common at the extremes of life.

**Occupation.**—Persons confined in an impure air, or in an air laden with irritating substances, are especially liable to bronchitis.

**Climate.**—It is most common in cold and damp climates.

**Season.**—It prevails most in the winter and spring.

**Constitution.**—The cachectic and debilitated are especially liable.

9

**Previous Attacks.**—Those who have already suffered from bronchitis are liable to repeated attacks.

**Other Diseases.**—Subjects of Bright's disease, tuberculosis, rachitis, as well as various pulmonary affections, are especially liable to attacks of bronchitis.

### Exciting Causes.

**Cold.**—Exposure to cold or chilling the body by cold and damp are the most common exciting causes.

**Acute Diseases.**—Bronchitis is a common accompaniment of the acute infectious diseases; more especially measles, influenza, whooping-cough, and enteric fever.

**Irritants.**—Irritating dusts and vapors act as excitants.

## PATHOLOGY.

### Catarrhal Inflammation.

There is primary paralysis of the blood-vessels, with congestion of the mucous membrane, accompanied by effusion of serous fluid and of mucus, the escape of leucocytes, cloudy swelling and degeneration of the epithelial cells and mucous glands; the mucous membrane is infiltrated with round cells. The inflammation may extend to the peribronchial tissue.

**Blood-vessels.**—The first change is hyperemia.

**Fibrous Coat.**—The fibrous coat of the bronchus becomes swollen, relaxed, and infiltrated with lymph-cells.

**Basement Membrane.**—It becomes edematous and wavy, and folded in appearance.

**Columnar Epithelium.**—The cells become swollen, loosened, and are thrown off in patches, leaving the basement membrane bare in spots. New cells of transitional form are produced and cast off.

**Muscular Coat.**—It becomes edematous and infiltrated.

**Mucous Glands.**—The cells desquamate, and there is abundant secretion and discharge of mucus.

**The Bronchial Tubes.**—The lumen becomes narrowed, from swelling of the lining membrane and the presence of secretion; the smaller tubes become occluded.

**Glands.**—The bronchial glands become swollen and hyperemic.

**Secondary Changes.**

**Pulmonary.**—There is general hyperemia and edema. There are some areas of emphysema; others of apneumatosis; and some of broncho-pneumonia.

**Cardiac.**—The right heart suffers from distention; after repeated attacks there may be permanent dilation.

## MORBID ANATOMY.

**Lungs.**—The lungs are large and heavy. Areas of collapse are deep purple in color. The bronchial mucous membrane is swollen and velvety. The large tubes contain muco-purulent secretion. The posterior parts of the lungs are almost solid from collapse, edema and congestion. From a cut surface frothy, watery fluid pours out on pressure. Emphysematous areas are sometimes present, especially along the borders.

**Heart.**—The right cavities are dilated and filled with blood. If an acute attack follows repeated attacks, there is usually hypertrophy of the right ventricle. There is dilation of the vena cava.

## SYMPTOMS.

**Onset.**—In some cases the attack is ushered in by a sense of chilliness; rarely, by a distinct chill. This is followed by aching pains in various parts of the body, and succeeded by the characteristic symptoms of the disease. In other cases the initial symptoms consist of an ordinary nasal or laryngeal catarrh.

**Fever.**—The temperature is usually moderate—ranging in the ordinary attack from 100° to 102° F.

**Cough.**—The early cough is short, dry and hacking, occurring sometimes in severe paroxysms; soon, however, the cough becomes moist and is accompanied by expectoration.

**Pain and Sensation.**—There is seldom sharp pain in the chest. There is usually a sensation of rawness behind the sternum and a sensation of tightness and oppression of the chest.

**Expectoration.**—Early, the sputum is a scanty, viscid, tenacious mucus; it is expelled with difficulty. Later, it is less viscid and becomes whitish or frothy and the cough "loosens." The sputum may be slightly blood-streaked. Still later, it becomes muco-purulent and of an opaque yellowish or greenish color, and is expelled in masses. The quantity, when free, may be six to eight ounces in the 24 hours. The sputum consists of mucus, serum, small oil globules, epithelial cells, leucocytes, various bacteria, and sometimes a small quantity of blood.

**Head.**—Early, there is usually headache; later, there may be drowsiness or apathy.

**Skin.**—In the early days it is usually dry; later, there is free perspiration.

**Pulse.**—The pulse rate is usually out of proportion to the temperature.

**Respiration.**—The rapidity of respiration and the degree of dyspnea are proportional to the size of the tubes involved; when only the large or medium tubes are affected, dyspnea is not great; following a paroxysm of cough or unusual exertion the respirations are quickened. If the temperature is high, the number of respirations to the minute is increased as an effect of the circulating blood producing increased activity by irritation of the respiratory center.

## PHYSICAL SIGNS.

**Inspection.**—Beyond increased frequency of respiration and moisture or dryness of the skin, little is revealed by inspection.

**Palpation.**—This confirms the signs noted on inspection; when the amount of secretition is great rhonchial fremitus may be felt.

**Percussion.**—The note may be little changed. If there is accompanying emphysema it will be hyper-resonant: at the bases and at the back there is dullness if there is congestion or edema.

**Auscultation.**—Early, the breath-sounds are harsh and exaggerated, especially over the upper portions of the chest. There is prolonged expiration. Later, when there is secretion, the characteristic sounds are sibilant and sonorous râles with, still later, fine and coarse moist râles. Over areas of collapse breath-sounds will be absent; also over areas of bronchial obstruction. Fine, crackling râles, especially at the base or in the back, indicate congestion or edema.

## DIFFERENTIAL DIAGNOSIS.

**Tuberculosis.**—In tuberculosis the fine, crackling râles are heard in the apex, and usually on one side; the temperature is high and there is great prostration.

**Pulmonary Edema.**—In this condition the râles are always moist, inclined to be uniform in size, and early confined to dependent portions of the lung.

**Bronchial Asthma.**—The râles are dry, squeaking and groaning, and chiefly expiratory.

**Broncho-Pneumonia.**—The dyspnea is excessive, all the symptoms more severe, and there are signs of cyanosis.

**Complications.**—Especially after repeated attacks there may be emphysema, asthma, and dilatation of the right heart. The attack may be accompanied or followed by capillary bronchitis or broncho-pneumonia.

**Course and Duration.**—In simple bronchitis, uncomplicated, the disease runs a mild course; it is not self-limited; according to the constitutional condition of the patient or the presence or absence of complications, it will vary in wide limits. Relapses are not uncommon. After repeated attacks it is inclined to become chronic. The presence of Bright's disease, cardiac dilation, emphysema or other pre-existing pulmonary affections renders it more persistent and protracted.

## PROGNOSIS.

**Favorable Signs.**—In a primary attack occurring in a previously healthy subject, the prognosis is always favorable. When uncomplicated, bronchitis of the larger tubes never threatens life.

**Unfavorable Signs.**—Conditions which may render the prognosis unfavorable, are the presence of complications affecting especially the lungs and the heart. There is slow recovery if emphysema is present. Over-distention of the right heart is unfavorable; also frequent, irregular and intermittent pulse. Bronchitis secondary to measles, influenza and whooping-cough is especially persistent.

## TREATMENT.

**Therapeutics.**

Aconite. (1x).—This is applicable only in the early stage; after the disease is once established, it is of no use. **Indications:**—Fever; dry, hot skin, restlessness and thirst; short, hard, tickling cough, with constant laryngeal irritation; dryness of the mucous membranes.

Bryonia. (1x).—Catarrhal inflammation of the mucous membrane of the trachea and larger bronchi; it is of no use when the smaller bronchi are invaded. **Indications:**—Dry cough, with stitches in the chest; short, labored respiration; feeling of oppression of the chest; with the cough, determination of blood to the head, with headache, and great turgescence of the face.

Belladonna. (2x).—When bronchitis sets in with violent fever, and intense congestion of the lungs, **Belladonna** will do more to control it than **Aconite** will. **Indications:**—Spasmodic cough, in short paroxysms; violent cough, worse at night; no expectoration, or, tenacious, blood-stained mucus; sensation of fullness in the chest.

Ipecac. (3x).—Especially for the bronchial catarrh of children. **Indications:**—Asthmatic breathing; much nausea; vomiting of mucus; rattling of mucus in the bronchial tubes; face livid during cough; loud, mucous râles, with wheezing respiration; severe gastric ailments and intestinal catarrh; pallid or bluish or bloated countenance.

**Kali bich.** (3x).—Cough, with expectoration of tough mucus, that can be drawn out in strings; thick coating on the tongue; loathing of food; burning pain in the trachea. For bronchorrhea with abundant purulent expectoration, give **Kali bi.**, 2 grains in 4 ounces of water, by inhalation, in a steam atomizer.

**Tartar emet.** (2x).—The chief indication for **Tartar emetic** is profuse secretion of mucus in the bronchial tubes, which is difficult to raise. **Indications:**—Great oppression of the chest, with suffocative breathing; extensive mucous râles; great rattling of mucus with the cough, but nothing is raised. Also, symptoms of incipient carbon-dioxide poisoning—sopor, delirium, pallor, bloated countenance. Also, profuse sweat without relief; disposition to vomiting and diarrhea; paroxysms of rattling cough, ending in vomiting. It is the leading remedy in capillary bronchitis of children, and for pneumonia notha of the aged.

**Antimonium ars.** (2x).—Abundant secretion of mucus, with loud râles; difficult breathing; skin cyanotic, with cool perspiration; the patient anxious and restless.

**Veratrum album.** (1x).—Especially in the later stages of capillary bronchitis of children, with failing strength; pulse rapid and irregular; abundant secretion of mucus, which the child is unable to raise; cold, moist skin.

**Bromine.** (2x).—Acute bronchitis, with catarrhal inflammation of the larynx and trachea, with hoarse, croupy cough; the patient is weak and perspiring; the cough is tight, hard and spasmodic. It is the spasmodic cough that is characteristic; it is attended by suffocative attacks, and rattling of mucus in the larynx.

**Ammonium carb.**—In capillary bronchitis of children, or in the bronchitis of the aged, **Ammonium carb.** is called for when there is marked failure of the respiratory or circulatory functions. **Indications:**—Accumulation of mucus in the bronchi, which it is difficult to raise; great oppression of the chest; loud, coarse râles; great prostration, with falling temperature. **Dose:**—Put grs. x. of **Ammonium carb.** in one-half glass water; give teaspoonful-dose every 15 to 30 minutes.

**Ferrum phos.** (2x).—The sputum may be blood-streaked. There are symptoms of engorgement, but without restlessness and irritability.

**Hyoscyamus.** (tr.)—Dry cough, worse at night and when lying down. Extreme sensibility of the larynx and trachea.

**Rumex.** (1x).—Cough is excited by inhaling cold air, and also by pressure over the trachea, or by air striking the neck or chest.

**Lachesis.** (6x).—Extreme sensitiveness of the bronchial mucous membrane, and of the neck externally

**Antimonium iodid.** (2x).—Abundant muco-purulent expectoration. Coarse mucous râles in the chest.

**Hepar sulph.** (2x).—Long paroxysms of loose cough, with muco-purulent expectoration.

**Drosera.** (tr.)—Loud, hoarse, cough in hard paroxysms.

**Pulsatilla.** (3x).—Loose, yellowish expectoration. Paroxysms of cough, exciting effort at vomiting, with sore pain in the chest. Sensation of dryness in the larynx and trachea. Cough excited by inspiration. Worse at night.

**Arsenicum.** (6x).—High fever, dyspnea, anxiety, tendency to asphyxia.

**General Measures.**

**Sick-room.**—The room should be well ventilated. The temperature should be kept at about 70° F. Keep the air moist by means of a steam generator of some kind, or a pan of hot water set on stove or register. Do not overdo in this respect; i. e., do not keep the room too warm or the air too moist. If the air becomes close, cover the patient well and ventilate freely at intervals, keeping the temperature maintained at 70° F.

**Fomentations.**—In the early stage if there is much hyperemia of the lungs and a feeling of oppression of the chest, hot applications to the chest will give relief. This may take the form of a hot linseed poultice or of a hot fomentation. A poultice should be lightly made, properly applied, and changed every two hours. The use of poultices in affections of the chest is worse than useless if not properly done. In applying or changing poultices or fomentations do not let the chest get chilled by exposure to the air, and never put on a poultice that will drip. After the pulmonary secretions have become loosened, a dry cotton jacket is preferable to fomentation or poultice.

**The Patient.**—Change the position of the patient from one side to the other at intervals. Do not let the patient lie constantly on his back. If there is much secretion difficult to raise, place the patient with the shoulders low and the hips and lower part of the body elevated, so that gravity will favor a removal of the secretion on cough. A patient who is not too ill to do so can lean over the side of the bed—his arms supported on a low chair—in order to accomplish this; it will greatly favor expectoration.

**Diet.**—Early, during the fever, the diet should be chiefly liquid, such as clear soup, chicken-broth, hot milk, gruels, and the like. To allay thirst, give barley-water flavored with lemon. For feeble patients in spells of exhaustion, hot milk with a little alcoholic stimulant is allowable.

**Bowels.**—Give daily attention to the bowels. Do not permit an accumulation. Use enemata of water or of **glycerin.**

## II. BRONCHITIS OF THE SMALLER TUBES.

**Synonyms.**—Bronchiolitis; capillary bronchitis; suffocative catarrh.

**Definition.**—It is catarrhal inflammation of the bronchioles and the smaller bronchial tubes.

**Note.**—It is probable that there is no case of bronchiolitis—so-called "capillary bronchitis"—without some degree of accompanying broncho-pneumonia, and there are many cases of intermediate forms in which the inflammation involves both the medium-sized bronchial tubes, the bronchioles and the alveoli; but there are cases occurring, especially in infants and young children, in which the condition of **bronchiolitis predominates** to such an extent as to make of them almost a clinical entity; and although this distinction has been abandoned by some high authorities, yet for convenience of description it is still retained by others.

**Age.**—Age is a most important factor in the incidence of this disease. It is confined for the most part to the **extremes of life.** The exceptions to this consist of those cases that occur in the extremely **debilitated,** in those who have suffered from many previous attacks of bronchitis, in **alcoholics,** and as a complication of acute **infectious diseases** in debilitated subjects.

**Constitution.**—The disease occurs especially in **cachectic** children and in **diathetic** conditions; feeble, ill-nourished and rickety children are especially liable to its attack. In such children, also, it occurs as a **complication or sequel** of the acute infectious diseases—measles, whooping-cough and influenza.

### MORBID ANATOMY.

**Bronchioles.**—The inflammatory congestion, the swelling, and the proliferation and casting off of the cellular elements and production of mucus, entirely **occludes the affected tubules.** The lining membrane of the tubule is markedly injected and its lumen is blocked by the secretion.

**Emphysema.**—There may be areas of acute emphysema, the air-cells beyond the occluded tubules becoming distended with air.

**Apneumatosis.**—Scattered through the lungs are areas of collapse. The areas **vary in size,** many being small. In some instances the collapse may involve the greater part of a lobe.

**Alveoli.**—Scattered alveoli which have shared in the inflammatory process are indicated by faint yellow areas.

**Bronchitis.**—The medium-sized and larger tubes show signs of catarrhal inflammation; the degree and **extent varies** in different cases.

**Heart.**—There may be over-distension of the right heart, as in other forms of bronchitis.

### SYMPTOMS.

**Note.**—The symptoms of bronchiolitis, while related to those of bronchitis of the larger tubes, are so much more severe in degree as to make of the disease almost a **distinct clinical picture.**

**Onset.**—The oncome of the attack is **gradual** when occurring by extension of a previously-existing bronchitis; in other cases, and in the greater number, the onset is **sudden.**

**Chill.**—The initial chill may be a distinct rigor, or repeated chills; in young children a **convulsion** often replaces the chill.

**Fever.**—The range of temperature is **usually high;** soon after the onset it may rise to 103° or 104° F. or more, and the attack throughout may be characterized by this high temperature. If the fever moderates, the invasion of **new areas** of lung tissue is announced by a sudden rise. Towards the end, with cyanosis, the temperature falls and may even become subnormal.

**Pulse.**—The pulse is **always rapid,** varying according to the patient's condition from 130 to 150, and it may even be so rapid as to be uncountable. It is of low tension, and sometimes so small as to be almost imperceptible.

**Cough.**—The cough is frequent, occurring often in paroxysms and attended by pain in the chest. Early it may be dry, and in some cases remain so throughout the attack. In the paroxysms of cough there is severe cyanosis. With deep cyanosis and the approach of a fatal issue the **cough subsides,** owing to obtunding of the senses.

**Expectoration.**—In some cases expectoration is absent throughout the attack; in others, it will be very scanty. The **sputum is viscid** and expelled only after severe effort and cough.

**Sputum.**—In character the sputum—when present—is mucous; and later, it is muco-purulent. The mass contains fine, short plugs, which are casts of the bronchioles. These casts hang down under the lower surface of the mass when the expectorated matter is made to float on water.

**Respiration.**—The breathing is always rapid, and severe **dyspnea** is characteristic. The number of respirations, according to the severity of the attack and the amount of lung tissue involved, will vary from 30 to 60 per minute, or, in extreme cases, the breathing becomes quick and panting; sometimes it goes on to **asphyxia.** The respirations are short and quick, and aided by the muscles of respiration. Orthopnea occurs early.

**Skin.**—There is pallor and a high degree of **cyanosis.** The face is livid and the lips purple.

**Perspiration.**—The skin is usually **moist,** sometimes there being profuse sweat.

**Nervous Symptoms.**—Early there is much **restlessness,** the patient tossing about. Later, as the blood becomes carbonized, there is **lethargy,** the patient showing great apathy; this may be accompanied by muttering **delirium.** In fatal cases, near the end, there is usually **coma.**

## PHYSICAL SIGNS.

**Inspection.**—When obstruction to the entrance of air into the alveoli is great, with effort at inspiration there is **sinking in** of the supraclavicular spaces, and **recession** of the lower intercostal spaces, and of the epigastric and hypochondriac regions. Strained effort at respiration with increased action of the thoracic muscles and also the abdominal muscles is revealed. The pallor and cyanosis of the skin are seen.

**Palpation.**—If there is accompanying catarrh of the larger tubes, rhonchial fremitus may be felt. Vocal fremitus is little changed.

**Percussion.**—The percussion note may be unchanged; over emphysematous areas it will be hyper-resonant. Over extensive areas of pulmonary collapse there is dulness.

**Auscultation.**—The respiratory murmur is usually harsh and rough in the upper and anterior parts of the chest; at the bases and the back it is feeble.

**Adventitious Sounds.**—The characteristic sounds are **crepitant rales,** hissing in character; there are also fine mucous râles. The râles are most abundant at the **back** and at the **bases** of the lungs. Sibilant and sonorous râles may be present, especially at the upper and anterior parts of the chest.

## COURSE AND DURATION.

In young infants a severe attack may end fatally in 24 hours; in older children it is usually more prolonged. In adults, when the disease is progressively worse, the fatal termination may come in four or five days. In the aged, again, as in infants, early fatal termination may also be expected. On the other hand, in the class of cases that go on to recovery the severe symptoms may persist for about a week before signs of improvement are shown; but even after this, the course of the disease is usually prolonged before complete convalescence is established. This is especially true in subjects of emphysema.

**Bacteriology.**

The specific micro-organisms found are the streptococci, the staphylococci, micrococcus lanceolatus (bacillus pneumoniæ).

## PROGNOSIS.

**Unfavorable Signs.**

**The signs calling for unfavorable prognosis are:—**Increasing dyspnea with accompanying cyanosis, indicating non-aëration of the blood. This is a sign of greatest gravity. Other signs and conditions calling for guarded or grave prognosis are:—Infancy and extreme old age; increasing weakness and frequency of the pulse, with weakness of the heart-action; sudden rise in the temperature; co-existence of Bright's disease, emphysema and heart-disease; in infants, rickets or other diatheses; in old age, arterio-sclerosis, or general debility.

**The signs of approaching fatal termination are:—**Increasing dyspnea, with cyanosis, delirium and coma. The respiration gradually ceases, with loud mucous râles in the chest; the patient sinks down with the head low and bent forward.

**Favorable Signs.**

As convalescence approaches, there is less dyspnea and cyanosis; the pulse becomes larger in volume and less frequent; the temperature gradually subsides; the tongue clears and the physical signs become less intense.

**Sequels.**—The attack may be followed by broncho-pneumonia, tuberculosis, or emphysema.

## DIAGNOSIS.

In making diagnosis consider the age of the patient, the predisposing and exciting causes, the high degree of dyspnea following the onset, the widely distributed fine râles,. and, with these symptoms, the retraction of the epigastrium and hypochondrium with inspiratory effort.

## DIFFERENTIAL DIAGNOSIS.

**Broncho-Pneumonia.**

If dulness on percussion is absent, as it may be in some cases of broncho-pneumonia, it is difficult to make a distinction between the two diseases. Moreover, the two conditions are often associated and the general symptoms are similar; dependence will have to be placed chiefly upon the physical signs.

### Acute Miliary Tuberculosis.

In this disease the onset is usually gradual; there are emaciation and general signs of tubercular affection of the cerebral meninges or of the abdominal organs. If there is expectoration, examination for bacilli will determine the nature of the attack.

### Lobar Pneumonia.

In this condition the physical signs determine the diagnosis.

### Pulmonary Edema.

This condition, being in most cases secondary to cardiac or renal disease, will suggest examination of the organs involved in the primary affections.

## TREATMENT.

### Therapeutics.

The medicines should be selected according to indications already given under Acute Bronchitis. **Tartar emetic** is chiefly to be relied upon, being indicated by the abundant secretion of mucus, which it is difficult to raise. In the early stage, that of congestion, **Belladonna** is the leading remedy. See also indications for **Veratrum alb.**, and especially **Ammonium carb.**

### General Measures.

**Fomentations.**—Hot fomentations may be applied to the chest when there is oppressed breathing. Do not use them constantly. Avoid the use of poultices. **Turpentine** may be added to the fomentation.

**Sick-room.**—Provide for good ventilation. Do not let a number of people crowd around the little patient. Keep the air moist. The temperature should be 70° to 75° F.

**Bathing.**—The child may be placed in a hot bath for a few minutes, then taken out and wrapped in a soft blanket; this sometimes has very good effect.

**The Patient.**—When there is cough with much expectoration, lower the head and shoulders so that gravity will favor the removal of the secretion.

---

# PLASTIC BRONCHITIS.

**Synonym.**—Fibrinous bronchitis.

**Definition.**—Plastic bronchitis is characterized by the exudation of a plastic fibrinous material, which forms either solid casts or hollow cylinders in the bronchi.

**Etiology.**—Of its specific cause nothing is known. The majority of cases occur in early middle life; it is more common in the male than in the female—2 to 1. It occurs in those who have been previously healthy, as well as in various diatheses; hence, the previous condition has no relation to the disease. It is a rare affection.

**Varieties.**—(a) Acute, (b) Chronic. The chronic is the more common.

## MORBID ANATOMY.

**Character.**—The casts are branched, having the formation of the bronchial tree. **Size.**—In size the casts vary from a mold of a few tubes, to an almost complete cast of the bronchial tree. A branched cast from one to two inches in length would be the most common form; they may measure from six to seven inches. **Color.**—In color they are pearl-gray or yellowish-gray; occasionally the cast is blood-tinged.

**Microscopic Appearance.**—The casts are made up of concentric layers of coagulated fibrin. The fibrin encloses in its meshes leucocytes, mucus, and epithelial cells; sometimes Charcot-Leyden crystals.

**Post-Mortem Findings.**—On post-mortem, casts are sometimes absent, even though casts were discharged during life. In some cases the epithelial lining membrane of the lung is intact; in others, the membrane is denuded. The peri-bronchial tissue is in some cases unaltered; in others, it shows inflammatory changes. The adjacent portion of lung may show emphysema or collapse.

## SYMPTOMS.

**Onset.**—There are two modes of onset. **(a)** The attack usually begins with signs of catarrh and abundant expectoration of mucus. The mucous expectoration may continue for several days before the cast is thrown off. **(b)** In other cases there is no premonitory catarrh; the attack sets in with rigors, high fever, dyspnea and paroxysmal cough.

**Cough.**—The entire course of the disease is marked by severe, spasmodic cough occurring in frequent paroxysms. After the fibrinous cast is raised and expectorated there is immediate relief of the cough and of all the other symptoms.

**Hemoptysis.**—The casts may be blood-streaked, or there may be a large quantity of blood raised, either preceding or following the expectoration of the cast.

**Pain.**—There may be sore pain in the insertion of the diaphragm, due to the violent cough. Sometimes there is localized pain over the affected portion of the lung.

**Fever.**—There is elevation of temperature from the onset of the attack until after the raising of the cast and subsidence of the accompanying symptoms.

**Duration.**—A single attack, from the appearance of the first symptoms until the cast is raised and expectorated with subsidence of the accompanying symptoms, may be from two to ten days.

**Recurrent Attacks.**—In some cases, after a cast has been expectorated, with accompanying relief, the symptoms will set in anew, only to subside after the formation and the expectoration of another cast. In other cases considerable intervals will separate successive attacks. These intervals may be short or may be very

long; in some cases but a few days; in others, several
years.

**Expectoration.—Quantity.**—The accompanying mucous expectoration is usually great; there may be as
much as a pint in the twenty-four hours. In the expectorated matter the fibrinous material may be found broken
up into larger or smaller pieces; when small, they may
escape attention unless searched for. The particles of
fibrin may be readily found by shaking up the sputum
with water.

**Digestion.**—In acute cases there is coated tongue, loss
of appetite, and disturbance of the stomach.

**Cyanosis.**—In severe attacks, with extensive formation of fibrin in the lungs, there is faulty aëration of the
blood, with cyanosis; this may go on to asphyxia.

## PHYSICAL SIGNS.

**Auscultation.**—The respiratory murmur is harsh, with
prolonged expiration. There are accompanying dry
râles. On palpation, dry or rhonchial fremitus may
sometimes be present. There are no other significant
physical signs.

## DIAGNOSIS.

Positive diagnosis can never be made except by finding the characteristic fibrinous casts in the sputum.
When the casts are broken up into small particles careful
examination is necessary in order to detect them. In
any case of paroxysmal dyspnea which is suddenly relieved by expectoration, the disease may be suspected
and the casts should be searched for in the sputum.

**Course.**—Subjects of this disease may have repeated
attacks at longer or shorter intervals extending over
many years. A fatal termination from the primary disease is rare; death is usually due to complications occurring secondarily, especially in cachectic subjects.

## TREATMENT.

Plastic bronchitis does not yield readily to treatment.
The line of agents used should include **Iodine, Kali bi-**

chromicum, Iodide-of-lime (B., C. & Co.). Favorable results have been reported from the use of **Carbonate-of-kreasote.** These agents should be used by inhalation, as well as by internal administration. In other respects, treat as in other forms of bronchitis.

---

# CHRONIC BRONCHITIS.

**Forms.**—Different cases of chronic bronchitis vary in degree from those which consist merely of recurrent attacks occurring in each successive winter season, to others which are continuous and accompanied by marked primary and secondary conditions.

Most attacks of chronic bronchitis are due to recurrent acute or sub-acute attacks of the disease.

## ETIOLOGY.

**Predisposing Causes.**

**Heredity.**—In some instances hereditary tendency is a predisposing factor; several members of the same family may be thus affected.

**Age.**—The disease is most common in the aged.

**Other Diseases.**—It is in many cases secondary to emphysema, alcoholism, Bright's disease, heart disease—especially lesions of the mitral valves—or any form which causes pulmonary congestion.

**Exciting Causes.**

The exciting causes are the same as in acute bronchitis; it occurs more especially in those who are exposed to sudden changes of temperature, or who breathe irritating particles in the atmosphere.

## MORBID ANATOMY.

**Fibrous Coat.**—The inner fibrous coat of the bronchi and the bronchial tubes is much thickened; there is cellular infiltration and dilatation of the blood-vessels. The outer fibrous coat is also infiltrated, and there is peribronchial thickening.

**Muscular Coat.**—After primary hypertrophy of the muscular fibers there is secondary atrophy.

**The Cartilages.**—In the aged the cartilage of the bronchial tubes may be calcareous; in others, they may be in process of absorption.

**Mucous Membrane.**—The mucous membrane is thickened, rough, and in ridges; in many places it is bare of epithelial cells.

**The Lungs.**—There are many emphysematous areas.

**Heart.**—There is usually dilation of the right heart.

## VARIETIES.

The character of the sputum varies in different cases to such an extent as to mark them as being of different types. These may be described under three varieties:—

**(a) Dry Bronchitis.**

This form is marked by scanty expectoration, which is viscid and tenacious. There are paroxysms of extremely severe spasmodic cough, the patient making violent effort to raise the scanty tenacious sputum. In time, emphysema and embarrassed circulation supervene.

**(b) Moist Bronchitis.**

In this form the quantity of expectoration is very great. In some cases the sputum is serous in quality; in others it is muco-purulent or purulent, but great in quantity. Emphysema and circulatory disturbances are not so common in this form as in dry bronchitis.

**(c) Putrid Bronchitis.**

In this form the sputum is very fetid; also the patient's breath. The expectoration is great in quantity and muco-purulent in character; the putrid odor is due to decomposition.

## SYMPTOMS.

**Temperature.**—Chronic bronchitis usually runs an apyrexial course; at times there is feverish action, which is usually due to the presence in the circulation of toxins from the retention of pus in the bronchial tubes.

**Pulse.**—The pulse rate is but little changed.

**Digestion.**—There is usually coated tongue, anorexia, and tendency to constipation.

**Heart.**—In time there is dilation of the right heart and embarrassed venous circulation, leading to cyanosis and eventually to general dropsy.

**Respiration.**—The patient becomes "out-of-breath" on slight exertion, and also after effort at cough.

**Cough.**—It is never absent. It varies in severity with the character of the secretion. In the dry form of bronchitis there are severe paroxysms; in the moist form it is loose, and accompanied by much expectoration. There is always a morning cough excited by the accumulated secretions of the night.

**Sputum.**—In the **dry form** it is viscid, tenacious, and grayish in color. In the **moist form** it is serous, frothy, nearly colorless, and contains few cellular elements; or, in this form, it may be muco-purulent with a large amount of cellular elements, the sputum almost like pus. The decomposed sputum in the **putrid form** is greenish-yellow in color, and contains fat globules, margaric and butyric acids. It is to the presence of these fatty acids that the fetid odor is due. The sputum in fetid bronchitis contains small bodies, called **Dittrich's plugs,** which are dirty-white or yellowish masses consisting of fatty detritus, micro-organisms, and crystals of margarin.

## COMPLICATIONS.

**Emphysema.**—After the disease has existed for some time a more or less extensive emphysema results; the patient then suffers from constant mild dyspnea which at times, especially at night, becomes urgent, with asthmatic breathing, giving rise to what is known as "bronchial asthma."

**Heart-Disease.**—As a result of the embarrassed pulmonary circulation the right heart becomes dilated, which is followed by the secondary conditions of static congestion of all the organs, and, eventually, edema and dropsy.

**Broncho-Pneumonia.**—Late in the course of the disease there may be sudden acute inflammation of the smaller tubes, leading to bronchiolitis or to bronchopneumonia. This complication is often fatal.

**Course and Duration.**—When chronic bronchitis is once established recovery is rare. For many years the patient may show no general signs of the existence of the disease, but in the advanced stage of chronic bronchitis there is emaciation, loss of strength and night-sweats. If no intercurrent malady ends the patient's life, towards the close there is constant cyanosis, the superficial fascia shows distention, the legs become edematous, the urine scanty and albuminous, and there is death preceded by dropsy due to cardiac failure; or death from asphyxia due to clogging of the bronchi with secretion which the patient is too feeble to remove. In the terminal event there is usually edema of the **lungs.**

## PHYSICAL SIGNS.

**Inspection.**—There is no change in the appearance of the chest until the disease has lasted for some time. In its more advanced stage, when emphysema has developed, there is "barrel-shaped" chest, fullness of the supraclavicular regions, and rounding of the shoulders.

**Palpation.**—Rhonchial fremitus is present if there is much secretion; vocal fremitus is diminished if there is much emphysema. It is increased over the bases of the lungs if there is much static congestion.

**Percussion.**—There is little change in the percussion note unless emphysema or congestion are present. With emphysema, the note is of lower pitch; with congestion, it is of higher pitch.

**Auscultation.—Respiratory Murmur.**—The breath-sound is harsh, with prolonged expiration. Owing to the presence of adventitious sounds the respiratory murmur is not easy to determine.

**Adventitious Sounds.**—These, as would be expected, are of great variety, according to the amount and character of the contained secretions. In various conditions the rhonchi may be dry or moist—sibilant, sonorous, fine and coarse mucous, crackling or bubbling. The character of the râles will differ in different parts of the chest, and will vary with the alterations of the nature of the secretions from day to day or even from hour to hour, and before and after coughing spells.

## DIAGNOSIS.

The diagnosis is usually not difficult. Take into consideration all the symptoms that have been enumerated. It may be necessary to distinguish it from pulmonary tuberculosis, but in this latter condition there is elevation of temperature, and the physical signs are more marked in the apices of the lungs. But the crucial test must always be by examination of the sputum for tubercle bacilii.

## PROGNOSIS.

If the disease is uncomplicated the patient will live for many years, until the development of the secondary conditions that have been described. If there is already extensive disease of the heart or of the kidneys, the prognosis must be modified accordingly. The prognosis is more favorable in the young than in the aged.

## TREATMENT.

**Therapeutics.**

**Sulpnur.** (3x).—Gouty subjects, or the tuberculous diathesis; bronchorrhea.

**Kali bi.** (2x).—"Dry" bronchial catarrh; hard cough; viscid sputum; hoarseness; aphonia.

**Iodine.** (1x).—Delicate, "phthisical" subjects; dry cough; sputum bloody; emaciation; night-sweats.

**Grindelia.** (1x).—Asthmatic breathing; dry râles.

**Kali hyd.** (1x).—In syphilitic subjects.

**Silicea.** (6x).—Sputum purulent; fever; night-sweats; emaciation; dyspnea. Rachitic children.

**Drosera.** (Tr.)—Hard paroxysms of cough, exciting vomiting; emphysema.

**Arsenicum.** (3x).—Dyspnea; debility; emaciation; dry, wheezing cough; scanty expectoration; heart-disease.

**Hyoscyamus.** (Tr.)—Dry, irritable cough at night.

**Phosphorus.** (3x).—Cachectic subjects; dry, hacking cough, with pain or "tightness" in the chest; hoarseness.

**Ammon. carb.** (1x).—Copious secretion; incessant cough. Heart or kidney affections.

**Rumex.** (Tr.)—Dry cough; irritable mucous membrane.

**Calcarea carb.** (6x).—With emphysema or bronchiectasis; purulent, fetid expectoration. "Scrofulous" diathesis.

**Mercurious sol.** (3x).—Diarrhea; stomach and liver involved.

**Hepar sulph.** (1x).—Loose cough; muco-purulent sputum.

**Aconite.** (1x).—Dry cough, with dyspnea.

**Arsen iod.** (2x).—Debility; anemia; emaciation.

**Sanguinaria.** (2x).—Fever; flushed cheeks; much sputum.

**Tartar emet.** (2x).—Moist râles; free expectoration.

**Stannum.** (6x).—Much muco-purulent expectoration.

**Spongia.** (3x).—Dry, laryngeal catarrh.

**Note.**—In making prescription in chronic bronchitis give attention to the constitutional condition and to the primary disease.

### General Measures.

**Inhalations.**—Use various inhalants: **Eucalyptus; Iodine; Kali bi.; Balsam; Creasote.**

**Hygiene.**—Avoid exposure to cold and damp; wear warm woolen clothing. Avoid vitiated air; seek warm, dry air and sunshine.

**Climate.**—In confirmed cases removal to a warm, dry, equable climate is of marked benefit.

# BRONCHO-PNEUMONIA.

**Synonyms.**—Lobular pneumonia; catarrhal pneumonia; disseminated pneumonia. (**Capillary bronchitis,** by some authorities, is considered as being identical with broncho-pneumonia. Others treat of these as separate conditions.)

**Definition.**—Broncho-pneumonia is an inflammation of the air-vesicles and the lung-parenchyma, the inflammation occurring in single lobules or in groups of adjacent lobules. The inflamed areas occur in isolated patches in different parts of the lungs; there is always more or less capillary bronchitis, as well as inflammation of the mucous membrane of the larger tubes.

**Varieties.**

(a) **Acute lobular pneumonia;** (idiopathic, or preceded by catarrhal bronchitis).

(b) **Secondary lobular pneumonia;** it follows whooping-cough, scarlet fever, measles, etc. **Aspiration-pneumonia** occurs after etherization or the coma of apoplexy, uremia, or other conditions in which the larynx loses its sensibility.

(c) **Embolic lobular 'pneumonia;** it follows ulcerative endocarditis, pyemia, etc.

## ETIOLOGY.

**Age.**—The extremes of life; it is most frequent in infants and young children.

**Conditions.—Environment:**—Exposure to cold; impure air. **Bodily:**—Rickets; chronic diarrhea; malnutrition; cachexia.

**Bacteriology.**—The local inflammation is excited by a pathogenic micro-organism. In most cases it is the streptococcus; in some, it is the bacillus pneumoniæ.

## PATHOLOGY.

**Early Changes.**—With inflammation of the lobules there is always accompanying bronchitis. There is associated bronchiolitis, as well as catarrhal inflammation of the mucous membrane of the larger tubes. The affected alveoli become filled with the products of inflammation, consisting of cast-off epithelial cells, leucocytes, and mucus. There is no fibrinous exudation. The bronchioles adjacent to the alveoli become filled with secretion, and the mucous membrane is soft and swollen and of a dark red color. Not only is the lining membrane of the alveoli inflamed, but it is characteristic of lobular pneumonia that the lung parenchyma shares in the inflammatory process. In the interstitial tissue the capillaries are enlarged, and there is round-cell infiltration.

**Bronchial Glands.**—These are enlarged and softened.

**Location of Affected Lobules.**—The affected lobules are irregularly scattered in both lungs; they are more abundant in the lower lobes and along the borders of the lobes. Some are deep-seated; others are at the pleural surface. The latter are wedge-shaped; the overlying pleura is inflamed.

**Resolution.**—When resolution occurs the contents of the alveoli undergo fatty metamorphosis. The fat is emulsified in serum and the liquefied product is absorbed or expectorated.

**Extent of Lung Involved.**—In mild cases there are widely-scattered lobules affected.

**Size of Affected Lobules.**—In a mild case the diseased area varies from the size of a pea to that of a marble. Between the affected areas there is healthy and crepitant lung tissue. With progressive inflammation many adjacent lobules share in the inflammation, and thus large areas of lung substance become involved.

**Degenerative Processes.**—In some cases the inflammation may result in suppuration and abscess. With this there may be destruction of lung tissue and formation of cavities. In other cases there is caseous degeneration; in others, gangrenous; in others, interstitial inflammation leading to chronic interstitial pneumonia.

**Embolic Lobular Pneumonia.**—In this form the inflammation is due to the lodgment of an embolus; or, in other cases, to the formation of a thrombus in the branches of the pulmonary artery. In pyemia and in ulcerative endocarditis the emboli are septic, causing inflammation and suppuration.

**Pathological Anatomy.**—The mucous membrane of the trachea and bronchi in some cases is normal; in others, it is congested. The small bronchi almost invariably show signs of inflammation. Irregular patches of consolidated lobules are found scattered throughout the lungs. The air-vesicles are found filled with detritus, epithelium and leucocytes. There is edema about consolidated spots; there are also scattered areas of collapsed lung, and some emphysematous areas.

**Nature of the Inflammation.**—In broncho-pneumonia the inflammation is productive; *i. e.*, there is a tendency to the formation of new tissue, especially interstitial and peribronchial tissue. It is this fact that gives a tendency to interstitial fibrosis as a sequel to broncho-pneumonia.

## SYMPTOMS.

**Onset.—Chill:**—An idiopathic case is usually ushered in by a slight chill or a succession of chilly sensations. There may be **repeated chills,** marking an extension of the disease-process in new areas of the lungs. **This symptom is always significant.**

**Fever.**—The temperature-range is of the continuous type, though marked by remissions and exacerbations. In some cases, after pursuing a moderate course for a time, the temperature will suddenly mount several degrees. This variability of the temperature, which denotes extension at intervals into new territory, is an important sign of the fever of broncho-pneumonia, and is to be taken into consideration in diagnosis and prognosis. The temperature often rises as high as 104° and 105° F.

**Skin.**—It is usually moist, with a tendency to perspiration.

**Pulse.**—The pulse is rapid—120, 130, and in extreme

cases, 150 and 160. There is increase in pulse rate with each extension of the disease and exacerbation of the temperature. The quality of the pulse is soft and compressible; it is sometimes irregular.

**Respiration.**—Respirations are always rapid—as high as 30, 40, and sometimes even more. There is severe dyspnea.

**Cough.**—Cough is almost always present; in young children it may be absent.

**Expectoration.**—It is generally present, but the sputum not great in quantity; in young children it is swallowed. In character it may be mucous, catarrhal, or muco-purulent.

**Cerebral Symptoms.**—Usually the mind is clear. With carbonization of the blood there may be obscuration of the mental faculties; in children there is sometimes delirium.

**Pain.**—There are sharp, stitching pains in various parts of the chest when the pleura is involved.

## BRONCHO-PNEUMONIA IN CHILDREN.

**Note.**—Owing to the more embryonic condition of the child's lungs broncho-pneumonia in infants pursues a course in some respects so different from that in adults as to merit separate description.

**Onset.**—Convulsions often replace the chill.

**Nervous Symptoms.**—There is great restlessness and extreme prostration.

**Respiration.**—It is very rapid—from 40 to 80 per minute.

**Fever.**—The temperature rises rapidly following the onset; it soon runs up to 104° or 105° F. Its course is marked by extreme remissions and exacerbations.

**Pulse.**—It is usually very rapid, varying from 120 to 170 or more.

**Tongue.**—Early, it has a white, heavy coating, which later becomes brown and dry.

**Gastro-Enteric Symptoms.**—The child takes nourishment with great difficulty. There is sometimes vomiting. In some cases there is diarrhea.

**Urine.**—The urine is scanty and high colored.

**Skin.**—It is moist and perspiring.

**Course and Duration.**—If the disease is extensive at the onset, involving a large number of lobules, with corresponding severity of the other symptoms, the case may end fatally in a few days. In other cases, with mild onset, the case may be progressing favorably when suddenly, with extension of the disease into new areas, the temperature, from 100°, may run up to 105° or more within a few hours, and the case be rapidly fatal. In severe cases the course of the disease is from one to two weeks. Some cases persist, with irregular remissions and exacerbations, for six or eight weeks before convalescence begins.

## PROGNOSIS.

The younger the child the more grave the prognosis. In older children in secondary broncho-pneumonia the prognosis is more favorable. The prognosis must always be guarded, for sudden extension of the disease to previously unaffected portions of the lung may at any time change the aspect of the case in a few hours.

**Resolution.**—The termination of the disease is always by lysis.

**Cerebral Symptoms.**—In some cases cerebral symptoms predominate. There may be great restlessness and delirium, interrupted by repeated convulsions. The accompanying symptoms are:—Rolling of the head; high fever; great prostration; vomiting; and other symptoms of meningitis.

**Strumous Cases.**—In children with tuberculous dia· thesis the lungs become much congested; there is great prostration, high temperature, great loss of flesh, and swollen lymphatic glands. Such a condition renders the prognosis grave.

## BRONCHO-PNEUMONIA IN THE ADULT.

**Onset.**—There is usually a distinct chill, or a succession of chills.

**Pain.**—There is pain in the chest; also headache and backache.

**Stomach.**—Vomiting sometimes occurs.

**Fever.**—The temperature soon runs to 104° and 105° F. In the very aged the range is usually more moderate, because there is on the part of the system a lessened degree of reaction to irritation. It may in such cases be no more than 102° to 103° F.

**Pulse.**—It is rapid and feeble.

**Cough.**—At first it is dry; in a few hours there may be profuse mucous expectoration; sometimes it is blood-stained.

**Urine.**—It is scanty; sometimes albuminous.

**General Condition.**—There is rapid prostration; great restlessness; sometimes delirium.

**Bowels.**—Usually there is constipation; sometimes diarrhea.

**Respiration.**—It is rapid; 30, 40 or more. Usually there is great dyspnea.

**Skin.**—It is moist and clammy; often there is free perspiration.

**Complications.**—In the aged there is usually much accompanying bronchitis; also, often emphysema, bronchial asthma, or cirrhosis of the lung.

**Course and Duration.**—In middle life the disease lasts from ten to twenty days; termination is by lysis. In the very aged many cases are fatal. In a case pursuing a mild course with moderate temperature and pulse, the entire aspect may be changed in twenty-four hours, owing to the invasion of new areas of lung tissue.

## PHYSICAL DIAGNOSIS.

**Inspection.**—This reveals rapid respiration, livid color of the skin, and moist surface.

**Palpation.**—It reveals vocal fremitus over consolidated

portions, if the area of consolidation is extensive; otherwise, the results are negative.

**Percussion.**—It reveals higher pitched note over consolidated areas. If the consolidated portion is slight there may be hyper-resonance.

**Auscultation.**—Crepitation is heard over the affected portion; also, according to the extent and degree of the accompanying bronchitis, subcrepitant and fine and coarse mucous râles. Between the points corresponding to diseased lung tissue, normal sounds may be heard; this is characteristic of broncho-pneumonia.

**Differential Diagnosis.**—From Lobar Pneumonia:—Note that there is absence of rusty sputum, of dry, hot skin, of extensive crepitation, and signs of consolidation. **From Pleurisy:**—In lobular pneumonia there is no friction sound, pains are less severe, and there are no signs which would accompany effusion. **From early Phthisis:**—There is no apical infiltration; no regular rise of evening temperature, and the sputum is of different character.

**Prognosis.**—Favorable:—In middle life; good constitutional condition; small extent of lung tissue involved; sthenic cases. **Unfavorable:**—Extremes of age; cachexia; great extent of lung tissue involved; asthenic cases.

**Causes of Death.**—Asthenia; asphyxia; complications.

**Sequels.**—Chronic bronchitis; phthisis; pulmonary cirrhosis.

## TREATMENT.

**Therapeutics.**

**Belladonna.** (3x).—Especially in children, and only in the early stages of the disease. Much accompanying congestion; active fever; moist skin; respiration rapid; moaning; cerebral excitement.

**Aconite.** (1x).—This is to be used when with the local inflammation there is accompanying systemic fever, with high temperature and circulatory excitement. Hence, it is most often called for early in the attack. But it need not be limited to this period, for so long as there continues to be febrile action, **Aconite** will aid the action of other medicines by calming the nervous erethism. **In-dications.**—Fever; rapid pulse; painful cough, with sensitiveness to inspired air; hoarseness; expectoration blood-streaked, the blood being bright red; respiration impeded; anxiety; stitching pains in the chest. **Special Indications.**—Feverish action, with vaso-motor disturbance; restlessness, from nervous erethism. Dry cough; or, expectoration tinged with bright-red blood.

**Ferrum phos.** (2x).—The action of **Ferrum phos.** is limited to the early stage, when there is active congestion of the lungs, with its attendant symptoms. This is the key to its use—a state of engorgement, before the later pathological changes, such as abundant catarrhal secretion, etc., have taken place. **Aconite** has a similar sphere, but the fever is more active, with restlessness and great nervous erethism, and a hard pulse. **Indications.**—Congestion of the lungs; moderate fever; pulse full and soft; the chest feels sore and bruised; scanty, blood-streaked sputum; sonorous and sibilant râles.

**Phosphorus.** (2x).—This is to be used especially when the disease occurs in cachectic, delicate subjects, and in secondary broncho-pneumonia after exhausting diseases; in subjects of Bright's disease, diabetes, and in fatty degeneration of organs. Also, in cases that sink into a low, typhoid-like condition. **Indications.**—Cachexia, or typhoid-like state; moderate fever; great oppression of the chest; rawness in larynx and trachea; expectoration purulent, or muco-purulent; mucus streaked with dark blood; abundant râles; sticky perspiration; weak, soft pulse; emaciation and prostration.

**Tartar emet.** (2x).—This is the most important remedy in the treatment of this affection. **Indications.**—Fine and coarse mucous râles; rapid respiration; oppressed breathing; cyanosis; lips blue; cool surface; sweat; feeble heart's action.

**Antimonium ars.** (2x).—Broncho-pneumonia of the aged, with loud râles and feeble heart.

**Byronia.** (1x).—Accompanying pleurisy, with stitching pains; soreness in the chest; children cry when coughing.

**General Measures.**

**Sick-Room.**—It should be well ventilated. Maintain a temperature of 70° F; keep the air moist.

**Patient.**—Change the patient's position frequently. When expectoration is difficult, lower the patient's shoulders and raise the hips, so that there may be a "down-hill" cough.

**Chest.**—Sponge the chest at intervals with hot water, and dry carefully. When there is high temperature, with dry, hot skin, use tepid sponging. Avoid the use of poultices. If there is local pain, the best application is a hot compress. If the fever is high and the skin of the chest is hot, do not bundle the chest in any way. Let the patient wear a light muslin shirt. On the other hand, if the surface of the chest is cool and moist, let the patient wear a cotton jacket. Kneading and manipulating the muscles of the chest will aid in the respiratory effort; this is especially important in young children and in the very feeble.

**Diet.**—With this disease there is generally great prostration; hence the patient should have a liberal and nutritious diet; good sustaining treatment is demanded.

**Heart.**—In threatened heart-failure give the usual cardiac stimulants; a hot compress applied directly over the heart, at intervals, is helpful at such times.

**Cough.**—When the cough is distressing, give mucilaginous drinks.

## ASTHMA.

**Definition.**—Asthma is a neurosis affecting the lungs, marked by the occurence of paroxysms of dyspnea due to spasmodic contraction of the bronchial tubes. The dyspnea is of the expiratory type. There is no discoverable characteristic pulmonary lesion. All morbid changes are secondary. The etiological factor may be

are repeated paroxysms of expiratory dyspnea, with absence of all symptoms or signs of the disease in the intervals between attacks.

**History.**—The disease received its significant name—
denoting "gasping for breath"—from Hippocrates.
Laennec first differentiated asthma from other conditions
attended by dyspnea.

**Nature.**—Asthma is looked upon as being a true
neurosis, dependent upon changes in the central nervous
system.

**Pathology.**—There is no discoverable **characteristic**
lesion in the lungs of an asthmatic subject. Whatever
pulmonary changes are found are **secondary.** The
paroxysm of dyspnea is believed to be due to spasmodic
constriction of the bronchial tubes through irritation of
the motor branches of the **vagus** supplying the muscular
fibers of the bronchi. It is believed, however, that this
one explanation does not account for all cases. The
hyperemia and inturgescence of the nasal and bronchial
mucous membranes in "hay-asthma" leads to the belief
that in such cases a similar condition exists in the finer
bronchial tubes, causing obstruction and consequent
dyspnea. In such case the effect would be produced
through the agency of the **sympathetic** nerves, which
are intimately associated with the cerebro-spinal nerves
and with the vagus in the pulmonary plexuses. Hence
it is probable that in different forms of asthma the
neurosis may belong to the vagus, or to the sympathetic
nervous system.

**Morbid Anatomy.**—The morbid conditions found post-
mortem are all secondary. In the lungs of old asthmatics there is hypertrophy of the circular muscular
fibers, with thickening of the walls of the bronchial
tubes and consequent diminished caliber. If the disease
has been of long standing there is always more or less
secondary emphysema. There is also in such case dilatation of the right heart. The bronchial glands are often
found to be enlarged.

### Varieties.

(a) **Spasmodic Asthma.**—In this form the **nervous** element is predominant; all other changes are secondary.

(b) **Bronchial Asthma.**—This term is applied to a class of cases in which the paroxysmal attacks of dyspnea occur in a subject who has previously suffered from **bronchitis** and emphysema.

(c) **Cardiac Asthma.**—To this variety belong cases occurring in those previously the subjects of **heart-disease,** either valvular or myocardial.

(d) **Renal Asthma.**—This term is applied to paroxysmal attacks of dyspnea as a result of **uremia** in subjects of acute or chronic nephritis.

(e) **Hay-Asthma.**—This is a variety of asthma in which the exciting factor is the pollen of plants, or other similar irritant.

## ETIOLOGY.

### Predisposing Causes.

**Age.**—No age is free. It has been known to occur in a baby fourteen days old. Eighty per cent of cases occur before the age of forty. It sometimes develops in old age.

**Sex.**—The proportion of cases in the male as compared to the female is about two to one. This is probably due to the fact that men are more exposed to the conditions that induce the disease. The influence of heredity is strongly marked; the tendency has been found in sixteen per cent of cases. Again, there is often family predisposition.

**Social Position.**—It is more common among the well-to-do than among the indigent.

**Phthisis.**—Those who have suffered from phthisis and made recovery are found to become asthmatics in some instances. It is supposed in such cases that enlarged bronchial glands may make pressure on the branches of the vagus. (It is a popular error that asthmatics have a degree of immunity from consumption.)

**Other Diseases.**—Diseases characterized by pulmonary complications—such as broncho-pneumonia, whooping-cough, measles, and the like—sometimes leave a predisposition to asthma. Also, diseased conditions of the pharyngeal and laryngeal mucous membranes, consisting of the presence of polypi, of hyperemia and of hypertrophy of these parts, in some cases predispose to asthma. Enlarged thyroid sometimes predisposes to this disease. Other diseases of a general nature also seem to bear an etiological relation to asthma. Among these may be named rickets, rheumatism, gout, skin-diseases (eczema, urticaria, herpes).

**General Consideration.**—The essential symptom of asthma—namely, **dyspnea**—is believed to be due to contraction of the bronchial tubes induced by spasm of the bronchial muscles. The muscular spasm is due to disturbed innervation. The nerve involved is the vagus. The irritant may be either central or peripheral. The vagi are excito-motor as well as inhibitory nerves of respiration. The respiratory center also has sensory communication with all parts of the body. Hence the asthma may be purely **central** in origin, or its exciting cause may be **peripheral,** and the effect on the respiration may thus be produced by reflex action.

**Exciting Causes.**

Exciting causes may be either central or peripheral.

I. **Central.**—(a) Mental emotion may excite an attack. **(b) Toxemia.**—Uremic poisoning: lead in the system.

II. **Peripheral.**—(a) **Nasal.**—The irritation may be due to:—(1) Nasal polypi; (2) Vascular turgescence of the cavernous tissue of the turbinates; (3) Chronic thickening of the mucous membrane; (4) Odors and gases (ipecacuanha; fumes of chlorin and of sulphurous acid, etc.).

(b) **Dental.**—The irritation of teething.

(c) **Bronchial.**—Bronchial inflammation is one of the chief etiological factors.

(d) **Gastro-intestinal.**—The excitant may be due to flatulence, constipation, or scybalous distension of the rectum; some special articles of diet.

(e) **Uterine.**—The uterus in some cases seems to be the source of the irritation.

(f) **Cutaneous.**—Cold to the surface; disappearance of eruptions.

(g) **Pneumogastric.**—Pressure on the vagus (neuroma; enlarged glands; exostosis).

## SYMPTOMS.

**Onset.**—In some cases the onset is sudden, with no previous warning; in others, there are premonitory symptoms, such as flatulence, nervous irritability, hyperesthesia, languor and drowsiness, profuse diuresis.

**The Attack.**—In most cases the attack comes on at night; often after the patient has fallen asleep. He is awakened by a sense of oppression of the chest, and at once is in the midst of severe dyspnea.

**Respiration.**—The effort at breathing is slow and labored, the dyspnea being expiratory. There is loud wheezing and rattling in the chest. The position is one of orthopnea. The patient fixes his arms against a firm support and brings into action all the auxiliary muscles of respiration.

**Skin.**—The face, at first pale, becomes livid, turgid, and later cyanotic. There is general perspiration, with cold extremities.

**Heart.**—There is acute dilation of the right heart, with surging and tumultuous action. The pulse is small and feeble. There is marked epigastric pulsation; also congestion of the base of the neck, with distended veins.

**Curschmann's Spirals.**—The sago-like pellets in the sputum consist of a minute thread running through a tubular contorted body formed in oblique spiral lines. The spiral portion consists of strands and fibers woven and plaited so as to form a tube-like body. The method of formation of these bodies is variously explained. They are not characteristic of asthma; sometimes they are found in bronchitis and in lobular pneumonia. They are formed in the minute bronchi.

**Charcot-Leyden Crystals.**—The sputum also contains microscopic crystals; in shape, pointed octahedra. They are composed of phosphoric acid with an organic base. They are not peculiar to asthma, being also found in other diseases, but they are found more constantly and in greater number in asthma than in any other affection.

**Blood-cells.**—The sputum contains a large number of leucocytes.

**Urine.**—With an attack there is often diuresis. After an attack the urine is scanty, high-colored, and loaded with urates.

**Temperature.**—It often becomes subnormal.

**Head.**—There is often severe headache.

**Muscles.**—The auxiliary muscles of respiration are generally fixed and rigid. In the extremities there are sometimes muscular cramps.

**Duration.**—A single paroxysm may last for from two to six hours, when the patient will become free from dyspnea. In other cases there may be labored breathing for a day or two.

**The Interval.**—In cases of uncomplicated spasmodic asthma, between successive attacks the patient is perfectly free from all symptoms of the disease.

## PHYSICAL SIGNS.

The chest is distended as in fixed inspiratory position, and it does not contract on effort at expiration. The prolonged distention of the lungs with consequent fixed expansion of the chest is due to the fact that with each act of inspiration the quantity of residual air is gradually increased. With the inspiratory effort a small quantity can be drawn into the alveoli, and it is there retained owing to the fact that it meets with obstruction on effort at expiration. This causes the accumulation which leads to over-distention.

**Palpation.**—Rhonchial fremitus can be plainly felt.

**Percussion.**—The note is hyper-resonant, owing to over-distention of the lungs with air. The superficial cardiac dulness is diminished or obliterated. The lower margin of the lung is displaced downward and its position is not appreciably affected by effort at expiration.

**Auscultation.**—A great variety of dry râles—wheezing, whistling, sonorous—are heard in all parts of the chest. Vocal resonance is diminished. Toward the end of the attack the râles become moist. The valvular heart-sounds of the right side are accentuated; those of the left side are feeble or inaudible.

**Cough.**—There is sometimes cough, which the patient makes every effort to restrain. As the attack subsides there is increased cough with characteristic expectoration.

**Sputum.**—The characteristic sputum is a thick, tenacious, glairy mucus, containing sago-like grains, Curschmann's spirals. In old cases the sputum may be muco-purulent, or purulent.

**Complications.**

**Pulmonary.**—In old cases of asthma secondary emphysema results. In the bronchial form of asthma bronchitis is always an accompaniment.

**Cardiac.**—In long-continued cases the heart becomes secondarily affected. There is dilation of the right heart, with reflex venous congestion, which in the end may lead to dropsy.

## DIAGNOSIS.

The **characteristic features** of asthma are:—(a) The sudden onset of the paroxysm of dyspnea, and its sudden cessation; (b) the respirations are "labored," with the expiratory act prolonged (two or three times as long as the inspiratory); (c) the sputum is characteristic—it is "pearly," containing small masses like pearls of boiled sago-grains; (d) the **physical signs** are:—Increased resonance over the entire chest, with sibilant and sonorous râles; (e) in the intervals the patient is entirely free from signs of the disease; (f) there is absence of demonstrable disease of the lungs.

In children the paroxysms of dyspnea are often attended by rise of temperature, and diagnosis is often difficult. The attack simulates broncho-pneumonia.

**Differential Diagnosis.**

**Tracheal Stenosis.**—In tracheal stenosis the dyspnea is of the inspiratory type.

**Laryngeal Obstruction.**—The dyspnea is attended by increased movement of the larynx. There is stridor with the breathing.

**Cardiac Dyspnea.**—It comes on after exertion. The respiration is "sighing," or "panting." Respiration is quicker than in asthma; the expiratory act is not prolonged.

**Emphysema.**—In primary emphysema there is dyspnea which is worse on exertion. There are demonstrable changes in the heart and in the lungs.

**Uremic Dyspnea.**—The character of the dyspnea is very much like that of asthma. It must be differentiated from asthma by examination of the urine.

**Hysterical Dyspnea.**—This sometimes closely resembles asthma, but there is always the absence of the sibilant and sonorous râles, and usually the dyspnea is not expiratory.

**Aneurism.**—Pressure of an aneurism of the arch of the aorta on the trachea may cause dyspnea resembling asthma, but "tracheal tugging" is almost always present, and the dyspnea is inspiratory.

## PROGNOSIS.

The earlier in life the disease occurs the more favorable the prognosis. In children recovery sometimes takes place; also in early adult life if the intervals between the paroxysms are long. Recovery is favored by removal of the exciting cause, and especially by residence in a suitable climate. If much emphysema has already developed, or if the right heart has become affected, the prognosis is unfavorable. Death during a paroxysm never occurs; and, although the patient may live for years, life is always shortened.

## TREATMENT.

In treatment the aim should be:—(a) To relieve the paroxysm; (b) to remove the exciting cause; (c) to treat the complications and improve the general condition.

**Treatment of the Paroxysm.**

**Palliative Measures.**—It is best to avoid the use of palliative measures, if possible, and direct all treatment to the removal of the exciting cause and to the patient's general condition, but in old-established cases it will be found that palliative treatment is demanded by the patient, and must be resorted to by the physician if he continues in charge of the case. There is a long list to select from. What will relieve one patient will fail with another. An "old asthmatic" usually knows the agent that will give him greatest relief.

**Potassium-nitrate.**—Soak heavy blotting-paper in a saturated solution of **Potassium-nitrate (Nitre)**. When thoroughly soaked take out the blotting-paper and let it dry. Use a small square of this paper; fold it in the middle so that it will stand tent-like; set it in a saucer and ignite it with a match. Let the patient inhale through a paper cone the fumes of the burning paper. This relieves in some cases.

**Stramonium.**—The smoking of dried stramonium leaves in a pipe, or in cigarettes, gives relief in some cases.

**Amyl-nitrite.**—The inhalation of **Amyl-nitrite** gives prompt relief in some cases.

**Coffee.**—In some cases drinking a cup of strong coffee gives relief.

**Nitro-glycerin.**—A dose of **Nitro-glycerin** (gr. 1-100) sometimes gives relief, especially in "cardiac asthma."

**Alcohol.**—A dose of brandy in some cases will relieve the paroxysm.

**Ipecac.**—Repeated one-drop doses of the tincture of Ipecac relieves in some cases.

**Menthol.**—The inhalation of **Menthol** sometimes relieves; also the inhalation of **Camphor,** or **Oil-of-Pine.**

**Electricity.**—The faradic current applied along the course of the vagus in the neck sometimes relieves.

**Hydrotherapeutics.**—The use of the cold shower-bath is valuable in fortifying the system against attacks of asthma. The bath should be given daily, or every other day, in the intervals between attacks. The bath should be followed by brisk rubbing in order to get up reaction.

**Hydrocyanic acid.**—The inhalation of the vapor of dilute **Hydrocyanic acid** sometimes · relieves the paroxysm; about three drops of the acid in half a pint of hot water. The patient inhales through a paper cone the rising vapor.

**Methyl-Chloride.**—Attacks have sometimes been· arrested by a spray of **Methyl-Chloride** applied rapidly over the back.

**Morphine.**—This is mentioned only to advise against its use. It will often relieve, but it does the patient no permanent good, and may do harm. Do not use it.

**Cocaine.**—The snuffing of a solution of **Cocaine** is resorted to by some, but it is a pernicious habit and should be forbidden absolutely by the physician. Its use is not unattended by danger.

**Note.**—The use of palliatives is of no permanent service. They should be avoided. In time each one loses its effect. Asthmatics who rely upon them may be said never to make recovery. Their use inclines the patient to neglect other treatment; they also depress the action of the heart and produce more or less pulmonary congestion. In taking charge of a case the physician should ·stop their use, letting the patient suffer a few paroxysms, while the physician directs attention to a search for and removal of the exciting cause and to improving the general condition.

**Surgical measures.**—Give attention to the condition of the nose. Remove polypi, enchondroses, or exostoses. Sometimes such measures are promptly curative.

**Climate.**—There are few cases that are not benefited by change of climate. The special character of the climate cannot be predetermined; some do well in one locality, others in another. Very singularly, some even do best in the smoky atmosphere of a city; but, as a rule, most cases receive benefit by a change to a dry, elevated region. Some patients obtain relief only by residence at the sea-shore or on an ocean voyage.

**Diet.**—Almost all asthmatics are dyspeptics, and careful attention must be given to the condition of the stomach and of the digestive organs. Regulate the diet. Meals must be taken at regular intervals. A patient must never over-eat; the evening meal, especially, should be light. An over-filled stomach often excites an attack.

**Hygiene.**—The patient must live under the best hygienic conditions; give proper attention to air, exercise, clothing, breathing, and regular habits.

**The Patient.**—Each patient seeks the position which he finds most comfortable. If in bed, raise the head and shoulders high by firm support rather than by soft pillows. If not in bed, the best position is in an arm-chair, with rather a hard seat or firm cushion.

**Therapeutics.**

**Grindelia.** (Tr.).—This drug is often useful in spasmodic asthma with all the characteristic symptoms. Dose of mother-tincture, five drops. Repeat at twenty-minute intervals until relief is obtained.

**Tartar emetic.** (3x).—Bronchial asthma with much secretion and rattling of mucus in the chest.

**Moschus.** (2x).—In nervous asthma; sensation of constriction in the chest.

**Aconite.** (1x).—For recent cases and those excited by exposure to cold; also for old cases occurring in strong vigorous subjects. There is heat; restlessness; perspiration; full bounding pulse; palpitation of the heart.

**Byronia,** (1x).—Recent cases only, with catarrhal bronchitis, and stiching pains in the chest. **Dose:**—1x, frequently repeated, during the paroxysm.

**Ipecac.** (Tr.).—Co-existing bronchitis. The attack excited by dust and odors; the cough causes gagging and vomiting.

**Arsenicum.** (3x or 6x).—This is to be given in the intervals between the paroxysms, for the primary condition. But in such cases it may also be tried during the paroxysm, in frequently-repeated doses. Chronic cases, with bronchitis; also, cases with co-existing emphysema or heart disease. **Indications:**—Arsenicum is indicated by the severity of the attack; loud wheezing; the patient seems to be on the point of suffocating. This is accompanied by livid countenance, cold sweat, frequent, small pulse, palpitation. Great prostration after the attack. **Dose:**—Persist in its use.

**Nux vomica.**—To be used for uncomplicated "spasmodic" asthma; no bronchial lesion; attacks excited by irritation of the pneumogastric, especially through the stomach. Coated tongue; irritable stomach; constipation; after the attack, disturbance of digestive organs; slight nausea and flatulence. **Dose:**—Tr. During the attack give frequently-repeated doses. In the intervals persist in its use. Strychnin is equally efficacious: 3x trituration.

**Lobelia.** (Tr.)—"Nervous" asthma; vertigo; nausea; vomiting; sensation of emptiness in the stomach. **Dose:**—Tr. Use at the time of the attack.

**Sambucus.** (3x).—The asthma of children; nightly attacks of dyspnea, with profuse perspiration.

**Sulphur.** (6x).—For gouty or lithemic subjects.

**Cuprum ars.** (3x).—Chronic asthma of the bronchial variety; more or less dyspnea constantly, with severe paroxysms at intervals.

**Quin.-bisulph.**—In "nervous" asthma. Old cases, with complications of heart, lungs or stomach. **Dose:**—One-grain pill, three times daily.

# PULMONARY EMPHYSEMA.

**Definition.**—Pulmonary emphysema is a condition of the lungs in which there is over-distention of the alveoli, with atrophy of the alveolar walls.

**Varieties.**

**Compensatory Emphysema.**—In this form the emphysematous area is local. The dilatation of the restricted portion of the lung is secondary to contraction, or interference with functional activity, elsewhere. It occurs secondarily to pulmonary cirrhosis, or to contraction of a part of the lung following the destructive changes of phthisis.

**Acute Vesicular Emphysema.**—In this form there is no atrophy of the vesicular walls. It is an acute dilatation of the alveoli occurring in bronchitis of the smaller tubes; also sometimes in cardiac asthma and angina pectoris, due to the strong inspiratory efforts made when the patient is suffering from these diseases.

**Interstitial Emphysema.**—This form has nothing in common with substantive pulmonary emphysema. (See p. 54.) Interstitial emphysema consists of the entrance of air into the connective-tissue spaces of the lung. The air appears as rows of beads in the substance of the lung and beneath the pleura. The air gains entrance through wounds of the lung or from rupture of air-vesicles following overstrain and violent coughing.

**Small-lunged Emphysema** (Senile atrophy of the lungs).—This is an atrophic change incident to advanced age, and is shared in by the lungs equally with other organs of the body. The slight degree of emphysema occurring in this condition is probably induced by the cough of a chronic bronchial catarrh.

**Large-lunged Emphysema** (Substantive emphysema). —This is the common form of the affection which is generally indicated when the term **Pulmonary emphysema** is used, and it is the form which alone will be considered in the following description of pulmonary emphysema.

# HYPERTROPHIC EMPHYSEMA.

**Synonyms.**—"Large-lunged emphysema;" substantive emphysema; idiopathic emphysema.

**Definition.**—Substantive emphysema, or idiopathic emphysema, is marked by enlargement of the lungs, with distention of the alveoli and atrophy of the alveolar walls; it is attended by imperfect aëration of the blood, marked dyspnea, and enlargement of the chest.

**Pathogeny.**—The force which acts to produce the distention of the alveoli has been variously explained, but the essential nature of the condition is over-distention of the alveoli with permanent loss of elasticity of the lung tissue. The doctrine is that lung tissue which yields to the persistently high alveolar tension is congenitally weak, or has become weakened as the result of disease. The nature of the congenital pulmonary weakness is believed to be a defect in the development of the elastic-tissue fibers of the lungs.

## ETIOLOGY.

**Age.**—It occurs in those of all ages. Marked cases are seen even in young children.

**Sex.**—Men are more often affected than women, for reasons connected with occupation.

**Heredity.**—Hereditary influence can be traced in a certain proportion of cases.

**Occupation.**—It occurs especially in those whose occupation calls for severe muscular effort, especially if performed with the lungs distended—such as glass-blowers, players on wind-instruments, and those who lift heavy weights. Those who work in a dust-laden atmosphere are affected as a result of the chronic bronchitis which such occupation induces.

**Diseases.**—It occurs secondarily in diseases characterized by severe dyspnea or persistent and severe cough, such as asthma, chronic bronchitis, whooping-cough, and the like. In children it may occur secondarily to asthmatic attacks due to adenoid vegetations.

## PATHOLOGY.

**Primary Lesion.**—The first change is dilatation of the alveoli, which are forcibly distended by air-pressure. This action puts the cells of the alveoli upon the stretch, and causes a diminution of the local blood-supply. As a result the alveolar epithelium undergoes fatty degeneration. The nuclei of the endothelial cells, as well as the connective-tissue cells, undergo division, granular degeneration, and waste. There results atrophy and destruction of the tissues, and in this way the vesicular wall is perforated with holes, and many adjacent lobules coalesce, becoming fused into round spaces. The process is accompanied by great destruction of the pulmonary capillaries.

## MÓRBID ANATOMY.

**The Lungs.**—When the thorax is opened the lungs are found to be distended, and even bulging out of the chest cavity. The apices fill the supra-clavicular region. The anterior margins are in contact. The precordial area is covered by the distended auricular process of the left upper lobe. The diaphragm is depressed.

**Color.**—The lung is pale-gray in color, marked by dots of black pigment.

**Consistence.**—The substance of the lung is dry and parchment-like in feeling. It is soft and non-crepitant, and when pressed a deep pit forms and remains.

**Distended Alveoli.**—The dilated air-vesicles and lobules vary in size, from those which are minute to those which by the coalescence of adjacent lobules form dilations from the size of a pea or a bean up to the size of an olive or of a walnut. In these larger ones the remains of the atrophied septa may be found as withered threads. Immediately underneath the pleura there are appearances as of a very thin froth, due to the presence of minute air-bubbles. The distended lobules are especially numerous along the margins of the lungs, forming rounded bullæ. Especially are the large bullæ found in the portion of the lung which occupies the hollow beside the spine.

**Section.**—On section the lung is dry and bloodless. Some edema may be present at the base.

**Pulmonary Artery.**—In advanced cases atheroma of the pulmonary artery is a common condition.

**Associated Lesions.**

**Lungs.**—Bronchitis:—A greater or less degree of bronchitis is always associated with the emphysema. **Phthisis:**—In some lungs areas of fibroid phthisis are present.

**Bronchi.**—Small bronchial tubes are often found obliterated, forming thin fibrous bands in large emphysematous bullæ. Rarely, limited lung collapse may be present, but this is by no means an essential accompaniment of emphysema.

**Heart.**—Displacement:—The heart is usually displaced; its axis is more nearly horizontal and the apex is carried to the left and downwards. **Right ventricle:** —From the obstruction to the pulmonary circulation the right ventricle becomes hypertrophied, with secondary dilation, followed by relative tricuspid incompetence. Following this there is dilation of the right auricle and systemic venous congestion. **Myocardium:** —There is usually fatty degeneration of the heart-muscle, due to impaired nutrition from obstruction to the return of blood by the coronary veins.

**Liver.**—The liver is enlarged, of the "nutmeg" character, from chronic venous congestion.

**Kidneys.**—The kidneys may be enlarged and cyanotic, or granular, from chronic interstitial nephritis.

**Abdominal Organs.**—There are evidences of venous congestion of all the abdominal organs, from portal stasis.

### SYMPTOMS.

**Dyspnea.**—This is the most constant and characteristic symptom. At first it is slight, occurring only on exertion. It becomes more urgent with the development of the disease. Later, it is constant, and much increased by any related causes, such as flatulent distention of the stomach, stooping, exertion, or the like. Every recurrent attack of bronchitis greatly increases the dyspnea, creating paroxysms of "bronchial asthma."

**Cyanosis.**—Evidences of interference with the proper aëration of the blood are common in advanced cases, even while the patient is still somewhat active. This condition is rare in any other disease.

**Cough.**—Cough is a common accompanying symptom. It usually occurs in paroxysms and is characteristically loud, hoarse and wheezy. It is especially troublesome in cold, damp weather.

**Expectoration.**—If bronchitis is present there may be profuse expectoration; otherwise there is but a slight quantity of mucus raised, the small mass being called "pearly."

**Hemoptysis.**—This is rare. When it occurs the amount of blood is usually small, though, rarely, it may be large and the attack prove fatal. It is due to rupture of a branch of the pulmonary artery from the associated atheroma.

**Digestive Sphere.**—There are symptoms of dyspepsia, impaired assimilation, flatulent distention of the stomach and intestines, and constipation, all due to portal congestion.

**Pulse.**—It is small and weak, owing to the poorly filled arteries.

**Head.**—There is often headache and drowsiness, from deficient aëration of the blood.

**Veins.**—There are signs of general venous stasis, and, late in the disease, edema and dropsy.

**Fingers.**—Late, there is clubbing of the fingers, and sometimes of the toes.

**Physiognomy.**—Early, the face is full, lips thick, and the mucous surface congested. Late, there is a drawn and careworn expression, with a bluish tint of the skin.

## PHYSICAL SIGNS.

**Inspection.—The Thorax:**—The general tendency is for the chest to become "barrel-shaped" or rounded in form; the antero-posterior diameter is much increased. The angle-of-Louis is prominent; the ribs become more horizontal; there is bulging of the sternum and of the infra-clavicular and mammary regions; the shoulders are elevated and brought forward; the spine is curved. The auxiliary muscles of respiration are hypertrophied and prominent. There is a line of venules girdling the body corresponding to the attachment of the diaphragm. In breathing, the inspiratory movements are seen to be restricted and the expiratory act is much prolonged.

**Palpation.**—Vocal fremitus is diminished. The cardiac impulse is feeble or absent, the edge being covered by a cushion of lung. The apex beat is imperceptible, or felt to the left and downward. There is epigastric impulse.

**Percussion.**—The percussion note is hyper-resonant, sometimes tympanitic. It varies but slightly between inspiration and expiration. The lower border of the lung is depressed one or two inches below the usual position on full inspiration. The area of cardiac dulness is obliterated.

**Auscultation.—Inspiration:**—The murmur is faint and feeble, and the act is short. **Expiration:**—The sound is prolonged and harsh. **Rales.**—According to the degree of accompanying bronchitis there may be sibilant or sonorous, or fine or coarse mucous râles. The respiratory sounds are exaggerated and harsh in quality. **Heart.**—The heart-sounds are feeble, and there is apex displacement. In cases of long standing there are signs of tricuspid incompetence.

## DIAGNOSIS.

In well-marked cases the diagnosis is not difficult. The condition may be masked by the accompanying bronchitis, broncho-pneumonia, or cirrhotic changes in the lung.

### Differential Diagnosis.

**Pneumothorax.**—In pneumothorax the affection is unilateral. There is absence of motion of the affected side. The note on percussion is amphoric. Pneumothorax develops more or less suddenly.

## PROGNOSIS.

When emphysema is once established the tendency is to become progressive; the rate at which it does so depends upon the continuance of the exciting cause, which, in most cases, is chronic bronchitis. In its chronic form it is of a serious nature. The patient may live for years, but is constantly exposed to danger from intercurrent diseases. In the absence of intercurrent affections the important factor in determining the probable duration of life is the effect upon the heart and circulation. The degree of dyspnea and of venous stasis, as shown by turgescence of the veins of the neck, are important elements to be considered. Renal complications are especially unfavorable. In uncomplicated cases death is due to heart-failure, with preceding dropsy and other evidences of cardiac insufficiency.

## TREATMENT.

**Prophylaxis.**—Every effort must be made to protect the patient from intercurrent diseases of the lungs. Every such attack aggravates the primary condition, and some forms, as pneumonia, may be rapidly fatal.

**Climate.**—During inclement seasons the patient should when possible, seek a climate which is equable, warm, dry and free from dust and winds. Those who are unable to make such changes must avoid fog, damp, and cold winds.

**Exercise.**—Straining, lifting, and any overwork must be rigidly avoided. Moderate exercise with an abundance of fresh air must be prescribed. Carefully avoid everything which would increase the dyspnea.

**Diet.**—These patients are often dyspeptic; the diet

requires careful regulation. Let the food be very **digesti-ble**, but nutritious in quality. Avoid sugars and starches. Prohibit alcohol and tobacco.

**Aero-therapeutics.**—The best results in the treatment of this disease by aëro-therapeutics have been obtained by the systematic use of the compressed-air bath.

**Medicinal.**—The medicinal agents to be used are such as are indicated for the complications and attendant conditions, rather than for the specific lung condition. Therefore the range of remedies will be those used for bronchitis, asthma, dyspepsia, and for weak heart, when this condition supervenes in the later stages.

**Weak Heart.**—In the late stages when the weak heart demands stimulant treatment, as in other conditions of the kind, use **Strychnin** (2x): **Sparteine sulph.** (1x); **Agaricine** (1x).

**Antimonium ars.** (2x).—Advanced stages, with excessive dyspnea, and severe paroxysmal cough; asthmatic attacks; also for the accompanying dyspeptic symptoms, when this condition is prominent.

**Antimonium tart.** (2x).—Moist cough; digestive disorders.

**Calcarea carb.** (6x).—Chronic bronchitis in fat subjects; much perspiration; in women, profuse menstruation.

**Calcarea phos.** (2x).—In advanced life, subjects of arterio-sclerosis.

**Phosphorus.** 2x).—Subjects of fatty **degeneration** of tissues.

**Lycopodium.** (6x).—Flatulent dyspepsia; lithemia.

**Aurum mur.** (3x).—In nervous subjects, with urine of low specific gravity; arterio-sclerosis.

**Glonoin.** (2x).—Asthmatic attacks, with high arterial tension.

## INTERSTITIAL EMPHYSEMA.

**Synonym.**—Interlobular emphysema.

**Definition.**—The presence of air in the connective-tissue of the lung.

**Nature.**—This condition has nothing in common with substantive emphysema. There is no dilation of the alveoli as in the other form. It is simply the presence of air in the connective-tissue spaces of the lung, as air may gain entrance to the connective-tissue of any organ or tissue of the body.

**Etiology.**—The air gains entrance through a wound of the lung or rupture of the air-vesicles as a result of overstrain or violent cough; also following tracheotomy in laryngeal diphtheria, or other similar conditions.

**Pathology.**—The conditions attending and supervening upon interstitial emphysema are chiefly—general emphysema, pneumothorax, and pulmonary collapse.

**Symptoms.**—Sudden, urgent dyspnea is the characteristic symptom. If pneumothorax occurs the dyspnea is extreme. Double pneumothorax is always rapidly fatal.

**Treatment.**—No direct treatment can be addressed to the lung condition. The most that can be done is to keep the patient quiet and try to prevent paroxysms of cough.

## BRONCHIECTASIS.

**Synonym.**—Dilation of the bronchi.

**Definition.**—Bronchiectasis is a chronic disease affecting the bronchial tubes in which their lumen is widened, forming cavities.

### ETIOLOGY.

The condition is scarcely ever primary. It occurs as a **secondary condition** after acute or chronic bronchitis, asthma, broncho-pneumonia, stenosis of the bronchi (syphilitic), cirrhosis of the lung, pleurisy, empyema, spinal curvature, and foreign bodies in the bronchi.

### MORBID ANATOMY.

**Varieties.**

(a) **Cylindrical.**—In the cylindrical form the bronchus is uniformly enlarged. When the enlargement tapers towards its extremities it is terms **fusiform.** Usually the cylindrical enlargement is not uniform in diameter. At intervals there are constrictions. The constricting bands are formed by a new growth of fibrous tissue.

(b) **Saccular.**—In this form the enlargement consists of a large number of rounded smooth-walled saccules, or globular-shaped cavities. In the wall is a small opening marking the site of the entering portion of the bronchus. Number and size of the saccules:—There may be many saccules—the size of an olive, the size of an egg, or larger—distributed throughout the lungs, separated by areas of normal lung tissue; or, an entire lobe may be transformed into a single large saccule. Rarely, the whole lung is so changed.

**Extent and Location.**—The dilation may affect but one lung, or in other cases both lungs. When secondary to bronchitis, broncho-pneumonia, or phthisis both lungs are affected. When secondary to pleural effusion, lobar pneumonia, foreign body, or stenosis of the bronchus, but one lung is primarily affected.

## PATHOLOGICAL ANATOMY.

**Mucous Membrane.—Acute stage.**—The mucous membrane in recent cases is swollen, reddened, showing its relation to acute inflammation. **Chronic stage.**—In chronic cases the mucous membrane is grayish and granular. The fibrous tissues of the bronchial walls are thickened, though in some cases the wall has become much thinned.

**Secretions.**—The dilated tubes may be empty, or may contain:—(a) A clear, gelatinous-like mucus; (b) a dirty-gray, stringy, curdy, inspissated mass of very foul odor.

**The Lung Tissue.**—The lung tissue adjacent to the dilation may be:—(a) healthy; (b) emphysematous; (c) collapsed; (d) edematous; (e) fibroid.

**Associated Lesions.**—With the bronchiectasis there may be—(a) general bronchitis; (b) pleuritic adhesions.

**Sequels.**—Dilation of the bronchus may result in—(a) Perforation of the pleura and pneumothorax; (b) penetration of the chest-wall secondary to pleuritic adhesion; (c) abscess of the chest-wall; (d) perforation into the cellular tissue of the mediastinum; (e) lardaceous disease following long-continued profuse purulent discharge.

## SYMPTOMS.

The symptoms will vary according to the nature of the primary disease to which the bronchiectasis is secondary, but there are certain symptoms common to all forms.

**Cough.**—This is a common symptom. The cough occurs in prolonged paroxysms, at first without result, but finally the patient expectorates a large quantity of very offensive greenish-yellow secretion. In the intervals between the paroxysms the patient is usually free from cough. The paroxysms occur usually on lying down at night and on rising in the morning. The act of expectoration is sometimes easy and sometimes difficult; the latter when there is advanced emphysema, stenosis of the bronchus, or marked induration of the lung.

**The Sputum.**

**Quantity.**—It is usually abundant; from 15 to 30 ounces daily.

**Consistency.**—Usually it is diffluent; rarely it is nummulated. On standing in a containing vessel. it settles into two or three strata; the **upper,** thin, brownish, frothy; the **middle,** a greenish fluid; the **lower,** a mass of purulent and granular matter.

**Color.** The color is usually greenish-yellow.

**Odor.**—It is unusually foul and fetid. The odor also taints the patient's breath.

**Elements.**—The sputum contains pus corpuscles, oil globules, fatty crystals, granular detritus, broken down connective-tissue, cholesterin crystals, Deitrich's plugs, sarcinæ, and numerous bacteria.

**Reaction.**—The reaction may be alkaline or acid; the latter from the presence of lactic, butyric, or acetic acids.

**Hemoptysis.**—The sputum sometimes contains blood, the quantity varying from a mere trace to large quantities. In rare cases the hemoptysis proves fatal. It is due to the ulcerative process in the bronchial wall extending to a branch of the pulmonary artery.

**Dyspnea.**—In the early stages there is but little dyspnea except upon exertion. Later, when much pulmonary tissue is destroyed, dyspnea is a constant symptom.

**Fever.**—Many cases run an apyrexial course. The temperature rises if secretion is retained and imprisoned.

**Pain.**—When pain is present it is due to inflammation of the overlying pleura.

**The Fingers.**—Clubbing of the fingers is sometimes a marked feature in old cases.

**Diarrhea.**—In advanced stages diarrhea may occur, either from septic infection or from lardaceous disease of the intestines.

## PHYSICAL SIGNS.

**Physical Signs,** in the main, will depend upon the character of the primary disease.

**Inspection.**—According to the form of the primary lung-affection the chest may be emphysematous, or there may be retraction, with diminished mobility.

**Palpation.**—Tactile fremitus is increased in cases accompanied by fibrosis.

**Percussion.**—The percussion sound is hyper-resonant when there is accompanying emphysema, or over a portion of the lung which has been converted into a mass of saccules. In this case the note may be tympanitic, or, if the saccules are large amphoric. There is dulness if there is much fibrosis. The characteristic signs are found most frequently posteriorly, at and below the roots of the lungs.

**Auscultation.**—On auscultation the sounds are many and varied, being chiefly those indicative of the presence of cavities. According to the size, shape, and contents of the cavities the sound may be tubular, cavernous, or amphoric. There will be also various moist râles, varying from fine and coarse mucous, to bubbling, and even gurgling. There is harsh vocal resonance and sometimes bronchophony or pectoriloquy. The veiled puff of Skoda is often heard.

## DIAGNOSIS.

**Diagnostic Symptom.**—The characteristic sign of the existence of bronchiectásis is the sudden expectoration of a large quantity of muco-purulent matter, usually very fetid, which is followed by the discovery of cavernous breathing over some part of the lung, and the disappearance of this sign as the cavity is refilled with secretion.

**Differential Diagnosis.**

**Fetid Bronchitis.**—The diagnosis must depend chiefly on the character of the expectoration, the mode of its evacuation, and the absence of signs of a cavity in the lung.

**Phthisis.**—Examination of the sputum with the finding of bacilli must aid in the diagnosis, though tuberculosis may be engrafted upon bronchiectasis. Also in phthisis fragments of pulmonary tissue will usually be found in the sputum when the disease has created such ravages as to suggest bronchiectasis.

**Limited Empyema.**—Dependence must be placed chiefly upon the character of the sputum. In empyema it consists chiefly of pus without the admixture of mucus, detritus, fibrinous casts and fatty crystals occurring in the secretion of bronchiectasis.

**Other Conditions.**—Other pulmonary conditions which must be differentiated from bronchiectasis are gangrene, carcinoma, carcinomatous ulceration, and syphilitic ulceration. The distinction is usually not difficult to make.

## PROGNOSIS.

The disease is almost always chronic. When it occurs as a sequel of measles, or whooping-cough in children, if the degree of dilation is moderate, recovery sometimes takes place.

## COMPLICATIONS.

The complications are many and various. There may be hemoptysis; metastatic abscess; broncho-pneumonia; pulmonary gangrene; empyema and pneumothorax; pulmonary fibrosis; cardiac and renal disease.

## TREATMENT.

Treatment must be directed to limiting the accompanying bronchitis and to the inhalation or injection of antiseptic preparations.

**Medicinal.**—The medicines that have been most used are **Silicea** (6x), **Stannum** (2x), and **Hepar sulph.** (in material doses).

**Inhalation.**—Inhalations and sprays of **Carbolic acid** and **Kali permang.** may be used.

**Injections.**—A method of treatment by intra-tracheal injection has given the most decided results. The preparation consists of **Menthol**, 10 parts; **Guaiacol**, 2 parts; **Olive oil**, 88 parts. One dram is injected twice daily. For this purpose a specially designed syringe is used. In giving the injection the patient grasps and holds the tongue, which is thrust forward. The nozzle of the syringe is carried back until the tongue and epiglottis are passed. The point of the syringe is then directed downwards and slightly forwards, and it must be made to pass below the larynx and into the trachea. The injection is then rapidly administered and the instrument quickly withdrawn.

**General Measures.**—The patient should frequently practice what is called "down-hill cough," that is, hanging the head dependent from the edge of a bed or couch so as to drain the cavities of the lung by gravity.

# SECTION II.

## PNEUMONIC FEVER.

**Name.**—From the Greek—**Pneuma**, air; **Pneo**, breathe.

**Synonyms.**—Pneumonia; Pneumonitis; Lobar pneumonia; Fibrinous pneumonia; Croupous pneumonia; "Lung-fever."

**Definition.**—Pneumonic fever is an acute, specific, infectious, self-limited disease, due to infection by the **micrococcus pneumoniae** (diplococcus lanceolatus) (Fraenkel). It has for its anatomical lesion inflammation of the vesicular structure of the lungs, with fibrinous exudation into the alveoli, the alveolar passages, and sometimes the larger bronchi; it is marked by chill, fever, headache, pleuritic pain, cough and characteristic "rusty" sputum. The blood shows hyper-leucocytosis.

**Primary Pneumonia.**—Pneumonic fever, when idiopathic, is called, also, primary pneumonia; **frank pneumonia.** It must be distinguished from **Secondary pneumonia.** Primary fibrinous pneumonia is an idiopathic and independent affection.

**Secondary Pneumonia.**—This develops, secondarily, in the course of acute infectious diseases—enteric fever, measles, scarlatina, etc.; also in the terminal stages of chronic exhausting diseases—diabetes, Bright's, paralysis, etc.

**Classification.**—Pneumonic fever, in the past, has been considered to be a disease of the lungs, and it has been so classified. But since it is now known to be due to general infection, constituting a true septicemia, it prop-

erly belongs among the acute infectious diseases, and
the preferable term is pneumonic fever. Owing, however, to the fact that its most characteristic lesion is in
the lungs, the old classification is still retained.

**Varieties:**—(Old nomenclature.)

I.   **Fibrinous Pneumonia** (Pneumonic Fever).

II.  **Broncho-Pneumonia** (Catarrhal Pneumonia; Capillary Bronchitis).

III. **Interstitial Pneumonia** (Cirrhosis of the lung;
Fibroid induration of the lung; Pulmonary fibrosis).

**Arbitrary sub-varieties:**—

"**Typhoid Pneumonia.**"—Attended by marked prostration and low delirium.

"**Bilious Pneumonia.**"—Accompanied by congestion of
the liver and jaundice.

"**Pleuro-Pneumonia.**"—Accompanied by pleurisy with
effusion.

**History.**—B. C.   Hippocrates affected to diagnosticate
the seat of this and allied diseases by the coating on the
tongue.

**1820.**—As late as this time no distinction was made
between pleurisy and pneumonia. The most absurd
theories prevailed. Brosieri taught that—"The first
changes are in the blood, which is converted into a gela-
tinous mucus."

**1836.**—Laennec first cleared up the diagnosis of diseases of the chest, and made it possible to differentiate
this affection.

**1884.**—Fraenkel described the diplococcus pneumoniæ, and demonstrated its relation to the disease.

## ETIOLOGY.

**Bacteriology.**—Pneumonic fever is of bacterial origin,
due to infection by the diplococcus pneumoniæ (micrococcus lanceolatus) (Fraenkel, 1884,) an oval-shaped
diplococcus with lancet-shaped links. The diplococcus
is readily found in ninety per cent of all cases; more
exact methods reveal its presence in all cases. (The

time of examination is important.) It is found in the hepatized portion of the lung, from which pure cultures may be made.

Experimentally, in lower animals, primary fibrinous pneumonia may be induced by injecting the diplococcus directly into the trachea.

The diplococci are found in other organs (spleen, liver, pleura, pericardium, endocardium, meninges) and also in the blood, thus constituting a true septicemia.

### Predisposing Causes.

**Prevalence.**—Pneumonic fever constitutes three per cent of all diseases of the globe. In Europe and America, 6.4 per cent. Hospital admissions are 2 to 3 per cent.

**Geography.**—It occurs in all countries and climates, being, however, most common in temperate regions.

**Altitude.**—Altitude predisposes (Leadville, etc.).

**Season.**—Winter and spring, two-thirds of all cases; summer and autumn, one-third.

**Out-Door Life.**—Lessens predisposition.

**Constitution.**—The cachectic are more frequently attacked than the robust. A strong constitution is protective.

**Sex.**—Men suffer from its attacks in greater number than women (but the disparity is not so great as generally stated).

**Age.**—It occurs at all periods of life. In infants and the aged its symptoms are often masked. Those in the prime of life are not especially predisposed.

**One Attack.**—Predisposes. Third, fourth, fifth and sixth attacks have been known.

**Lower Animals.**—True pneumonia is of frequent occurrence in the lower animals.

**Hygiene.**—Unsanitary surroundings, by lowering the vital energy, predispose.

**Traumatism.**—Injury to the chest may lower the vitality of the parts so as to favor the development of the disease.

**Dust.**—Inhalation of dust is not of itself an exciting cause.

**Endemic.**—In tenements, and in localities where the conditions are such as to favor predisposition, there may be endemic appearance of the disease.

**Epidemic.**—At times so many cases occur as to constitute an epidemic, chiefly related to weather and climatic influences.

**Alcoholism.**—Alcoholics are especially predisposed to pneumonic fever.

**"Cold."**—"Taking cold" acts only as a predisposing cause, rendering the system susceptible to development of the disease on invasion of the lungs by the specific cause.

**Rate.**—Pneumonic fever constitutes six and six-tenths (6.6) per cent of the total mortality (secondary pneumonia not included). In recent years, attending the great increase in and the more crowded condition of urban population, the percentage of deaths from pneumonic fever in all countries is steadily increasing.

**Immunity.**—The patient's blood contains a pneumotoxin and an anti-pneumotoxin; blood-serum containing the latter injected into the healthy subject produces a condition of immunity (Klemperer).

## PATHOLOGY.

**Stages, Three.**

  I. **Engorgement** (Congestion) ;
  II. **Red Hepatization** (Consolidation) ;
  III. **Resolution** (Gray Hepatization).

I. **Engorgement.**—There is increase of blood to the part; the vessels are dilated. On the alveolar walls the vessels are tortuous; they project, and narrow the alveolus. The epithelial cells swell, and desquamate; from the dilated vessels a viscid, fluid, coagulable lymph exudes; it is rich in albumin. Red and white blood-corpuscles migrate (sometimes there is extravasation of blood).

**Morbid Anatomy.**—The lung is increased in size; intensely red; floats on water, since it still contains a small amount of air. It is fragile and easily torn; on pressure of a cut section a bloody, viscid fluid exudes, which, early, contains some small air-bubbles.

II. **Red Hepatization.** (Consolidation).

The lymph thrown out coagulates; the alveoli are filled with fibrillated fibrin, enclosing red blood-corpuscles, leucocytes and large, nucleated cells—changed epithelium. The bronchioles and the small bronchi, up to those one-fifth inch in diameter, are filled with fibrinous plugs. The proportion of these elements varies in different cases. The blood-vessels are still hyperemic, and distended with closely-packed corpuscles. The pleura is inflamed. The color (red) is due to the abundance of red blood-corpuscles, both in the distended vessels and in the exudate. The diplococci are now most numerous.

**Morbid Anatomy.**—**Consistency:**—The lung is firm and solid; it sinks in water; it is easily torn; it does not crepitate. **Color:**—It is dark, brownish-red; it may be uniformly red, or mottled, the pale inter-lobular tissue and the bronchial and pulmonary vessels appearing in streaks, giving an arborescent appearance. **Volume:**—The organ is enlarged, the surface showing imprints of the ribs. **Section:**—The cut surface is granular, due to the appearance of minute plugs of fibrin' expressed from the cut openings of bronchioles. **Pleura:**—The surface is covered with fibrin. **Micro-organisms:**—Diplococci are always present, and sometimes staphylococci and streptococci.

III. **Resolution.** (Gray Hepatization).

The red blood corpuscles disintegrate, the hematin disorganizes; the elements in the bronchioles and alveoli (corpuscles, leucocytes, fibrin) undergo granular and fatty degeneration, and are emulsified in lymph now thrown out by the blood. At the termination of the process the affected portion of the lung is filled with a yellowish fluid, rich in leucocytes, which is removed partly by expectoration, but mostly by absorption by the lymphatics.

**Morbid Anatomy.—Consistency:**—Early, much the same as in the preceding stage; later, as the contents liquefy, the lung becomes soft and friable, and exudes a yellowish, opaque, viscid fluid. **Color:**—Early, grayish; later, yellowish, or mottled, resembling granite; the change in color is due to destruction of red blood corpuscles, fatty degeneration of the various elements, and to the greatly increased number of leucocytes.

The processes characteristic of the several stages are not sharply defined, but merge into one another.

**Exudation.**

**Source.**—The exudation is from the blood—its fibrin and formed elements, the red corpuscles, the leucocytes. There is an alteration in the walls of the blood-vessels, as a part of the inflammatory process, permitting their passage (Cohnheim). The coagulable lymph has the same source.

**Color.**—Grayish-yellow—is favored by the more abundant transudation of the leucocytes. The red have no power of locomotion, hence they remain near the seat of transudation, while the white crowd past them, and fill all the vesicles.

**The vessels** remain pervious, however much compressed. They never become obliterated. When the vessels are released from pressure the blood-current resumes its flow. The liquefaction of the previously solid fibrinous mass releases the pressure on the vessels, and thus the circulation is restored.

When resolution takes place the liquefied contents of the affected portion of the lung are removed, partly by expectoration, but mostly by absorption, through the medium of the lymphatics. New epithelial cells are formed, and cover the denuded walls of the alveoli; the circulation is re-established, and the entire lung-structure regains its integrity.

**Other Modes of Termination.**

**Purulent Infiltration.**—The inter-alveolar tissue and the air-cells become filled with pus, rendering the lung-stroma soft and friable.

**Abscess.**—Local abscess is very rare in pneumonic fever. It follows purulent infiltration. It occurs only in the cachectic. The abscess may become encapsulated, or open into a bronchus, or into the pleura.

**Gangrene**—Necrosis and gangrene occur in rare instances.

**Induration.**—Induration of the lung occurs as a sequel in a small number of cases.

**Other Forms.**

**Central Pneumonia.**—In central pneumonia the pulmonary lesion is confined to the region of the hilus, never reaching the surface of the lung. This variety is unattended by pain, and the diagnosis is often obscure. Examination of the blood, revealing a condition of leucocytosis, will aid in establishing the diagnosis, if other symptoms point to the existence of the disease.

**Migratory Pneumonia.**—This term is applied to cases in which new areas of lung tissue, adjacent to that already affected, are successively invaded. Sometimes the newly invaded areas may be remote from those already affected.

## MORBID ANATOMY.

**Bronchial Glands.**—The bronchial glands are congested and swollen; red and soft.

**Bronchi.**—The bronchi show more or less catarrhal inflammation; the mucous membrane is red and swollen—later, paler. The terminal tubes contain exudation.

**Heart.**—The right heart is distended with blood, and filled with coagula; the left is empty.

**Muscles.**—They are flaccid, brittle and pale; the fibres are granular; some individual fibres show fatty degeneration.

**Liver.**—It is enlarged—gorged with blood, and the cells are cloudy.

**Spleen.**—It is enlarged and flaccid.

**Rigor Mortis.**—It is well marked.

**Duration of Stages** (approximate):

    I.   Engorgement—one to two days.

    II.  Hepatization—four to eight days.

    III. Resolution—in favorable cases, two or three days. It may be two weeks, or, in some cases, much longer.

**Early Resolution.**—In the first stage the process may be arrested, and the congestion subside. Even in the second stage it is thought that arrest of the process may occur.

**Side Affected:**

    The right lung, in 60 per cent. of cases.

    The left lung, in 24 per cent. of cases.

    Both lungs, in 16 per cent. of cases.

**Lobe affected,** in order of frequency:—

    1.  Lower lobe of the right lung.

    2.  Lower lobe of the left lung.

    3.  Middle lobe of the right lung.

    4.  Upper lobe of the right lung.

    5.  Upper lobe of the left lung.

Location of the lesion: It begins at the hilus and extends to the surface. Central pneumonia is rare.

## PHYSICAL SIGNS.

**First Stage.**—Engorgement.

**Inspection.**—There is restricted motion of the affected side; costal breathing is the type in double pneumonia; tension of sterno-cleido-mastoid and the upper portion of the trapezius.

**Palpation.**—Vocal fremitus is pronounced according to the degree of congestion.

**Percussion.**—The lung tissue still contains air, hence the note is little changed from normal; it may be higher pitched, unaltered by opening and closing the mouth. Towards the end of this stage there is slight dulness.

**Auscultation.**—The Respiratory murmur is feeble; in quality broncho-vesicular; over the unaffected portion of the lung the murmur is exaggerated; there are subcrepitant râles if there is an associated bronchitis; crepitant râles (crepitatio indux).

### Second Stage.—Consolidation.

Inspection.—There is no expansion of the affected region on inspiration; there is increased expansion of the opposite side; the skin is cyanotic.

Palpation.—Vocal fremitus is markedly increased, except in central pneumonia, or when there is pleuritic effusion; "palpatory percussion" gives a distinct sense of resistance, especially in children.

Percussion.—There is marked dulness over the consolidated lung; there is change of pitch with opening or closing the mouth; there is sense of resistance to the finger; there is no flatness unless pleurisy with effusion accompanies; in basic pneumonia, Skoda's sign appears in the infraclavicular region. Caution.—In consolidation of the left lower lobe, beware of being misled by sounds coming from the stomach and intestines.

Auscultation.—There is loud, tubular breathing; bronchophony (have the patient say "999" as loud as possible); there is egophony if there is slight pleuritic effusion. If a large bronchus is obstructed, the tubular breathing may be temporarily absent, but coughing often dislodges the accumulation and restores the sound. Pleural friction-rub sometimes is heard; there are sub-crepitant râles if bronchitis accompanies. It is not true that the crepitant râles are always absent in this stage; they may be present in the region adjacent to the solidified portion of lung.

### Third Stage.—Resolution.

Inspection.—There is a gradual return of expansive motion.

Palpation.—There is gradual disappearance of fremitus.

Percussion.—There is gradual loss of dulness, generally in patches; some dulness in spots; dulness often lingers late in convalescence.

**Auscultation.**—Bronchial breathing is succeeded by broncho-vesicular, and later by normal respiratory murmur. Crepitant râles **(crepitatio redux)** again appear; also subcrepitant râles. In purulent infiltration there are coarse and gurgling râles. The crepitant râle has been known to persist three weeks after defervescence, but it generally disappears in one week.

## GENERAL SYMPTOMS.

The characteristic lesion is the only constant feature. The other symptoms vary greatly. The pathognomonic signs are: (1) The lung lesion, as demonstrated by physical diagnosis. (2) The disproportion between the frequency of the respiration and of the pulse.

Errors in diagnosis are most commonly made in children and in the aged.

### Individual Symptoms.

**Onset.**—Usually there are no premonitory symptoms. The attack begins with sudden—

**Chill.**—The patient shivers; the teeth chatter; the skin is blue and cold; there is oppression of the chest; difficult respiration; cough, without expectoration; soon, the

**Reaction.**—Flushed face; headache; vertigo; the alæ nasi work; anxious expression; pain in the side; rapid, full pulse; intense thirst; hot and dry skin. In a few hours the disease is at its height.

**Fever.**—The temperature rapidly rises, soon reaching 103° to 105° F. Except for the daily remissions, it remains sustained to the time of the crisis, when there may be hyperpyrexia—107° F. or higher. At the end of the crisis—10 or 12 hours—it becomes subnormal, 95° or 96° F.

**Variations from the Regular Course.**—Early there may be a sudden fall of temperature (pseudo crisis) with quick return to a high range. In the cachectic and in alcoholics, the temperature range may be moderate. Immediately before death there may be extreme hyperpyrexia—109°,

110° F. The period of decline of the temperature may be prolonged, which is usually due to complication. After falling, it may rise again, due to extension of the pneumonic process (migratory pneumonia), or to a complication. A sustained high temperature after the tenth day indicates purulent infiltration. Apex pneumonia has the highest temperature.

**Hyperpyrexia.**—A temperature of 106° or 107° F. is occasionally seen, generally just before the crisis.

**Tuberculosis.**—Persistent fever after the eighth day, not due to extension, leads to the suspicion of tuberculosis.

**Crisis.**—Crisis generally occurs on the fifth or seventh day; exceptionally, it may occur on any day from the third to the fourteenth. The duration of the crisis is usually from eight to twelve hours; it may be prolonged, which denotes complication. At the end of the crisis, the temperature becomes temporarily subnormal, 98°, 97° or 96° F. Eighty-five percent. of cases of pneumonic fever terminate by crisis; fifteen per cent. by lysis. It is not true that the crisis is always on odd days.

## THE HEART.

**Cardiac Paralysis.**—A greater number of deaths than formerly suspected are due to paralysis of the heart. There may be heart-failure from two different causes:

(a) **Paralysis of the right heart,** due to extensive consolidation of the lung, over-distension of the pulmonary artery, passive congestion of the venous system, formation of heart-clot, and arrest of the heart in diastole.

**Symptoms.**—Muffled first sound, and poorly accentuated second-sound heard over the area of the pulmonary valves; increased area of dulness to the right; a low systolic murmur; epigastric impulse. Pulse small and weak.

(b) **Gradual Failure of the Heart** as a whole when the toxemia is intense, with extreme hyperpyrexia, nervous symptoms pronounced, and great prostration—a general adynamic condition.

**Symptoms.**—All the heart-sounds are faint; in rhythm they approach each other; irregularity; a soft, low-pitched murmur; the pulse soft and weak.

## PULSE.

**Volume.**—During chill, the pulse is small; in the succeeding fever it is full and bounding. With extensive consolidation there is small pulse.

**Rate.**—There is increased pulse rate with primary rise of temperature: 100 to 110 is ordinary, 120+ is serious; 130+ is always grave. Slow pulse at the height of the fever points to complication—cardiac or cerebral. With the **crisis** the pulse may temporarily become subnormal, 40—30.

**Rhythm.**—The pulse is generally regular. Any irregularity is unfavorable; it points to weakness and disturbed innervation of the heart. Before and following the crisis there is sometimes slight irregularity without grave significance.

## BLOOD.

**Bacteriology.**—In some cases the diplococcus lanceolatus is found in the blood; generally when there is secondary diplococcus infection (endocarditis, etc.) or, severe generalized infection.

**Fibrin.**—The fibrin is increased: from 4:1,000, it may be as high as 10:1,000; coagulation is rapid and the clot is very firm.

**Red Corpuscles.**—During the fastigium, the red cells are approximately normal in number; after crisis there is slight anemia (this is not peculiar to penumonia—it is true of fevers generally). Poikilocytosis is marked. There are many pale cells, taking but little stain.

**Leucocytes.**—In the majority of cases, there is hyper-leucocytosis.

**Number.**—From 7,500 per cmm. (normal) the leucocytes may be as high as 90,000 per cmm., or more.

**Time.**—The leucocytosis begins at the time of the chill; it remains active through the fastigium; it falls with and after the crisis; it is one or two days after the crisis before normal is reached.

**Variations from the Usual Course.**—Leucocytosis continues in (1) delayed resolution; (2) purulent infiltration; (3) abscess; (4) empyema; (5) gangrene.

**Degree of Leucocytosis.**—In cases of mild infection, with vigorous reaction, leucocytosis is slight; with severe infection and vigorous reaction leucocytosis is marked (this includes nine-tenths of all cases).

**Absence of Leucocytosis.**—In cases of severe infection, with feeble reaction, there is no leucocytosis (these cases almost invariably die).

## SPUTUM.

**Character.**—Early, it may be purely catarrhal. Soon, it is viscid, adhesive, gluey. It contains mucin in large amount.

**Color.**—It is rust-colored; the color is determined by the red blood-corpuscles; it is of various shades, due to action of the oxygen of the air on the hematin.

**Elements.**—Mucin; red blood-corpuscles, intimately intermixed and uniformly diffused; dichotomous fibrinous casts from the smaller bronchi; altered epithelial cells; leucocytes.

**Time of Appearance.**—The sputum appears on the first day in about one-half the cases; in other cases it may appear on the second or third day.

**Quantity.**—The quantity is not great; a total quantity of two ounces per diem is large.

**Anomalies.**—"Prune-juice" sputum is in color chocolate-brown; it is less viscid than the "rusty sputum; its character is due to decomposition. It contains large air-bubbles, when there is collateral edema.

**Note.**—The "rust-colored," viscid sputum is not pathognomonic unless it contains fibrinous casts; sputum of like character may occur in general miliary tuberculosis.

**Fibrinous Casts.**—If a mass of sputum is floated on the surface of water in a glass, fibrinous casts may some-times be seen depending from the lower surface.

## URINE.

**Quantity.**—The urine is diminished in quantity; there may be 1,000—800 cc.; sometimes even 400 cc. With the crisis there is increase, but restoration to the normal quantity is generally delayed several days.

**Specific Gravity.**—1,025—1,030.

**Color.**—Dark; (4-6, Vogel).

**Reaction.**—Acid.

**Sediment.**—On cooling there is a sediment consisting of: amorphous acid-urate-of-soda; uric-acid crystals; crystals of oxalate-of-lime; epithelium.

**Chlorides.**—The chlorides are absent (they reappear after resolution). Absence of the chlorides from the urine is characteristic of pneumonic fever.

**Albumin.**—A trace (a large quantity of albumin is unfavorable).

**Bile.**—In so-called "bilious pneumonia" bile is often present in the urine.

## THE X-RAY IN DIAGNOSIS.

**The X-Ray.**—The extent of consolidation can be determined with a degree of accuracy. The diminution of the consolidated area, as the disease progresses toward convalescence, can be noted. The diminished movement of the diaphragm can be demonstrated. Central pneumonia can be readily diagnosticated.

## COMPLICATIONS.

The complications may be considered under

Three Groups:
    I.    **Respiratory;**
    II.    **Circulatory;**
    III. **Other than Respiratory and Circulatory.**

**I. Respiratory.**

**Pleurisy.**—There is always inflammation of the pleura over the affected area of the lung, except in that rare condition, central pneumonia. The **diplococcus lanceolatus** is present in the product of the pleural inflammation.

**Pleurisy with Effusion.**—This occurs in about five per cent of cases. The effusion is serous, rich in fibrin. Diagnosis is usually possible on the fourth or fifth day. The physical signs are obscure; in the absence of paracentesis the only certain sign is displacement of the adjacent organs, especially the heart; this never occurs in uncomplicated pneumonia. After resolution of the pneumonia the pleurisy usually runs a shorter course than when it is the primary disease. The **prognosis** is generally favorable, except in the aged.

**Empyema.**—When empyema occurs it is generally due to secondary infection by the streptococcus; empyema primarily due to the diplococcus is rare. The time of appearance is generally several days after the crisis. **Symptoms:** Rapid rise of temperature; chills; sweat; dulness replaced by flatness. The diagnosis can always be confirmed by use of the needle.

**Bronchial Catarrh.**—When extensive, bronchial catarrh is a serious complication; the pneumonic process does not run a typical course; resolution is delayed and the temperature remains sustained; there is loss of flesh and strength; death often from cardiac paresis or asthenia. The expectoration is mucous; there are sibilant and sonorous râles; increased dyspnea.

**Edema.**—Collateral pulmonary edema is a serious, often a fatal complication. **Symptoms:** Coarse, bubbling râles; expectoration watery and frothy; intense dyspnea; cyanosis.

**Emphysema.**—Dyspnea is excessive; bronchial catarrh generally accompanies; the heart's action is seriously embarrassed; the physical signs are often obscure—dulness is not pronounced; tubular breathing is absent; resolution is slow; the prognosis is always grave.

## II. Circulatory.

**Endocarditis.**—This is the most common cardiac complication; usually the endocarditis is of the ulcerative variety; it is often due to the presence of the diplococcus. The symptoms are obscure; murmurs may be present or not. Fever, chills and sweat, and especially secondary meningitis, point strongly to the existence of ulcerative endocarditis.

**Pericarditis.**—It is generally due to extension of inflammation from the pleura; the form may be plastic, sero-fibrinous or purulent. **Symptoms:**—Increased dyspnea and pain, together with physical signs, which, however, are masked in left-sided pneumonia.

**Heart-clot.**—Almost always there is ante-mortem clot from slowing of the blood-current; the location of the clot is generally in the right heart.

### III. Other Organs.

**Meninges.**—Meningitis occurs secondarily; due to invasion by the diplococcus lanceolatus. Diagnosis is often difficult, masked by symptoms of the primary affection. **Symptoms:**—Delirium, tonic muscular spasm; cephalalgia; later stupor and coma. Ulcerative endocarditis usually precedes the meningitis.

**Liver.**—Jaundice, when present, is most often due to congestion and pressure on distended veins or biliary ducts. Catarrhal jaundice may occur.

**Kidneys.**—Acute Bright's is rare. Usually the lung affection is the terminal event in chronic Bright's.

**Parotids.**—Inflammation, enormous swelling and often suppuration of the parotids is sometimes a complication. It is due to local diplococcus infection, through Steno's duct, from the mouth.

**Joints.**—Purulent arthritis sometimes occurs; the pneumococcus has been found in the affected joint.

**Intestines.**—Diarrhea is due to pseudo-membranous colitis, in some cases.

**Nutrition.**—It usually suffers but little, and the patient does not greatly emaciate.

**Digestion.**—There is anorexia, as in febrile states generally; the urgent dyspnea interferes with swallowing. Thirst is usually great.

**Vomiting.**—Sometimes occurs with the chill. Vomiting in the course of the attack may be from (1) cerebral irritation; (2) the spasmodic cough; (3) indigestion.

**Bowels.**—Generally there is constipation, rarely diarrhea.

## PROGNOSIS.

In uncomplicated cases of primary frank pneumonia the prognosis is always favorable.

**Favorable.**—Favorable conditions are:—Fever, moderate; the pulse moderate and regular; the respirations infrequent; the ratio of pulse and respiration not much altered; deep respirations possible; paroxysms of cough, mild; the accompanying bronchial catarrh mild, and not extensive; a lower lobe affected; no tendency to extension; the expectoration rusty-brown; leucocytosis.

**Unfavorable.**—Unfavorable elements which will modify the prognosis are:—Absence of the initial chill; extremes of life; persistent high temperature, 105°+; previous cachexia, or alcoholism; pregnancy; previously-existing heart-disease; irregular and weak heart; extensive consolidation; bilateral pneumonitis, "prune-juice" expectoration; early gastro-intestinal disturbance; pulse-respiration ratio much altered; active delirium; asthenia; extensive bronchitis; endocarditis; absence of leucocytosis; in general, all complications.

**Caution.**—The degree of toxemia is the most important element to be taken into consideration in the prognosis of pneumonic fever.

In the majority of cases the toxemia has no direct relation to the extent of lung-tissue involved.

## DIFFERENTIAL DIAGNOSIS.

**Pleurisy with Effusion.**—Onset, "chilliness;"—pain, "stitchlike;" — cough, without expectoration; — fever, moderate, terminating by lysis;—prostration, not great; —countenance, pale; herpes, absent. **Physical Signs:**— Thorax, distended; fremitus, absent; flatness on percussion; displacement of neighboring organs;—auscultation, friction-sound; vocal resonance, absent.

**Crucial Test.**—The hypodermic or aspirator-needle will draw serum; in pneumonia, thick blood. (This is not a scientific method of making a diagnosis and should be avoided.)

**Broncho-Pneumonia.**—Usually it is secondary to bronchitis and other respiratory affections. Onset, gradual; —fever, irregular, declines by lysis;—sputum not "rusty," but sometimes streaked with blood;—dyspnea intense;—cyanosis marked;—sweat common;—signs of consolidation, bilateral;—upper lobes often affected;— tubular breathing rare;—duration of the disease indefinite.

**Important Test.**—No leucocytosis; absence of the diplococcus.

**Acute Pneumonic Phthisis.**—This generally occurs in a "tuberculous" subject, and in children, and early life; often it follows a "cold." Onset, repeated slight chills; —fever remittent in type;—profuse sweats;—emaciation rapid;—sputum may be "rusty," but it contains elastic-fibres and bacilli;—consolidation usually begins at the apex;—signs of cavity appear;—prognosis, fatal.

**Crucial Test.**—The presence of yellow elastic-fibres, . and of bacilli in the sputum.

**Typhoid.**—"Typhoid-pneumonia," so-called, sometimes closely resembles enteric fever with severe involvement of the lungs. In the absence of right-iliac tenderness and the characteristic roseloa rash, the presence of leucocytosis will determine the diagnosis in favor of pneumonia.

**Crucial Test.**—Widal's test is conclusive.

**Meningitis.**—The presence of pneumonia may be obscured by symptoms simulating meningitis. Careful examination of the lungs should exclude error. In meningitis note:—Occipital headache; rigidity of the cervical muscles; exaggerated reflexes; hyperesthesia; slow and irregular pulse.; pulse-respiration ratio not markedly altered.

With early cerebral symptoms there is probably no meningitis; their late appearance, especially if developing suddenly, favors a diagnosis of meningitis, which is secondary to the pneumonitis.

**Caution.**—The presence of leucocytosis is of no aid, for it occurs in both conditions.

## DURATION.

Some cases of pneumonic fever terminate in twenty-four or thirty-six hours. A case of primary, frank pneumonia in a vigorous subject often runs its course in fourteen days. This is rare. Some cases may linger for months. The attack dates from the initial chill.

## PNEUMONIC FEVER IN CHILDREN.

In children many symptoms differ in so marked a degree from corresponding symptoms as they occur in the adult as to warrant separate consideration.

**History.**

**1823.**—Not until this year was bronchitis distinguished from pneumonia in children (Leger).

**1844.**—Atelectasis was first proved to be a different pathological condition from hepatization (Legendre and Bailly).

**Etiology.**

**Primary.**—In children the disease is primary oftener than in the adult.

**Constitution.**—Children in previously good health are attacked in a majority of instances.

**Age.**—It occurs even in the new-born; in a child of three months it has been known to run a typical course. From the end of the first year the number of cases increases. In childhood the greatest number of cases occur from the ages of four to seven years.

**Other Diseases.**—In children pneumonic fever sometimes occurs as a complication in whooping-cough, measles, scarlatina, typhoid and diphtheria.

**Seat of Lesion.**—The upper lobes are more often affected than in the adult.

## SYMPTOMS.

**Onset.**—In children the **chill is absent** in a large majority of cases.

**Vomiting.**—In about half the cases vomiting replaces the chill.

**Convulsions.**—In some cases (5 to 10 per cent) convulsions replace the chill.

**Diarrhea.**—Especially in hot seasons, diarrhea sometimes marks the onset.

**Cough.**—It is not generally so marked as in adults.

**Expectoration.**—Under five years expectoration is seldom seen, the sputum being swallowed. The sputum may sometimes be found in the vomited matter.

**Pain.**—A peculiarity of the pain in children is that it is often referred to points distant from the chest—to the loin, epigastrium, or to any point in the distribution of the intercostal nerves.

**Respiration.**—This is "jerky," with a characteristic expiratory moan.

**Pulse.**—It is relatively more rapid than in the adult.

**Temperature**—It has a high range; also it often departs from the typical course.

**Gastric Disturbance.**—It is more common than in the adult.

**Delirium.**—It is far more common than in the adult.

**Diagnosis.**—With care the diagnosis is generally clear. One of the most misleading features is late appearance of the physical signs. But in children the combination of (1) high temperature, (2) rapid respiration, (3) rapid pulse, points almost invariably to this disease.

In the chest-examination never fail to auscultate high in the axilla, between the spinal column and the scapula, and in the sub-clavicular space.

**Observation.**—When a child cries lustily while being examined, the chances are all against its having pneumonia.

**Prognosis.**—It is generally favorable. Unfavorable features are:—Under three years of age; complications;

great extent of lung involved; late convulsions; late vomiting and diarrhea; temperature-range steadily above 105° F.

## PNEUMONIC FEVER IN THE AGED.

**Prodromata.**—In the aged premonitory symptoms occur in sixty per cent of cases, consisting of malaise, anorexia, headache, dull pains in the limbs and in the chest.

**Chill.**—In about one-half the cases chill is absent. When present it is seldom a distinct rigor; generally it is a protracted shivering.

**Early Symptoms.**—When chill is absent the attack generally sets in with slight pyrexia, increased frequency of respirations, short, hacking cough, and great prostration. In other cases the oncome is marked by nausea, vomiting, diarrhea and collapse, the patient early sinking into a semi-comatose condition.

**Location of Lesion.**—In the aged the process begins in the upper lobes in a large number of cases.

**Physical Signs.**—Crepitant râles are often absent in the stage of engorgement.

**Fever.**—The temperature-range is lower than in middle life. Some cases run an apyrexial course.

**Pain.**—In the aged pain is seldom severe. It is a dull, uneasy feeling, not distinctly localized.

**Cough.**—In the aged cough is not, as a rule, severe; in some cases there is no cough.

**Expectoration.**—Rarely it is absent; only in about one-third the cases is it the characteristic "rusty" sputum; in the others it is catarrhal or "frothy."

**Respiration.**—The breathing is panting, but without great increase in rapidity of respiration, no more than 22 to 26 per minute; dyspnea is not common.

**Pulse.**—It is never as high as in earlier life—generally 76 to 80; seldom 120; an intermittent pulse is common. In the aged do not depend upon counting the pulse at the wrist; take it at the heart.

**Lysis.**—Termination is by lysis oftener than when the disease occurs in middle life.

**Prognosis.**—Generally it is unfavorable; but very severe cases sometimes make good recoveries.

**Mortality.**—After the age of sixty-five a large proportion of all deaths are due to pneumonic fever.

## TREATMENT.

**Therapeutics.**

**Veratrum viride.**—This is the most important drug to be given in the stage of engorgement, to which its use must be limited. In my own experience, and in that of others, it has apparently cut short oncoming attacks of pneumonia. It must be given early, immediately following the chill. It is of no avail after hepatization has begun.

**Symptoms.**—Stage of engorgement; severe and long-lasting chill, followed by intense pulmonary congestion, with great arterial excitement; dyspnea; full, hard pulse; throbbing headache; livid face; dry tongue; vertigo.

**Special Indications.**—Intense pulmonary congestion, with full, hard, bounding pulse.

**Dose.**—Five minims is a maximum dose; 1 to 3 usually enough. In children, ¼ to 1 minim.

**Caution.**—If it produces nausea, reduce the dose. Watch the action carefully to avoid cardiac depression. ("Norwood's Tincture" is the best preparation.)

**Aconite.**—This medicine is of but very limited use in pneumonia. It is of no value whatever after the process of exudation has begun, and in the period prior to the exudative, in most cases **Veratrum vir.** has greater power. Its use must be confined to the stage of engorgement, immediately succeeding the chill.

**Symptoms.**—Sthenic cases, in subjects previously robust; attack excited by exposure to cold; sharp chill, with quick reaction, rapid rise of temperature, oppression of the chest, dry, hot skin, great thirst, dry cough, or cough with blood-tinged sputum, great nervous erethism, anxiety and restlessness.

**Special Indications.** Sthenic cases; pulmonary hyperemia, with restlessness and nervous apprehension which is not due directly to the suffering caused by the embarrassed respiration.

**Dose.**—Three drops of the first decimal dilution in a little water, repeated every half-hour or hour.

**Bryonia.**—This is by far the most important remedy for the second stage, that of fibrinous exudation and consolidation, and especially for the pleuritic inflammation, with its characteristic sharp, stitching, cutting pain.

**Symptoms.**—The period of restlessness has passed; the patient is inclined to remain quiet; there is great anxiety, not from nervous erethism, but from the dyspnea; severe, shooting, cutting pains, painful cough, with scanty expectoration of bloody sputum; tongue with thick coating of white fur; mouth dry; great thirst; stomach inactive; liver engorged; constipation; pulse hard and tense; urine red and scanty.

**Special Indications.**—The presence of the pleuritic pains, which cause aversion to the slightest motion.

**Dose.**—First decimal dilution; three drops at a dose, repeated every one or two hours.

**Ferrum phosphoricum.**—The action of this agent is limited to the stage of engorgement; it is of no use after exudation has set in, nor is it of use in sthenic cases. It belongs to the treatment of the initial stage of pneumonia when occurring in the aged, or in subjects who are feeble, cachectic, and reduced by previous exhausting diseases, more especially by the zymotic diseases which are attended by bronchial catarrh; hence, in secondary pneumonia, such as that following measles, phthisis, typhoid, and similar conditions. There is but moderate reaction to slight chill, the patient is listless and apathetic, there are extensive râles, with blood-streaked expectoration.

**Symptoms.**—In cachectic subjects; slight chill, or only chilly sensations; mild reaction; moderate fever; extensive crepitant, subcrepitant and mucous râles; dyspnea; cough, with early bloody expectoration; the patient listless, sometimes drowsy.

**Special Indications.**—Cachectic subjects; moderate re-action to slight chill; tendency to accompanying bronchial catarrh.

**Dose.**—The second decimal trituration, two grains, repeated at one-hour intervals.

**Iodine.**—This drug has a special, though distinct, sphere in the treatment of pneumonia. Its place is in the stage of consolidation. Before this it is of no use. It takes the place of **Bryonia** in a certain class of subjects. There is fever, with high temperature, but an absence of the pleuritic pains of **Bryonia**. It belongs to the treatment of pneumonia in so-called "scrofulous" subjects, those with "delicate" skin, soft flesh, and enlarged glands.

**Symptoms.**—Fibrinous exudation and inflammation of the lungs, with high temperature, in "scrofulous" subjects; absence of pain; rapid emaciation; enlarged glands; excessive irritability and sensitiveness; albuminuria. Also an accompanying pericarditis or endocarditis.

**Special Indications.**—The diathesis of the patient, as already given, determines the choice.

**Dose.**—First decimal dilution, three drops in a little water, repeated every one or two hours.

**Precaution.**—Always use a fresh preparation of **C. P. Iodine.**

**Phosphorus.**—This, in importance, is second only to **Bryonia.** A pneumonia that runs an uncomplicated course can readily be carried through with **Bryonia,** but when pneumonia deviates from its typical course, **Phosphorus** must then be considered. It belongs to the treatment of the second stage, that of consolidation, and also its use extends into the period of resolution. It finds its chief sphere in pneumonia in delicate, feeble or cachectic subjects, and those cases in which there is great exhaustion and depression. With **Bryonia** the attack may have been brought on by "catching cold;" with **Phosphorus** there is an absence of such exciting cause. With **Phosphorus** the pains are not intense and acute, but are moderate, and vaguely localized. In the third stage of the disease it favors fatty metamorphosis of the formed elements. It should also be given when there are signs of suppuration, indicated by muco-purulent expectoration, with some blood, sweats and hectic. When the pleura is especially affected **Phosphorus** is not indicated.

**Symptoms.**—Stages of hepatization and resolution. Pain not very severe—vaguely localized stitches. Great prostration. Great weight and oppression of the chest; severe embarrassment of respiration; extensive mucous râles; cough, with bloody, muco-sanguinolent, or sanguineo-purulent, difficult expectoration. Very useful in severe cases, asthenic pneumonia, and "typhoid-pneumonia." Collateral edema.

**Special Indications.**—Asthenic cases in cachectic subjects; vague pains; much accompanying bronchitis; muco-purulent sputum.

**Dose.**—Second decimal dilution, two drops in a little water, every two hours.

**Precaution.**—Always use a fresh preparation of **Phosphorus.**

**Phosphorus** is also a remedy of first importance in— (a) Bronchitis; (b) Typhoid-pneumonia; (c) Bilious-pneumonia; (d) Collateral edema.

(a) **Bronchitis.**—When the fibrinous exudation is not great in amount, and consolidation is not extreme, but the accompanying bronchitis is severe and extensive, **Phosphorus** is the chief remedy.

(b) **"Typhoid-Pneumonia."**—In those low and asthenic cases called "typhoid-pneumonia," **Phosphorus** is the all-important remedy. This is when, instead of pursuing the typical course, the patient sinks into an adynamic state; there are extensive mucous râles; the tongue becomes brown and dry; the mind clouded and dull; or, if this condition supervenes in the third stage.

(c) **"Bilious Pneumonia,"** so-called, when from blood-changes, producing hematogenous icterus, **Phosphorus** is the remedy.

(d) **Collateral edema,** complicating pneumonia; in this condition **Phosphorus** is the most important remedy.

**Ammonium carb.**—This drug may be used as a cardiac stimulant and expectorant, when there is loud rattling of mucus in the lungs, with weak heart's action. **Dose:**—2 to 5 grains, repeated.

**Tartar emetic.**—This remedy is scarcely ever indicated in typical or uncomplicated pneumonia. It is only when the disease deviates in certain respects from its normal course, or when it occurs in subjects who are greatly debilitated, or who are feeble from the exhaustion of disease, or from infancy or extreme age, that **Tartar emetic** is called for. Its place is in threatened pulmonary paresis, when the lungs are embarrassed by the abundance of its secretions, as indicated by extensive coarse râles and rattling of mucous, while, at the same time, owing to weakness, notwithstanding the loose cough, but little sputum is raised; this condition is accompanied by great dyspnea, oppression of the chest, general prostration, cyanosis, cold surface, and clammy sweat; also, collateral edema.

In general, **Tartar emetic** belongs to the treatment of asthenic cases of pneumonia complicated by bronchitis, with profuse secretion, and pneumonia secondary to influenza, measles, whooping-cough, and other affections of the respiratory mucous membrane.

**Symptoms.**—Commencing resolution. Increased frequency of pulse; great anxiety and restlessness; copious, cool perspiration; pallid countenance; cyanosis; suffocative spells, great dyspnea; loose, rattling cough, as if much would be expectorated, but nothing comes. Impending paralysis of the lungs. Collateral edema.

**Special Indications.**—Impending pulmonary paresis, with profuse secretion, and great prostration.

**Dose.**—Second decimal trituration, one grain, repeated every one, two, or three hours.

**Precaution.**—This remedy must not be used in doses large enough to produce its depressing toxic effects.

**Arseniate of antimony.**—This is another important remedy. In referring to it Goodno calls it "a rival of **Tartar emetic.**" The class of cases to which it belongs are the pneumonias of elderly people, especially those cases secondary to epidemic influenza. It is especially applicable to cases in which there is precedent organic disease of the heart or kidneys. It is also indicated in pneumonia secondary to emphysema. The condition demanding its use is threatened "paralysis of the lungs."

**Symptoms.**—Intense dyspnea; loud rattling in the bronchial tubes; frothy, watery sputa, expectorated with difficulty; inability to clear the bronchial tubes; feeble, rapid pulse; failing circulation.

**Special Indications.**—Impending "paralysis of the lungs," in secondary pneumonia, or in the aged and cachectic.

**Dose.**—Second decimal trituration, two grains, repeated every half-hour or hour.

**Sulphur.**—The indications for the use of **Sulphur** are best expressed by the two words, **delayed resolution.** Hence, it belongs to the treatment of the latter part of the second stage, and the third stage. The second stage is prolonged, the crisis does not occur on the seventh or eighth day, as it should; or, there has been a pseudo-crisis, and all the symptoms are again at their height, and remain so. This condition is accompanied by great vascular excitement. **Sulphur** will now hasten the accession of the desired crisis. Again, in the third stage, after the crisis, resolution is slow; from day to day the patient's condition is unchanged; the affected portion of the lung remains solid, with no signs of clearing. **Sulphur** will now bring about a reaction, and promote prompt resolution. **Phosphorus** is the remedy from which it is most important to differentiate **Sulphur**, since each has its chief sphere in the treatment of the third stage.

The distinction to be made may be best expressed in the following manner:—

| Sulphur: | Phosphorus: |
|---|---|
| 1. Amount of exudative material great. | 1. Amount of exudative material small. |
| 2. Consolidation pronounced. | 2. Consolidation not extreme. |
| 3. Catarrh not marked. | 3. Much mucous secretion. |
| 4. Vascular symptoms prominent. | 4. Nervous symptoms prominent. |
| 5. Little or no expectoration. | 5. Muco-purulent expectoration. |
| 6. Sthenic state; it is a condition of suspense; reaction does not promptly occur. | 6. Adynamic state; typhoid-like symptoms; or, signs of suppuration. |

**Symptoms.**—Sthenic cases, with delayed resolution; vascular excitement; fever; disposition to perspire; dyspnea; sensation of heat in the chest; "flushes" of heat, hot hands and feet; aggravation in the forenoon. Meningitis.

**Special Indications.**—Delayed resolution; the case "drags," without decided change.

**Dose.**—The second or third decimal dilution, three drops, repeated every one or two hours.

**Meningitis,** complicating pneumonia, is another condition calling for **Sulphur.** There are the usual symptoms —great irritability; opisthotonos, or rolling the head; strabismus, stupor or coma.

**Rhus tox.**—In so-called "typhoid-pneumonia" this is the chief remedy. There is auto-intoxication, from retrograde tissue metamorphosis, with active fever, loss of flesh and great prostration.

**Symptoms.**—Low delirium, with nervous restlessness; lips and tongue dry, brown and cracked; besotted expression; swelling of the parotids; bronchial catarrh; "prune-juice" expectoration; emaciation; weak pulse;

rheumatoid pains in various parts; tympanites; sensitiveness of the abdomen; putrid diarrhea.

**Special Indications.**—An aydnamic condition, with low delirium, due to profound toxemia.

**Dose.**—Third decimal dilution, three drops in a little water, repeated every hour.

**Hepar sulph.**—This remedy is limited in its use to the treatment of purulent infiltration, or abscess; hence, it is applicable only in the third stage, or in chronic pneumonia.

**Symptoms.**—Fever; emaciation; spasmodic cough, with purulent and fetid expectoration; perspires freely; great sensitiveness to drafts of air; the chest is sore, and sensitive to touch; loss of appetite; an accompanying diarrhea.

**Special Indications.**—It is the presence of the suppurative process that calls for this remedy; the extreme sensitiveness to air, profuse secretions, and easy perspiration are characteristic.

**Dose.**—The third decimal trituration, two grains, repeated every two hours.

**Precautions.**—The lower potencies promote suppuration; the higher have a tendency to check it.

**Silicea.**—This is the most efficient remedy for abscess of the lung, one which **Hepar** has failed to arrest; the symptoms resemble those of **Hepar,** but the suppurative process is of longer standing.

**Symptoms.**—Scrofulous subjects; muco-purulent expectoration; emaciation; hectic; profuse sweat about the head.

**Dose.**—Sixth centesimal trituration; two grains every three hours.

**Hyoscine hydrobromate.**—This preparation is also very useful in controlling the condition of nervous and mental excitement; the patient is wakeful, the face is haggard, the pulse failing, from the weak and tired heart.

**Dose.**—Give a one-grain powder of the 3x trituration,

repeated every hour. Continue its use at longer intervals after the patient has become quieted.

**Belladonna.**—This remedy has no direct action on the pneumonic process. It is of use only in those cases in which there is intense delirium, as a symptom of cerebral congestion or inflammation. Also, in children, for the convulsions attending the onset.

**Symptoms.**—Dilirium, violent, with injected and protruding eyes; dilated pupils; strong pulsation in carotids; full, hard, frequent pulse; garrulity; anxiety, with desire to flee. Head drawn back; intolerance of light and noise. In children :—Onset, convulsions, with intense pulmonafy congestion. Dry cough.

**Special Indications.**—Active delirium, with cerebral congestion. Convulsions in children; intense pulmonary congestion. Dry cough.

**Dose.**—Third decimal dilution, ten drops in one-half glass water; dose, teaspoonful, repeated every quarter-hour to every hour, according to the severity of the symptoms.

**Hyoscyamus.**—This remedy will not specifically affect the croupous inflammation of pneumonia, but in two other conditions that sometimes arise it is of signal service. One of these is in affections of the sensorium. It is called for when there are cerebral symptoms; the delirium is sometimes violent, resembling that of mania a potu; the patient may attempt to strike and bite those about; attempt to get out of bed; uncovers himself; loquacious; busy with his hands, picking, working and clutching; sits up and looks about in a vacant way, then, at command, lies down again and becomes quiet.

The cerebral irritation of **Hyoscyamus** is non-inflammatory. Unlike the **Belladonna** condition, the head is not hot, and there is no throbbing of the carotids. The **Hyoscyamus** cases, post mortem, show no signs of inflammatory action in the cerebrum or in the cerebral meninges. The irritation of the cortical cells is from toxins.

**Symptoms.**—Acute mania; delusions and hallucinations; refuses food and medicine, declaring he is being poisoned; suspicious of those about; attempts to get out of bed to escape an imaginary foe; refuses to remain covered, and throws off the bed-clothing; loquacious; at times lies quietly for hours, but is easily aroused to violent mania. Distressing paroxysms of cough at night, without expectoration.

**Special Indications.**—Acute mania, not due to cerebral inflammation.

**Dose.**—Three drops of the first decimal dilution, in a little water, repeated every hour.

The other condition calling for **Hyoscyamus** is a cough, without expectoration, which is especially troublesome at night.

Some authorities recommended Hyoscyamus in low delirium, stupor and coma, dry tongue, involuntary stools, etc., but in this condition it has always disappointed me, and I have abandoned its use.

**Agaricus.**—This remedy is called for when there is a high grade of delirium, especially when accompanied by cardiac weakness. Like that of **Hyoscyamus**, the delirium is not due to inflammation, but to the toxic condition of the blood. In pneumonia of alcoholics, with mania, it is a leading remedy.

**Symptoms.**—Restlessness; insomnia; constant desire to get out of bed; tremor; tremulous tongue; anxious expression; face pale; free perspiration; weak heart.

**Special Indications.**—Wild mania, with restlessness, tremor, and effort to escape are characteristic.

**Dose.**—Use the mother-tincture; three drops, frequently repeated. **Agaricin,** first decimal trituration, two grains, hourly, may also be used.

**Opium.**—This drug is to be used in so-called "typhoid-pneumonia." Sopor bordering upon stupor. The patient sinks down in bed; the lids half closed; the eyeballs are turned upward; snoring with the mouth open; tongue thick and trembling; jerking of the limbs; face dark red. When the patient is in this condition **Opium** will sometimes bring about a reaction. **Dose:**—Give one-drop doses of the tincture, repeated every half-hour or hour.

**Veratrum alb.**—This remedy is useful in states of collapse, with cold surface, and weak heart's action, due to general exhaustion, especially when from diarrhea.

**Symptoms.**—Weak heart, with general exhaustion, due to toxemia, asthenia, or to inability to take food on account of gastric disturbance. Emaciation; anorexia; diarrhea; pulse, weak, soft, compressible, irregular, and its rapidity increased; all the heart-sounds feeble; low temperature; pallor of the skin; cold extremities.

**Special Indications.**—Weak, small pulse; emaciation; exhaustion; cold surface; diarrhea.

**Dose.**—Three drops of the tincture, repeated every half-hour.

## CARDIAC PARESIS.

In pneumonia the burden thrown upon the heart, from the embarrassed pulmonary circulation, or the effect of toxins and impaired nutrition, often causes primary failure of this organ. This condition creates an emergency which must be met by prompt stimulation. The agents that may be used are several. But discrimination must be used, and a different remedy applied, according as the threatened heart-failure is from engorgement of the right heart, or enfeeblement of the entire organ.

**Pulse.**—The character of the pulse is the index for the use of stimulants.

**Symptoms.**—A dicrotic pulse, or a rapid, weak, compressible, irregular or intermittent pulse, calls for stimulation of the patient.

**Effect.**—The results of stimulation are to be judged by improvement in the character of the pulse.

**Period.**—Following the crisis is the time when stimulation is most apt to be demanded. But in alcoholics, in the feeble and the aged, stimulation may be called for from the onset.

### Heart-Stimulants.

**Alcohol.**—This stimulant is to be used when the heart shares in the condition of general asthenia, as in secondary pneumonia, typhoid-pneumonia, and pneumonia of the aged, as well as the corresponding condition occurring in the course of the disease in children.

**Indications.**—Weak heart, with general exhaustion, due to toxemia, asthenia, or to inability to take food on account of gastric disturbance. Emaciation; anorexia, diarrhea; pulse, weak, soft, compressible, irregular, and its rapidity increased; all the heart-sounds feeble; low temperature; pallor of the skin; cold extremities.

**Forms.**—Brandy; whisky; wine (sherry, tokay, champagne); wine-whey.

**Dose.**—Brandy or whisky: the dose may vary from a dram to an ounce, according to the urgency of the symptoms and the results obtained; repeat at intervals of one, two, or three hours. Do not give in too concentrated form—dilute with four to eight parts water. If the stomach will permit, it may be given in milk-punch or egg-nog.

**Sherry** or **tokay** may be given in a similar manner to the above, but in correspondingly larger doses.

**Champagne.**—When the stomach is intolerant of other forms of alcohol, champagne can often be taken.

**Dose.**—A pint may be given, in divided doses, inside of five or six hours, or, in urgent cases, as high as a quart.

**Caution.**—Better results will follow the administration of full doses of alcohol than to drag along with the use of insufficient quantities.

**Wine-whey.**—This is a good form for use in the case of children.

**Glonoin.**—This is the best stimulant when the embarrassment is from engorgement of the right heart.

**Symptoms.**—Extensive consolidation of the lungs; cyanosis; signs of general venous congestion; jugular veins full; small radial pulse; faint pulmonic second-sound.

**Dose.**—The first decimal dilution, five drops in a little water, repeated every hour or half-hour, according to effects.

**Strychnin sulph.**—This is a powerful and promptly acting stimulant; it should be used in urgent cases. It is adapted both to cases in which there is threatened failure from engorgement of the right heart, and in weakness of the entire organ from the poisonous effects of toxins, or from asthenia.

**Dose.**—In the most urgent cases a dose of one-fiftieth grain may be given subcutaneously at intervals of every two or three hours, lengthening the interval, and reducing the dose to one-hundredth grain as the desired effect is produced.

**Oxygen.**—This agent is of service when there is deficient oxydation of the blood from respiratory failure, in extensive consolidation with accompanying bronchial catarrh, or collateral edema, as evidenced by severe dyspnea, cyanosis, cold surface, feeble pulse, and mental hebetude.

**Dose.**—Give the gas freely; several gallons per hour may be administered. If the patient is much depressed, do not demand any effort on his part, but let the gas escape in such manner that he will inhale it freely.

## GENERAL MEASURES.

**Sick-room.**—Let this be a large, well ventilated apartment. Never let the air become "close" or vitiated, which is especially harmful in diseases of the lungs.

**Temperature.**—Keep the air at about 70° F.; slightly lower rather than higher.

**Humidity.**—Keep the atmosphere moist by the use of a steam-atomizer, or an evaporating dish on stove or register.

**Rest.**—Absolute rest is all-important, in order that the strength may be conserved. Permit no exertion on the part of the patient.

**Applications to the Chest.**—Do not use poultices; they confine the heat, they are uncomfortable, untidy, disturb the patient by frequent changing, and are of no direct benefit. Cold applications (ice, cold-bath, etc.) have not enough in their favor to warrant the possible risk of harm in some cases. All that is necessary is to keep an equable temperature by the use of a soft muslin jacket, open in front and tied with tapes, thus permitting ready access to the chest.

**Relief of Pain.**—The sharp pleuritic pain of the early stage is best treated by hot compresses to the painful spot. Put on as hot as can be borne. Do not use a wet compress that will drip. The best is a compress consisting of several folds of flannel; sprinkle one surface with warm water, and quickly run a hot flat-iron over it until it steams. Apply quickly and change frequently.

**Hydrotherapy.**—For purposes of cleanliness, as well as for sedative effect, sponging with warm or tepid water may be employed, according to the demands of the case.

**Bathing for Antipyretic Effect.**—When there is high temperature, hot skin, nervous erethism, severe dyspnea, and commencing cardiac weakness, sponging of the surface with cool water (70° F.) for ten or fifteen minutes will reduce the temperature, quiet the patient, and have a tonic effect. If, without too much distress to the patient,—embarrassing the respiration or the heart's action,—he can be turned partly on one side, and then on the other, so that the back can receive cool sponging, this will do most to reduce temperature. In any event, the front and sides of the chest, and the axillæ, should be bathed in the manner indicated. Repeat the cool sponging as often as the indications, as above given, require it.

**Diet.**—This is all-important, especially in asthenic cases, with great prostration. Feed carefully and systematically. The main reliance may be on milk, first removing the cream. Also give nutritious broths, and farinaceous foods. When the patient can take nothing else, give an egg-lemonade. Recipe:—Make a glass of lemonade with one-third of a lemon. Sweeten with sugar. Drop in one fresh egg and stir. This is both refreshing to the patient and it affords nutrition. **Salt-broth.**—When milk disagrees, or is distasteful, salt-broth can often be taken. **Recipe:**—Make a broth by stewing a quantity of dried-beef, or of codfish, in water. Add a portion of milk, but do not thicken. Feed the broth with a spoon. Many patients will take this with relish.

**Demulcents.**—Demulcent drinks are often grateful to the patient. Slippery-elm water, or gum-Arabic water, are best. The addition of a little lemon-juice is often desirable. If stimulation is sought, a little rock-candy and whisky may be added.

**The Bowels.**—Strict attention should be given to the state of the bowels. An overloaded colon or rectum will seriously depress the heart's action. Let an enema be given daily. The morning is the best time for this unless the patient's natural habit is late in the day.

## PULMONARY FIBROSIS.

**Synonyms.**—Interstitial pneumonia; Chronic pneumonia; Cirrhosis of the lung.

**Definition.**—The condition to which the term "pulmonary fibrosis" is applied is marked by a state of induration of the lung due to the development of new connective-tissue in any of the structures of the lung, in the walls of the alveoli, in the peri-bronchial or peri-vascular connective-tissue, in the inter-alveolar or in the inter-lobular tissues. Usually all the structures are involved, but the hyperplasia may predominate in any one of them.

### ETIOLOGY.

Hyperplasia of the connective-tissue of the lung, resulting in fibrous induration, is always a secondary lesion. Any irritation in the lung, if it be sufficiently long-continued, will finally cause connective-tissue growth and pulmonary induration. Hence, cirrhosis of the lungs may follow a variety of primary conditions, the most prominent of which are:—

(a) **Pulmonary Tuberculosis.**—This is the most common cause, producing the form known as fibroid phthisis.

(b) **Pneumonia.**—In extremely rare instances it is believed to follow lobar pneumonia, especially the variety called "subacute indurative pneumonia." This form of pulmonary fibrosis is rare, because the irritation, viz., the subacute indurative pneumonia, is usually of but short duration.

(c) **Broncho - Pneumonia.** — Broncho - pneumonia in some cases is followed by induration of the lung, occurring especially in children.

(d) **Bronchiectasis.**—Induration of the lung often occurs in connection with bronchiectasis, but as a rule the pulmonary lesion is primary.

(e) **Pleurisy.**—In some cases inflammation of the pleura results in the extension of the irritation to the lung-stroma, and consequent induration. This form is called **pleurogenic fibrosis.**

(f) **Syphilis.**—Induration of the lung occurs in infants in congenital syphilis. In adults, the induration may result after the absorption and disappearance of gummata.

(g) **Irritative Substances.**—Cirrhosis of the lung in knife-grinders, stone-cutters, etc., is secondary to chronic bronchitis or to the tuberculosis induced by the inhalation of irritative substances. Foreign bodies in the air-vesicles, if long retained, may also produce local induration.

(h) **Bright's Disease.**—In subjects of chronic interstitial nephritis there may also be cirrhosis of the lung, as well as cirrhosis of other organs. The connective-tissue hyperplasia in this condition is due to irritants in the blood acting upon the fibrous tissue of the blood-vessels, and through this extending to the adjacent fibrous tissue.

## PATHOLOGY. ·

**Tissue-Changes.**—As a result of the primary inflammation and irritation there is hyperemia of the interlobular and inter-cellular tissue, with small-celled infiltration and the formation of fusiform cells which develop into fibrous tissue. At first the new tissue is vascular, but later, when it contracts, the blood-vessels are obliterated and the new tissue forms a dense, fibrous mass, with compression of the air-cells and induration of the part. The contraction of the tissues is usually followed by secondary bronchiectasis in the affected portion of the lung.

## MORBID ANATOMY.

**Varieties.**

(a) **Lobar Form.**—The lobar, or massive, form affects usually but one lobe of a lung; generally the lower lobe.
(b) **Insular Form.**—In this form the fibroid areas are scattered in various parts of the lung. Broncho-pneumonia is the most common primary condition. Sacculated bronchiectasis often occurs in connection with it.
(c) **Reticular Form.**—In this form fibrous bands are scattered symmetrically throughout both lungs. The condition is exceedingly rare.

**Microscopic Appearance.**—Microscopical examination of a thin section of the affected portion of lung shows thickened alveolar walls. The air-vesicles may be obliterated, or compressed, containing epithelial cells, leucocytes, and sometimes granular matter and fat-granules. There is fibrous thickening of the peri-bronchial tissue.

**Section.**—The lung is firm, hard, solid, and on section it creaks under the knife.

**Color.**—It may be dull red, bluish, or marbled.

**The Bronchi.**—In advanced cases the bronchi are more or less dilated, sometimes forming cavities, thus creating a condition of bronchiectasis.

**Mucous Membrane.**—The mucous membrane is sometimes ulcerated, especially in the dilated portions of the bronchi. Ulceration is due to irritation of the retained secretion.

**Gangrene.**—In some advanced cases gangrene may follow putrid ulceration.

**Pleura.**—The overlying pleura is almost invariably thickened. In chronic cases it may be almost cartilaginous.

**Extent Involved.**—Generally the condition is unilateral. It may involve only a portion of one lung. When this is the case, it is usually the apex. An entire lung may be involved. It is bilateral in the forms due to inhalation of dust or irritating particles, and in those forms due to irritating agents in the blood.

**Pigmentation.**—The cirrhotic lung usually contains an excessive amount of pigment. It renders the tissues marbled and mottled, and in extreme cases the tissues will be uniformly and intensely black.

## SYMPTOMS.

**Early Symptoms.**—The early symptoms vary according to the nature of the primary affection; later, according to the subsequent changes in the lung. The character of the symptoms varies according to the degree of bronchiectasis that develops in the different cases. Early in the disease process the diagnosis may not be clear. In any case of broncho-pneumonia if the symptoms of inflammation of the lung continue long after resolution should take place, interstitial pneumonia may always be suspected. Especially is this to be looked for in children.

### The Established Disease.

**Dyspnea.**—Dyspnea is a constant symptom. When the disease is unilateral the dyspnea is relieved by lying on the affected side.

**Cough.**—Cough always accompanies. It is usually violent, and occurs in paroxysms.

**Expectoration.**—In the early stages it is the expectoration of bronchial catarrh; later, when there is bronchiectasis, it is usually abundant, and is muco-purulent, or brownish and fetid.

**Hemoptysis.**—If there is ulceration of the mucous membrane in the dilated bronchial tubes there is often hemoptysis, but usually the blood is small in quantity.

**Fever.**—For long periods the disease may run an apyrexial course. Sometimes there is evening temperature of 100° to 102° F. If the putrid secretions become confined it causes rise of temperature. Late in the disease the fever often assumes the hectic type.

**Fingers.**—Late, there may be clubbing of the fingers.

**Course.**—With the progress of the disease there is gradual loss of flesh and strength, night-sweats, disturbances of digestion, and diarrhea.

## PHYSICAL SIGNS.

**Inspection.**—When the affected lung is shrunken there is marked contraction of the chest-wall, with great displacement of the heart and diaphragm, curvature of the spine, and depression of the shoulder. There is enlargement and increased respiratory movement of the opposite side.

**Palpation.**—There may be increased tactile fremitus over the affected lung. If, however, the bronchial tubes are obliterated the fremitus may be diminished.

**Percussion.**—The signs on percussion differ with the various conditions. They may denote solidification (high-pitched, "wooden" note); bronchiectatic cavity (tympanitic or amphoric resonance); or other sounds according to the relative amount of healthy and diseased lung tissue.

**Auscultation.**—Since the lung changes are of such varying character, the sounds on auscultation may be many and various. According to the condition of the lung corresponding to the area examined, there may be absence of respiratory sounds; tubular breathing; bronchophony; increased bronchial whisper; rales of various

character, usually moist râles. On the unaffected side
there is exaggerated respiratory sound.

**Pulse.**—At first it is but little affected. Late, it is
small in volume, rapid, weak, and irregular.

**Heart.**—Late, there is dilation of the right heart.

**Course.**—Pulmonary fibrosis is always a chronic affection, lasting for years. The final symptoms, unless some
intercurrent disease occurs, are those of cardiac-failure,
with weak circulation, edema, and dropsy, the immediate cause of death being heart-failure.

## DIFFERENTIAL DIAGNOSIS.

**Pleurisy.**—Pleurisy with effusion may be followed by
retraction of the chest-wall when the lung does not
expand after absorption of the fluid. In this case the
retraction of the chest-wall is more localized, with absence of respiratory and adventitious sounds. After
pleurisy the retraction is uneven, and the ribs are
twisted. In interstitial pneumonia the retraction is more
uniform; there is absence of fetid expectoration and
pyrexia.

**Phthisis.**—From chronic phthisis it is to be differentiated by the result of the examination of the sputum.
In tuberculous phthisis the affection is usually bilateral;
in fibrous it is unilateral. In fibrosis there is want of the
extension from the upper to the lower lobes, which is
so characteristic of the progress of pulmonary tuberculosis.

**Malignant Growth.**—Malignant growth of the lung or
of the mediastinum sometimes resembles fibrosis of the
lung. Look for pressure-signs, pain, currant-jelly-like
expectoration, and the area of dulness approaching the
median line; also, note the extreme degree of cachexia.

## PROGNOSIS.

The duration of the disease is usually one of years,
even extending to ten or twenty or more. Death may
be due to intercurrent affection, to a septic broncho-

pneumonia, or, as the terminal event, to cardiac failure, with dropsy.

## TREATMENT.

**Prophylaxis.**—Especial care should be observed in cases of broncho-pneumonia which do not undergo prompt resolution. Protect the patient from catarrhal affections of the lung. Causes attending occupation must receive attention.

**Climate.**—Early, much benefit may be derived from a residence in a mild climate with equable temperature and pure air, free from dust.

**Diet.**—The strength should be conserved and nutrition promoted by an abundant nutritious diet.

**Medicinal.**—Consult the medicinal measures recommended in chronic bronchitis, bronchiectasis, phthisis, and other allied lung affections.

# BROWN INDURATION OF THE LUNGS.

**Synonym.**—Chronic passive congestion of the lungs.

## ETIOLOGY.

Brown induration of the lung is due to long-continued obstruction to the flow of blood from the pulmonary veins to the left cavities of the heart. The heart condition in which it occurs in its most typical form is **mitral stenosis.**

## MORBID ANATOMY.

**Lungs.**—Both lungs are alike affected. They are small in size. The lung tissue is firm; it contains but little air; the lung does not collapse on opening the thorax.

**Pleura.**—The pleura is generally thickened, pigmented, and adhesions are often present. The vessels on the surface of the pleura are much distended, and in places there are extravasations of blood.

**Color.**—The color of the lung is of a rusty brownish-red tint. It is shown best on section. The color is due to **pigmentation** by hematoidin.

**Section.**—A section of the lung shows that the discoloration is not uniform. The dense, dry pigmented tissues merge into tissue of lighter color. The changes are most marked in the **lower** lobes. Hemorrhagic **infarctions,** wedge-shaped, may be found in various parts of the lung.

**Microscopic Appearance.**—The walls of the alveoli are thick and pigmented. The capillaries are distended, varicose, and engorged with blood. The air-vesicles contain many free epithelial cells. The lymph-spaces contain black and brown pigment. The connective-tissue is thickened and pigmented.

**Mucous Membrane.**—The bronchial mucous membrane is congested, the vessels dilated, tortuous, and filled with blood. It is in great part denuded of epithelial cells. The basement membrane is edematous and thrown into folds.

**Pulmonary Vessels.**—Patches of atheroma may be found in the pulmonary artery and in the pulmonary veins.

## SYMPTOMS.

The symptoms are not distinctive. They are such as belong to the heart condition to which the chronic congestion of the lungs is secondary. Late in the course of a case of mitral stenosis the occurrence of **hemoptysis** would indicate that the lung is in a condition of brown induration, the hemoptysis being due to hemorrhagic **infarct.**

**Physical Signs.**—The breath-sounds are weak, and broncho-vesicular in quality. There is dulness on percussion, most marked at the bases.

**Treatment.**—Treatment must be directed to the primary cardiac condition.

# COLLAPSE OF THE LUNGS.

Definition.—It is of two forms:—(a) **atelectasis**, or congenital collapse; and (b) **apneumatosis**, or acquired collapse.

**Atelectasis.**—The condition of atelectasis is congenital, the lungs not being expanded at birth.

**Apneumatosis.**—This is an acquired collapse, and is due to obstruction to the entrance of air into the lungs, or into a portion of a lung.

## ETIOLOGY.

**Atelectasis.**—The failure of the air to enter the lungs may be due to congenital weakness, as in strumous, rickety, or syphilitic subjects, or to bronchial obstruction. Obstructive agents may be the presence in the air-passages of mucous or meconium, the pressure of enlarged bronchial glands, or want of action of the diaphragm.

**Apneumatosis.**—The conditions which may cause obstruction to the entrance of air into the affected portion of lung are of several classes:—(a) Obstruction of the upper air-passages; (b) Obstruction of the bronchi; (c) Impaired expansion of the chest; (d) Compression of the lung; (e) Pneumothorax.

(a) **Upper Air-Passages.**—The conditions may be enlarged tonsils; adenoids; new-growths; laryngeal stenosis.

(b) **The Bronchi.**—Obstruction may be caused by the presence of viscid mucus or other secretions in bronchitis; capillary bronchitis; broncho-pneumonia; diphtheria (extension into the bronchi); edema; whooping-cough.

(c) **Impaired Expansion.**—Impaired expansion of the chest may be due to paralysis or weakness of the respiratory muscles. Weakness of the muscles may be present in rickets; extreme old age; prolonged fever.

**(d) Compression.**—Compression of the lung may be due to fluid in the pleural cavity; pericardial effusion; cardiac hypertrophy; aneurysms; tumors; ascites.

**(e) Pneumothorax.**—An opening into the pleural cavity allows partial collapse of the lung, due to the elasticity of the organ.

**Mode of Collapse.**—When a bronchial tube is obstructed, thus preventing the entrance of air beyond the point of obstruction, the air which is imprisoned undergoes gradual absorption and the elasticity of the lung produces a state of collapse in the area involved.

**Kyphoscoliosis.**—In deformity of the thorax the lungs are compressed and hindered in their expansion, and aplasia results.

## MORBID ANATOMY.

**Lung-Tissue.**—The collapsed portion of the lung is solid, non-crepitant, and more or less fibrous to the touch, resembling the tissue of the spleen. If the collapsed portion of the lungs is on the surface, the affected area is sharply defined, angular in outline, shrunken and depressed.

**Section.**—On section the lung tissue is dry, non-crepitant, the surface smooth and glistening.

**Color.**—The color is generally dark violet, or pale slate-blue.

**Extent.**—There may be numerous small patches, or considerable areas.

**Location.**—The collapsed areas most commonly found are at the base of the left upper lobe, and in the middle lobe of the right lung; also the posterior parts of the lungs, beside the bodies of the vertebræ. Sometimes, especially in children, the entire **middle lobe** of the right lung may be found collapsed.

## SYMPTOMS.

**Atelectasis.**—In cogenital collapse if the child lives for a short time after birth there is severe dyspnea, shallow respiration, cyanosis, drowsiness, twitchings, and sometimes convulsions.

**Apneumatosis.**—In acquired collapse occurring as a complication of bronchitis, broncho-pneumonia, or other affection with obstruction of the smaller bronchi, the onset is often sudden, marked by dyspnea, rapid breathing, quick and feeble pulse, weak cough, gradual cyanosis, increasing weakness, and finally loss of consciousness.

## PHYSICAL SIGNS.

**Inspection.**—On effort at inspiration there is sinking in of the supra- and infra-clavicular spaces, the interspaces, and the lower part of the chest.

**Percussion.**—If the area involved is large the note is high-pitched. If the condition is associated with emphysema the physical signs may be masked.

**Auscultation.**—There is absence of vesicular murmur over the affected area. In collapse from pleural effusion there is distant tubular breathing on the affected side.

## PROGNOSIS.

**Atelectasis.**—In atelectasis the probable duration of life in the child may be forecast by the **degree of cyanosis.** If this is great, death usually occurs in a few days; if less severe the child may live for several weeks or sometimes months, with gradual failure and death.

**Apneumatosis.**—In this condition also the **degree of cyanosis** is the index to the gravity of the case. If the cyanosis gradually increases the prognosis becomes grave or fatal. On the contrary, if it diminishes the prognosis is so much the more favorable. As a rule, the condition calls for **grave prognosis.** The symptoms to be considered are the patient's strength, the amount of inspiratory recession, the degree of dyspnea and of cyanosis.

## TREATMENT.

**Apneumatosis.**—In acquired collapse the indications are to maintain the strength of the patient and to promote expectoration.

Keep the patient at rest in bed and apply warmth to the extremities. Aid the patient in the respiratory act by massage and manipulation of the chest. Give nourishing food and stimulants.

**Medicinal.**—The medicinal agents will be such as are applicable to the primary conditions—bronchitis, broncho-pneumonia, or obstruction of various kinds.

The treatment of congenital atelectasis belongs to works on obstetrics.

# PNEUMONOCONIOSIS.

**Synonyms.**—Anthracosis (coal-dust); siderosis (metal-dust); chalicosis (stone-dust); miner's lung; miller's lung; knife-grinder's phthisis; stone-cutter's phthisis.

**Definition.**—It is an occupation-disease of the lungs, with fibrosis and pigmentation, progressive in character, due to the inhalation of dust of various kinds.

## ETIOLOGY.

There are a great many occupations in which the artisan breathes a dust-laden atmosphere. The dust acts as an irritant to the lungs, producing inflammation, degeneration, and tissue-changes of various kinds. An enumeration of such occupations would include coal-miners; charcoal-burners; graphite-workers; stone-cutters; marble-polishers; quarrymen; potters; masons; plasterers; knife-grinders; file-cutters; iron-workers; millers; bakers; workers in saw-mills, in cotton factories, jute factories, tobacco factories, and other industries creating a dust-laden atmosphere.

## PATHOLOGY.

The inhaled dust is first deposited on the bronchial mucous membrane and in the air-cells. Some of it is absorbed by the lymphatics and carried into the bronchial glands and tissues.

The dust which is inhaled acts as an irritant to the bronchial mucous membrane, setting up diffuse chronic bronchitis. This is followed by interstitial inflammation and hyperplasia of connective-tissue, which leads to cirrhosis, emphysema, and bronchiectasis. In many cases there is secondary infection by the bacillus tuberculosis, and the case then becomes one of pulmonary tuberculosis, of the fibroid variety. In all cases in which pneumonokoniosis results in destructive changes and the formation of cavities it is due to the tuberculosis which has occurred secondarily to the primary lung condition. In uncomplicated pneumonokoniosis destructive changes do not occur.

## MORBID ANATOMY.

**Pigmentation.**—The lung is discolored according to the nature of the inhaled dust. When the dust consists of carbon, as in coal-miners, the lung is of a deep black. In workers in oxide-of-iron the lung is red. In workers in ultramarine the lungs are violet in tint. The pigmentation may be uniform, or in speckles and streaks. It is darkest in parts which are indurated.

**Fibrosis.**—This is the most characteristic lesion. The fibrosis is due to new tissue in the alveolar walls, and in hyperplasia of connective-tissue generally. The fibrous areas are densely indurated. Bands of pigmented fibroid tissue may traverse the lung in various directions.

**Emphysema.**—This change is usually present. It may be general over the lungs, or confined to the neighborhood of the induration.

**Bronchi.**—There is chronic inflammation of the bronchial mucous membrane, with thickened bronchial walls and fibrous changes in the peribronchial tissues.

**Cavities.**—Cavities with black ragged walls, due to tissue-necrosis, may be found. They are the result of tubercular processes.

**Bronchial Glands.**—The bronchial glands are enlarged and deeply pigmented.

**Pleura.**—There is usually thickening and pigmentation of the pleura, with adhesion of the pleural surfaces.

**Heart.**—The heart is secondarily affected, becoming hypertrophied, with, later, dilatation.

## SYMPTOMS.

**Cough.**—This is an early and constant symptom. It is due to the irritative bronchitis.

**Dyspnea.**—This also is a constant symptom. Late in the disease there may be bronchial asthma.

**Expectoration.**—Early, the sputum is mucoid; later, it becomes purulent and profuse, sometimes amounting to a bronchorrhea. The sputum is pigmented; sometimes, as in coal-miners, being almost as black as ink. In other cases the sputum is white (cotton); red (oxide-of-iron); blue (ultramarine). Gritty and stony masses have been found in the sputum of grinders and stone-cutters. In bronchitectasis the sputum is fetid.

**Heart.**—The symptoms attending dilation of the heart and consequent obstructed pulmonary circulation appear late in the disease.

**General.**—Late in the disease there will be emaciation, night-sweats, diarrhea, and dropsy.

**Course.**—The course of the disease is extremely chronic. For years there may be only the cough and a moderate degree of emaciation, the latter becoming more rapid towards the close.

**Physical Signs.**—The physical signs are suggested by the conditions described. They are such as are found in bronchitis, in pulmonary fibrosis, in emphysema, in softening, and in cavity-formation.

## PROGNOSIS.

If the case is taken in hand early the prognosis depends entirely upon the removal of the cause by change of occupation. If the pathological changes are well established the prognosis is bad. In any case, even if the changes have not gone very far, it is not a safe risk for life insurance. A patient showing symptoms of the affection, even though the lungs become somewhat tolerant, if he continues at his trade seldom lives to pass middle life.

## TREATMENT.

**Prophylaxis.**—The one radical method is to cease the unhealthy occupation. If this cannot be done something can be accomplished by providing free ventilation and a moist atmosphere. In some occupations the use of the respirator is a necessity.

**General.**—The general measures indicated include nourishing diet, plenty of sunshine, and as much fresh air as can be provided. The lung conditions call for treatment belonging to bronchitis, emphysema, bronchiectasis, and the other changes present.

## PULMONARY SYPHILIS.

**Forms.**—Pulmonary syphilis is of two forms:—**(a)** Congenital, and **(b)** Acquired. The acquired form is an exceedingly rare condition.

**Congenital Pulmonary Syphilis.**

**Lesion.**—The lung lesion may be **(a)** Circumscribed; or **(b)** Diffuse. The circumscribed form is termed **gumma**; the diffuse is described as a **pneumonia**. Generally, however, the two forms are associated.

**Gumma.**—The circumscribed lesion does not differ in character from the gumma found in the acquired disease.

**Pneumonia.**—The syphilitic lung lesions to which the term **gumma** is applied are of two forms:—**(a)** White pneumonia; and **(b)** Interstitial pneumonia.

**(a) White Pneumonia.**—In its true form this lesion is found only in the lungs of still-born children, or in children that have survived but a short time. Usually birth is premature. **Morbid anatomy.**—The lung is increased in size. It is solid, dry, white, or grayish-white in color; sometimes it is reddish-marbled. The cut surface is smooth and shining. **Microscopic appearance.**—The alveolar walls are thickened. The alveoli are much enlarged and filled with masses of cells undergoing fatty degeneration.

**(b) Interstitial Pneumonia.**—This is more common than the white pneumonia. **Morbid anatomy.**—The lungs are large, hard, and of grayish-red tint. A single lobe may be affected, or it may be universal. **Microscopic appearance.**—The inter-alveolar and inter-lobular connective-tissue is increased, forming broad meshes; the alveoli are crowded or completely obliterated. The alveolar epithelium shows desquamative changes.

### Acquired Pulmonary Syphilis.

**Time of Appearance.**—Acquired syphilis of the lung makes its appearance generally from four to five years or more after primary infection. The symptoms are often obscure, and are easily confounded with other similar lung conditions.

**Forms.**—The lesions may consist of (a) Gumma; (b) Broncho-pneumonia; (c) Fibroid induration; (d) Changes in the lymphatics; (e) Syphilitic phthisis.

**(a) Gumma.**—Gummata have been found in those who in life gave no signs of lung affection. **Symptoms.**—In those cases in which the gummata cause irritative symptoms they consist of:—Paroxysmal cough, with difficult expectoration, with but little emaciation and no pyrexia. Pleuritic pains are common. **Physical signs.**—The physical signs are those of localized pulmonary induration. Such symptoms, uninfluenced by ordinary treatment, with a previous history of syphilitic infection, would serve for diagno

**(b) Broncho-pneumonia.**—In some cases there are signs of bronchitis or broncho-pneumonia resisting ordinary treatment and responding only to anti-syhpilitic treatment.

**(c) Fibroid Induration.**—In this variety indurated tissue forms, extending over the hilus around the bronchi and vessels; there may also be scattered masses of fibroid tissue.

**(d) Changes in the Lymphatics.**—In this form the bronchial glands are enlarged and the lymphatics leading from the lungs to the glands are dilated and distended with a creamy fluid.

(e) **Syphilitic Phthisis.**—In this variety there are destructive changes in the lungs, with general symptoms resembling phthisis, but the diagnosis can be made only by examination of the sputum for the bacillus tuberculosis, and excluding that condition. Again, it must be kept in mind that tuberculosis may be implanted upon syphilitic lesion of the lung.

## DIAGNOSIS.

There is nothing pathognomonic in the symptoms or physical signs attending syphilitic lesions of the lungs. The symptoms do not differ from similar non-syphilitic lesions; hence in most cases the diagnosis must depend upon suspicion or knowledge of the syphilitic taint, the simultaneous existence of other syphilitic lesions, and response to anti-syphilitic treatment.

## PROGNOSIS.

The prognosis will depend upon the extent of the pulmonary lesions, evidences of syphilis in other parts, and the general condition of the patient.

## TREATMENT.

**Early Stage.**—If the condition is recognized early the usual course of specific treatment with **Mercury** and **Kali hyd,** is the only method to pursue.

**Late.**—If the disease is in an advanced stage, and the patient emaciated, the **Iodide** treatment, together with measures directed to improving the strength and general nutrition of the patient, is called for.

# TUMORS OF THE LUNGS.

**Varieties.**—The most common forms are sarcoma and carcinoma. The growths are in most cases secondary.

**Morbid Anatomy.**—Primary growths may occur as definite tumors, or as infiltrations; the latter are the more common. The pulmonary lymphatics are usually infiltrated in the neighborhood of the growth. Secondary tumors are often multiple, but a single mass may be present. If softening occurs there may be destruction of tissue, the formation of cavities, and the collection of pus.

**Symptoms.**—Growths have been found after death, their presence not having been revealed by symptoms during life. In other cases the symptoms are such as are common to many chronic pulmonary diseases—cough, dyspnea, expectoration, hemoptysis, emaciation, fever. The expectoration is sometimes of prune-juice or currant-jelly character, which is characteristic. The physical signs are those of lung consolidation. If the growth extends to the mediastinum its pressure upon important vessels and nerves gives rise to more active and urgent symptoms than when confined to the lung.

**Prognosis.**—A fatal termination is inevitable. Treatment can be but symptomatic and palliative.

# SECTION III.

## PULMONARY TUBERCULOSIS.

**Varieties.**

I. Acute Pneumonic Tuberculosis.
II. Chronic Pulmonary Tuberculosis.
III. Fibroid Phthisis.

### I. ACUTE PNEUMONIC TUBERCULOSIS.

**Synonyms.**—Acute Pneumonic Phthisis; "Galloping Consumption;" Phthisis Florida.

**Definition.**—A specific inflammation of the lungs, running an acute course.

**Etiology.**—It is due to infection by the bacillus tuberculosis in a very susceptible subject.

**Types.**—A. The Pneumonic Type; B. The Broncho-Pneumonic Type.

### A. THE PNEUMONIC TYPE.

**Forms.**—(a) Primary; (b) Secondary.

(a) **Primary.**—The primary form occurs in those in previously good health; or it may be preceded by a "cold."

(b) **Secondary.**—The secondary form may follow localized tuberculosis of other parts; or, it may follow measles, whooping-cough, influenza, or debilitating diseases.

**Age.**—The pneumonic type is usually a disease of adult life; it is rare in children.

121

## PATHOLOGY.

### (a) Penumonic Type.

**Area Involved.**—Usually but a single lobe is involved, but in some cases an entire lung may be affected.

**Source of the Bacilli.**—(a) The bacilli may enter from without, by inhalation; or, (b) from within, by the discharge of old caseous foci.

**Naked-eye Appearance.**—The affected portion of lung is solid; it is deeply congested.

**Section.**—A section shows on the cut surface a variegated appearance; scattered over the dark, congested surface are nodules (the size of shot); in color, translucent, pearly, gelatinous-like. These are tubercles. They are located in the inter-lobular septa, especially at their points of junction.

**Caseation.**—Older areas show caseous masses, which are located in the peri-bronchial tissue, resulting from diffuse infiltration of the peri-bronchial and perivascular lymphatics. The lung-tissue is yellowish and consolidated.

**Cavities.**—There are scattered small cavities, produced by the breaking down of the caseous matter; they have irregular, ragged walls.

**Pneumothorax.**—A superficial cavity may rupture, and cause pneumothorax, subsequently becoming a pneumopyothorax.

**Fibrin.**—There are masses of fibrinous exudate in the alveoli.

**Differentiation.**—In some cases the consolidated lobe may, in gross appearance, be hard to distinguish from fibrinous pneumonia. In such case examine other parts (the opposite lung, the bronchial glands, the peritoneum) for tuberculous foci.

**Pneumococcus.**—The pneumococcus is sometimes found, but it is not a necessary agent in the production of acute pneumonic phthisis.

**The Pleura.**—There is usually pleuritis, with the characteristic changes.

## PHYSICAL SIGNS.

**Location.**—In most cases, the upper lobe is the part affected.

**Examination.—Early:**—Pleuritic friction-sounds; fremitus; absence of respiratory murmur; crepitant râles; bronchial breathing; dulness on percussion. (Note that these signs are the same as occur in lobar pneumonia.) **Later:**—After the first week or ten days, the signs belonging to softening and cavity-formation make their appearance.

## SYMPTOMS.

**Onset.**—The disease is usually sudden in onset.

**Chill.**—It is ushered in abruptly by a severe chill.

**Fever.**—There is rapid rise of temperature following the chill; it soon reaches 104° or 105° F. The course of the fever is of the continuous type, but more especially in severe cases there are remissions of 1.5° or 2° F. In some cases there is hyperpyrexia—106°-107° F.

**Pain.**—There is often sharp pain in the side (due to the pleuritic complication).

**Cough.**—It appears early, and remains throughout as a marked feature of the disease.

**Expectoration.**—At first it is mucoid; then rust-colored (it now generally contains bacilli); later, muco-purulent, and greenish (this greenish sputum is characteristic).

**Hemoptysis.**—In some cases there is bronchial hemorrhage.

**Dyspnea.**—It is an early symptom; usually it is severe; the respirations are rapid (30-40 or more); superficial; sometimes there are suffocative attacks.

**Night-Sweats.**—Night-sweats usually begin about the end of the first week; the sweats are profuse and exhausting.

**Emaciation.**—Emaciation is usually first markedly apparent about the end of the first week, and after that is rapid and extreme.

**Vital Powers.**—From the first there is great prostration, and finally extreme exhaustion.

**Mind.**—The mental state is cheerful and hopeful, even to the last.

**Duration.**—Usually the duration of the disease is from two to six weeks; in rare cases it extends to three or four months.

**Prognosis.**—Always grave; recovery is very rare.

## DIAGNOSIS.

Acute pneumonic phthisis must, in the first week, be differentiated from **lobar pneumonia.** The chief distinguishing features in favor of acute pneumonic tuberculosis are:—The apex is usually first involved; the type of fever is often remittent; there are profuse sweats; sometimes hemoptysis. After the first week the signs usually become distinctive. There is absence of the crisis belonging to pneumonic fever. At any period examination of the sputum and detection of the bacillus tuberculosis will establish the diagnosis.

**Termination.**—In the few cases that do not end fatally there is proliferation of cicatrical tissue in the necrosed lung, with contraction and slow recovery.

## B.  THE BRONCHO-PNEUMONIC TYPE.

**Pathology.**

**Naked-eye Appearance.**—The cut surface of the lung shows:—Disseminated areas of consolidation corresponding to lobules, or groups of lobules, with crepitant lung tissue between. Here and there are zones of collapsed lung tissue, or emphysematous areas. The adjacent lung is congested and slightly edematous.

**Color.**—Early the solidified masses are grayish-red; later, opaque white, or yellowish caseous.

**Cavities.**—The caseous matter softens, breaks down, and leaves small cavities. Pneumothorax may result if the cavity is superficial.

**Microscopic Appearance.**—The solidified matter in the lobules consists of tubercular masses, caseous matter, and proliferated epithelial cells.

**Termination.**—If recovery takes place (which is rare) encapsulation may occur, or, breaking down, with subsequent cicatrization.

## PHYSICAL SIGNS.

**Early.**—The early signs are similar to those occurring in catarrhal bronchitis—moist râles, with or without pleuritic pains. Later, in scattered areas there will be impaired percussion resonance, sub-crepitant râles, and broncho-vesicular breathing. Still later—signs of softening and cavity-formation. The lesions are usually located, for the most part, at the apices, and extend downwards. Usually the changes are bilateral.

## SYMPTOMS.

**Onset.**—The mode of onset varies in different cases:— (a) It may attack those in previous good health, but suffering from temporary exhaustion from overwork; (b) hemoptysis is the initial symptom in a few cases (showing a previously-existing tubercular focus); (c) repeated chills initiate other attacks; (d) in children it often follows measles, whooping-cough, or other infectious diseases.

**Age.**—This type (the broncho-pneumonic) occurs most frequently in children and young adults. It is most common from the sixth month to the fifth year.

**Fever.**—Early the temperature is usually high—103°-104° F., but its course is irregular, with frequent remissions.

**Pain.**—Pain is present or absent according to the involvement of the pleura.

**Cough.**—This occurs early, and is a constant symptom.

**Expectoration.**—First it is mucous; then, muco-purulent; later it contains elastic fibres; also, at times, it is blood-stained; sometimes it is fetid.

**Hemoptysis.**—This is a late symptom in some cases.

**Perspiration.**—There are drenching night-sweats.

**Exhaustion.**—With the progress of the case the exhaustion becomes extreme.

**Emaciation.**—There is progressive loss of flesh, and finally extreme emaciation.

**Course and Duration.**—In the acute cases, by the end of about three weeks the patient is much emaciated and exhausted, and in a low, typhoid-like state, with delirium, dry, coated tongue, and high fever, and the case ends fatally. Other cases pursue a tedious course for six or eight weeks, when the symptoms abate in severity and the disease becomes chronic, with secondary infection, destruction of lung tissue, cavity-formation, and death as in chronic pulmonary tuberculosis. A few cases finally recover, with cicatrization of the affected lung tissue.

**Diagnosis.**—It must be differentiated from simple, non-tuberculous broncho-pneumonia. The crucial sign is the discovery of elastic-fibres or bacilli in the sputum.

**Prognosis.**—The prognosis is almost always unfavorable; recoveries are few.

## TREATMENT.

**General Remarks.**—The treatment of acute pneumonic tuberculosis is, as a rule, very unsatisfactory. The measures adopted make but little impression on the disease, and the mortality rate is high. Still, in every case, effort should be unremitting.

**Medicinal.**—The remedies to be used are those which are most efficacious in the treatment of the chronic form of the disease:— Arsenicum iod.; Phosphorus; Baptisia; Iodine; Ferrum phos.; Antimonium iod., etc.

**General Measures.**—The nursing should be as in acute fevers generally, with a sustaining diet.

# CHRONIC PULMONARY TUBERCULOSIS.

**Synonyms.**—Phthisis Pulmonalis; Chronic Ulcerative Tuberculosis of the Lungs; "Consumption."

**Prevalence.**—Phthisis pulmonalis is the most prevalent of all diseases. It is the cause of about one-seventh of all deaths. Of late years, owing to modern methods of treatment, because phthisis is now recognized as being a curable disease, the mortality-rate is being gradually reduced.

## ETIOLOGY.

**Specific Cause.**—The specific cause of tuberculosis is the invasion of the tissues by the **bacillus tuberculosis**—the bacillus of Koch.

**Avenue of Entrance.**—The bacillus tuberculosis gains entrance to the lungs by:—(a) Inhalation in the inspired air; (b) Conveyance to the lungs (by the lymphatics or veins) from a tuberculous focus in other parts, the bronchial glands, the pleura, or other tissue or organ.

**Predisposing Cause.**—The predisposing cause is the possession of a constitution having a low equation of resistance to the infective action of the **bacillus tuberculosis**. The low equation of resistance on the part of the constitution may be the result of—(1) Heredity; or, it may be—(2) Acquired.

(1) **Heredity.**—The constitution having a low equation of resistance may be due to **heredity** when one or both parents have been tuberculous, or otherwise cachectic.

(2) **Acquirement.**—The constitution with low equation of resistance may be acquired by:—(a) Confinement in a vitiated atmosphere, especially when due to overcrowding by human beings; unsanitary surroundings; deficient food; depressing emotions.

(b) The **acquired** predisposition (low equation of resistance) follows as a result of acute or chronic diseases which are attended by bronchial catarrh, such as:—bronchitis; broncho-pneumonia; measles; whooping-cough; influenza; diabetes; Bright's; and other maladies. A certain number of cases of pulmonary tuberculosis are preceded by pleuritis; in such cases it is probable that the pleuritis, from the first, is tubercular. As a sequel of typhoid, pulmonary tuberculosis is extremely rare. Also, lobar pneumonia is very rarely followed by tuberculosis. Contrary to a view that has prevailed in the past, the subjects of mitral lesions do not enjoy comparative immunity from tuberculosis.

## PATHOLOGY.

**The Tubercle.**—The tubercle is the histological **unit** of the process (though there can be tuberculosis—especially in the acute pneumonic form—without the formation of "tubercles;" also, "tubercles" are not peculiar to "tuberculosis").

### Formation of Tubercles.

**Irritation.**—The specific irritant to the lung-tissue is the **bacillus tuberculosis,** or its toxins.

**Reaction.**—There is reaction to the irritant (bacillus, toxin) on the part of:—(a) the fixed connective-tissue elements; and (b) the vascular system.

**(a) Reaction of the Fixed Connective-Tissue.**—At the point of infection and irritation there is proliferation of round cells, called "epithelioid" cells. **Epithelioid cells** are so called because of their resemblance to epithelial cells in possessing a large amount of protoplasm.

**(b) Reaction of the Vascular System.**—There is round-cell infiltration about the focus of irritation, the leucocytes coming from the surrounding blood-vessels, forming a lymphoid tubercle. A **lymphoid tubercle** is one in which the lymphoid cells greatly preponderate in number and amount over the epithelioid cells.

**Giant Cells.**—In the tubercles there are large, irregularly-shaped cells, with numerous nuclei; these cells are called "giant" cells. They are enlarged epithelioid cells, or epithelioid cells "run together." Giant cells are not peculiar to the tubercular process. But in no other pathological products are they so numerous. They occur also in tubercular growths of syphilitic origin.

**Naked-eye Appearance.**—At this stage the tubercles appear as grayish, pearl-like bodies; there may be an aggregation of many into a mass (tubercular* mass).

**Location.**—Tubercles may form in:—(a) The bronchial mucous membrane; (b) the peribronchial tissue; (c) the walls of the alveoli; (d) the lung-substance.

**Micropscopic Structure.**—The tubercle is non-vascular; it is crossed by a few connective-tissue fibres, forming a fibrous stroma. There are bacilli in all the cells (most numerous in the giant-cells). Hence, the tubercle consists of (a) epithelioid cells; (b) lymphoid cells; (c) giant-cells; (d) bacilli; (e) a light connective-tissue stroma.

**Degenerative Changes.**

(a) Coagulation-necrosis; (b) caseous necrosis; (c) fatty metamorphosis.

(a) **Coagulation-Necrosis.**—The formed cells lose their structure and outline, and become converted into a homogeneous mass; in color, opaque waxy, or gray. The degeneration is due to the non-vascularity of the tubercle, as well as to the direct action of the toxins of the bacilli.

(b) **Caseation. — Caseous Necrosis. —** Caseation is a subsequent process to coagulation-necrosis, which always precedes it. The caseous mass is yellowish, of

---

*The term "tuberculous" is preferably to be used in referring to the disease process excited by the bacillus tuberculosis, in all its forms and manifestations. The term "tubercular" is to be confined in its application to the histological structures called "tubercles."

cheesy consistence. It can never undergo resolution; it can be cast off (by communicating with a bronchus, through ulceration); it can be reabsorbed; become encysted; or, calcified. Caseous matter contains many bacilli.

**Fatty Metamorphosis.**—The tubercle may undergo fatty metamorphosis. The biochemic change which is involved in the process of fatty metamorphosis is caused by the direct action of the toxins, which interfere with the gaseous cell metabolism; that is, the interchange of carbon-dioxide and oxygen.

**Course.**—When the tubercle has formed, and become caseous, the tissues are subject to the action of two opposing forces, a tendency to the limitation of the tuberculous process—(1) **Encapsulation**; and, a tendency to spread of the process—(2) **Dissemination.**

(1) **Encapsulation.**—There is hyperplasia of surrounding connective-tissue, resulting in the formation of a dense, fibrous wall ("limiting-membrane"), which completely encloses the caseous mass.

**Subsequent History:**—(a) The caseous mass may remain enclosed in its capsule for an indefinite period (one year, or many years), the bacilli remaining latent. (b) At any time the fibrous capsule may "break down" (due to streptococcic invasion), thus liberating the contained caseous matter, and the bacilli thereby invade the surrounding lung-tissue, thus setting up afresh the tuberculous process in new territory.

(2) **Dissemination.**—If encapsulation does not take place, the tendency is for the tuberculous process to spread, by means of the dissemination of the bacilli from the original focus, to surrounding structures.

**Modes of Dissemination.**—(a) **Mucous Membrane:**—If the original focus is seated on the bronchial mucous membrane, particles of the tubercular nodule may become detached as the result of violent cough, or from ulceration (streptococcus invasion); then inspiratory effort carries these particles into the bronchioles, thus establishing new foci of tuberculosis. (b) **The lung struc-**

ture:—When the original focus is in the lung structure, bacilli are conveyed to other parts of the lung by (1) the flow of lymph; (2) the phagoctyes, which take up bacilli from the edge of the tubercle, migrating with them; in the new location the phagoctye perishes and the bacillus is liberated. In this way bacilli are conveyed not only to other parts of the affected lung, but they may be carried to distant parts of the body, to the cerebral meninges, to the joints, etc., thus creating new foci and setting up a tuberculous meningitis, arthritis, etc.

**Calcification.**—Tubercles may undergo calcareous degeneration. The salts of the blood (chiefly the phosphates and carbonates of calcium) form an insoluble combination with the proteids of the neoplasm. **Subsequent course:**—(a) The calcerous mass may become encapsulated, and so remain throughout a life-time; or (b) at a later period the fibrous wall may ulcerate, by suppuration of the surrounding structures, due to streptococcus invasion, thus liberating the calcareous particles, which may appear in the sputum.

**Consolidation.**—Consolidation in pulmonary tuberculosis is due to the infiltration of the lung tissue by masses of tubercles.

**Cavity-Formation.**—The formation of cavities is due to secondary streptococcus invasion of the infiltrated tissue, with resulting suppuration, necrosis, and loss of substance. The abscess communicates with a bronchus, the pus escapes, and is removed from the lungs by expectoration. Absorption of the toxins by the lymphatics and venules causes septicemia, with all the symptoms belonging to secondary infection.

## EARLY DIAGNOSIS.

### The Bacillus Tuberculosis.

The detection of the bacillus tuberculosis in the sputum renders the diagnosis positive.

## The Sputum.

Have the patient, preferably on first waking in the morning, wash the mouth thoroughly with pure water. After the first spell of cough and expectoration (to clear away bronchial mucus), have the patient make a second effort at cough, and what is raised is to be expectorated into a clean, wide-mouthed bottle. **Caution:**—Avoid obtaining "mouth sputum."

## Time of Examination.

Results are best if the examination of the specimen is made inside of twenty-four hours from the time it is obtained.

## The Specimen.

Deposit a quantity of the sputum on a clean glass slide, and spread it slightly. Hold it over a black surface; there will usually be found a number of grayish-yellow, irregular, translucent granules (caseous matter), smaller than the head of a pin. Pick up a granule with a clean pointed instrument; spread it over the surface of a clean cover-glass. If the granules of caseous matter cannot be found, a particle of pus is next best; the mucus rarely contains bacilli.

## Exact Method.

If specimens obtained in this way fail to reveal bacilli, take the mass of sputum and partially digest it with **caustic-potash**; collect the solid portion by the centrifuge. If a few bacilli are present this will usually secure them.

## Glass-plate Method.

In the early stage of the disease, when there is no expectoration, take a clean plate of glass, three inches wide and six inches long; hold it about six inches from the patient's mouth; have him make forcible effort at cough, a number of times. On the surface of the glass there will be deposited a fine spray; here and there may be found some fine pellets of matter that have come from the alveoli; select one of these, remove it to a slide, and stain it in the usual method.  Often the bacilli may be detected by this means.

### Staining.

1. Spread the cover-glass with a thin (not too thin, yet not too thick) layer of the sputum to be examined.

2. Dry it in the air.

3. Fix it by passing through the flame three times.

4. Stain in **Para-fuchsin.**

5. Pass it through the flame ten times, keeping it steaming.

6. Wash with water.

7. Wash with solution of **Sulphuric acid** (10 per cent).

8. Again wash with water, washing out thoroughly.

9. Counter-stain (30 seconds) with **Methylene-blue** (don't overstain).

10. Wash with water until very faint blue remains.

11. Mount in **Canada-balsam.**

12. Examine with oil-immersion lens (1-12 in.).

### Identification.

**Shape.**—The bacillus is rod-shaped, with rounded ends, and a slight curve; they often appear in pairs, placed end-to-end, or overlapping; many have a "beaded" appearance, which indicates old bacilli, of low degree of virulence.  The bacillus tuberculosis has no spores. **Size:**—Length, 1.5—3.5 u; breadth, 0.2—0.5 u (micromillimeter).

### Diagnosis.

The detection of the bacillus in the expectorated matter is absolutely diagnostic of tuberculosis.  At times a number of specimens will be examined before the bacilli are detected.

**Differentiation.**—The **bacillus tuberculosis** must be distinguished from the **smegma bacillus** (placed in 60 per cent alcohol the smegma bacillus parts with its stain), and from the **bacillus leprae** (exclude it clinically).

### Vital Capacity.

Marked reduction in the vital capacity of the individual denotes lowered equation of resistance to tuberculosis. The vital capacity (amount of air, in cubic inches,
that the lungs will contain, as measured by the spirom-
eter) of a man five feet eight inches in height (5 ft. 8 in.)
is 230 cu. in. If this should be reduced to 200 or less, it
denotes low equation of resistance to tuberculosis. In
connection with suspicious physical signs it has diagnostic value. The vital capacity of woman is about 38
cu. in. less than in a man of the same height. There is,
normally, an increase of 8 cu. in. vital capacity for every
increase of an inch in height.

### "Corpulence."

What is called "corpulence" takes into consideration
the relation of the individual's weight to his height.
**Rule**:—Divide the weight by the height. **E. g.**:Weight,
160 lbs; height, 5 ft. 10 in. One hundred and sixty divided by 5.83 equals 27.44, which expresses the "corpulence" of the individual. The standard corpulence is 26.
The standard for women is 23. If the "corpulence" is
reduced two points (1 to 24 in men, or 1 to 21 in women)
it is "abnormal leanness," and favors tuberculosis.

### Perspiration Test.

The sweat of the subject of tuberculosis contains
**tuberculin.** If the sweat be recovered and injected into
a tuberculous guinea pig the characteristic tuberculin-
reaction will take place. Serum secured by creating a
blister on the skin can be used instead of the sweat.

### Location of the Lesion.

In the vast majority of cases (500 to 1) the initial
lesion is in the apex of the upper lobe of the lung. **Exact location**:—An inch or an inch and a half from the
summit of the apex, near the posterior and external border.

### Side Affected.

The right apex is more often invaded than the left (of
427 cases, right apex 178; left, 134; both, 115). The

right bronchus affords a more ready avenue of entrance than does the left.

### The Apex.

The conditions that determine primary invasion of the **apex** of the lung are:—Less functional activity '(the weight of the shoulder is upon it, and the first, second and third ribs are more restricted in motion than the lower ones) ; greater exposure to the air; less ventilation; greater difficulty in removing secretion; the secretion becomes inspissated. On the right side the divisions of the bronchial tree—the bronchial tubes—which extend into the upper lobe leave the main bronchus at a right-angle; in other parts of the lung the angle is obtuse. This arrangement favors freer ventilation in the apex of the left lung than in the apex of the right.

### Order of Distribution of the Lesions.

**Upper Lobe.**—Initial lesion.—The primary lesion, in the vast majority of cases, is in the apex of the upper lobe of the lung. **Location on the chest-wall.**—The location on the chest-wall corresponding to this initial lesion in the apex is, **anteriorly,** a spot just below the center of the clavicle; **posteriorly,** over the supra-spinus fossa of the scapula. From this initial point the usual line of extension is downward along the anterior aspect of the upper lobe of the lung, its line of extension corresponding to a vertical line on the **anterior** aspect of the chest-wall about an inch-and-a-half from the sternal ends of the first, second and third interspaces.

**Middle Lobe.**—The middle lobe is rarely the site of a primary lesion; sometimes it escapes altogether. When secondarily affected after the upper lobe the lesion follows the line of extension of the upper lobe.

**Lower Lobe.**—The lower lobe on the affected side, right or left, is usually early involved, often long before the disease has made much progress in the upper lobe of the same side, and before the apex of the opposite lung is affected. **The initial lesion** starts in the lower lobe about an inch-and-a-half below the highest point of the apex of the lobe. On the chest-wall this point corresponds to a spot, **posteriorly,** just to the right of the spine of the fifth dorsal vertebra. From its initial point near the apex the usual **line of extension** is downward and outward along the inter-lobar septum. On the chest-wall this line corresponds to the vertebral border of the scapula as it is in position with the arm raised behind the head.

**Blood Changes.**—The blood changes in pulmonary tuberculosis are quite varied, one type of cases early taking on the characteristic changes of chlorosis, with a marked diminution of hemoglobin and only slight reduction of red cells. Another type gives such changes as are found in other secondary anemias (a parallel reduction of red cells and hemoglobin), with more or less marked hyper-leucocytosis. In the more chronic form the consumption of the liquid together with that of the cellular elements produces a condition which approaches the normal, and repeated blood-examinations will often show an increase of the hemoglobin and red cells, while the tuberculous process is making continued progress. The blood recovers rapidly from the effects of hemoptysis. Normoblasts appear, but not in numbers found after hemorrhages caused by other conditions.

**Extension Towards the Base.**—In its further progress towards the base the lesion does not advance along any special line, but extends by scattered nodules of infiltration.

**Exceptions.**—There may be various departures from the lines of extension in the several lobes, as above indicated, but the usual order is as here given.

**X-Ray Examination.**—The X-ray gives little information of the lung-changes in the incipient stage of tubercular infiltration. The tissues are not sufficiently dense to cause the appearance of a shadow. After the changes have become sufficient to be revealed by the X-ray they can be detected by other methods of diagnosis. The only thing that the X-ray shows in the early stage is restricted motion of the diaphragm.

## TUBERCULIN TEST.

**Value.**—Response to this test is absolutely diagnostic of tuberculosis, and it is available at the earliest stage of the disease-process, when the physical examination is inconclusive.

**Method.**—Two days before the test, take the patient's temperature every two hours, in order to get correct knowledge of the range.

**Time of Injection.**—Make the injection at 6 or 8 o'clock a. m., or 10 to 11 o'clock p. m.

**Site of the Injection.**—Observing the usual aseptic precautions, make the injection deep in the tissues of the back, in the space between the scapula and the spinal column.

**The Reaction.—Time:**—The reaction begins usually about 12 hours after the injection (it may occur in 8 or 9 hours; or, rarely, be delayed to 24 hours). **Symptoms:**— A characteristic pyrexial curve; malaise; pains in the head, back and limbs; sometimes nausea and vomiting. **The temperature curve:**—There is an abrupt rise to the maximum, whatever that may be in the individual case; the maximum temperature is sustained for 2 or 3 hours; then there is a gradual decline to normal, which is reached in 24 to 36 hours; it is followed by a sub-normal temperature, lasting for some time, when the patient returns to his usual condition.

**Indications for Use.**—The tuberculin test should not be used indiscriminately; only in what appears to be the early stages of phthisis, when other methods of diagnosis have failed to establish the true nature of the case and it is desired to determine positively whether it is of tubercular origin.

**Examination.**—Make physical examination of the lungs at the time of reaction; sometimes it is possible to detect by auscultation some of the early signs, which before the injection of the tuberculin were absent.

**The Dose.**—Begin with a very small dose of tuberculin; if no reaction occurs, repeat with a larger dose in 2 or 3 days. **Initial dose:**—One-half (½) a milligramme; if no reaction occurs, in 2 or 3 days repeat with one (1) milligramme; if no reaction, in 2 or 3 days repeat with two (2) milligrammes; if no reaction, the next time three (3) milligrammes, and so proceed. A dose of ten (10) milligrammes must not be exceeded.

**What the Test Indicates.**—Reaction to tuberlin indicates that there is a tuberculous focus somewhere in the patient's body; it does not necessarily imply that existing symptoms are due to its presence, nor does it render it certain that the tubercular focus is in the lungs.

**Exceptions.**—In some cases (the proportion not determined) syphilis may give a reaction to tuberculin; non-tuberculous subjects may react at some dose, but the reaction is not typical.

**Caution.**—The tuberculin test should be used with great caution. It sometimes arouses a latent tuberculosis to great activity.

## SYMPTOMS.

**Mode of Onset.**—The initial symptoms of different cases of pulmonary tuberculosis show various forms, as: (a) Hemorrhagic form; (b) Catarrhal form; (c) Pleuritic form; (d) Laryngeal form; (e) Fever-and-chill form; (f) Glandular form.

**Hemorrhagic Form.**

In some cases the initial symptom is pulmonary hemorrhage:—(a) repeated slight losses of blood, for weeks, coughed up; or, more frequently, (b) an abundant hemorrhage.

**Preceding Condition.**—There is, doubtless, tuberculosis in all these cases before the hemoptysis occurs.

**Subsequent Course.**—(a) In some cases other pulmonary symptoms do not appear; (b) in others, the chronic condition gradually develops; (c) in still others, signs of consolidation at once appear and the course of the disease is rapid.

Note.—Hemorrhage as an initial symptom is not, as a rule, of grave import. Such cases are often amenable to treatment, and recovery is not infrequent.

### Catarrhal Form.

It follows repeated "colds," taking the form of bronchial catarrh; either (a) primary; or, (b) secondary—to measles, whooping-cough, influenza, or other debilitating disease; there are accompanying weakness, loss of flesh, fever, and the usual physical signs over the apex (defective expansion; broncho-vesicular respiration; high-pitched percussion-note; fremitus). This form is usually very gradual in onset.

### Gastro-enteric Form.

Irritability of the stomach; vomiting; acid eructations; diarrhea (sometimes); malaise; emaciation; palpitation of the heart; anemia; slight afternoon fever. These cases, through error in diagnosis, and failure to examine the lungs, are sometimes treated as "dyspepsia."

### Pleuritic Form.

It may be (a) Primary (dry pleurisy at the apex, with friction murmur); (b) Secondary to pleurisy with effusion (about one-third such cases later develop pulmonary tuberculosis).

### Laryngeal Form.

Throat and larynx symptoms; hoarseness, aphonia; scanty expectoration (containing bacilli); tubercles or ulcers (revealed by the laryngoscope). Cases of this mode of onset are rare. It is probable that there is a preceding slight tuberculosis of the lung, though it is rarely detected.

### Fever-and-Chill Form.

Recurring paroxysms of chill, fever and sweat, resembling malarial fever (in malarial regions the error in diagnosis is often made).

**Glandular Form.**

The pulmonary symptoms are preceded for a long period by enlargement of the lymph-nodes of the neck, axilla, and, doubtless, of the mediastinum (the glands of the anterior portion of the mediastinum are most frequently affected).

## INDIVIDUAL SYMPTOMS.

**Cough.**

It is one of the earliest symptoms, and is seldom absent at any period.

**Character.**—Early, short, dry, hacking. Later, with expectoration; most troublesome—after meals, after exertion; on lying down at night; in the morning. Still later—severe paroxysms, sometimes causing vomiting.

**Cause.**—The early cough is due to irritation from the presence of tubercles; later, to the secretion; it may be due (especially in children) to pressure of enlarged bronchial glands on the trachea.

**Expectoration.**

It appears early (rarely delaying more than two months.

**Character.**—Early, clear, viscid, glairy mucus, or sometimes watery; later, it contains small gray or greenish purulent masses (caseous matter); still later, profuse, muco-purulent, yellowish or greenish.

**Quantity.**—Early, but scanty expectoration; later, there may be 8 to 10 ounces, or more.

**Taste.**—"Sweetish," or, "salty."

**Odor.**—Faintly sweet, or it may be putrid.

**Elements.**—Mucus, tubercles; bacilli; caseous matter; pus; elastic fibres; blood (sometimes).

**Elastic Fibres.—Character.**—A curled or branched network. In order to detect it, compress some of the purulent matter between two glass plates about three inches square; on a black background the fragments of elastic tissue appear to the naked eye as greenish-yellow spots. Or, boil some of the sputum for a few minutes with an equal volume of solution of caustic soda (20 grs. to the oz.); let the fluid stand in a tall conical glass for 24 hours. Examine the sediment under the microscope and the elastic fibres can be demonstrated.

## Pain.

Pain in the chest is present in almost all cases.

**Location.**—Usually the pain is in the supra- or infra-clavicular regions; or, in the lower axillary or mammary regions.

**Cause.**—The pain is due to inflammation of the underlying pleura or lung; or, stretching of old adhesions in coughing.

**Pain in the Joints.**—Tubercular synovitis is accompanied by severe articular pain.

**Nutrition.**—There is early emaciation, which is progressive; it is interrupted by periods of gain in weight, due to temporary arrest of the disease-process in the lungs.

**Respiration.**—The respirations are increased in frequency; they become more rapid as the disease of the lung extends in area, and when the disease is very extensive there is urgent dyspnea.

## Pulse.

There is increase in the pulse rate, and the pulse is "excitable," easily influenced by exertion.

**Diurnal Periods.**—The quickest pulse is usually in the morning; it falls after 9 p. m.

**Variations.**—The frequency of the pulse is influenced more by the condition of the patient with reference to his strength than it is by the pyrexia.

**Rate.**—Early, with but mild fever, it is 90 to 100; later, 100 to 110 or more.

**The Pulse of Weakness.**—A rapid pulse with low temperature is a sign of exhaustion.

**Digestion.**—Usually there is loss of appetite; thirst; coated tongue; symptoms of gastric catarrh. Vomiting occurs in some cases, due to (a) paroxysms of cough, or (b) irritant lesions of the pneumogastric.

**Diarrhoea.**—In some cases diarrhœa is an early symptom; in others, it occurs late, as a result of ulceration of the intestines.

## PHYSICAL SIGNS.

**Inspection.**

**Chest.**—The "phthisical" chest is long and narrow; the ribs are inclined towards the vertical; wide intercostal spaces; acute costal angle; antero-posterior flattening; prominent costal cartilages and depressed sternum; a deep concavity over the xiphoid cartilage. Phthisis is by no means confined to those having chests of this shape. But such chest, which usually contains a heart small in size, predisposes its possessor to tuberculosis on invasion by the bacillus.

**Clavicles.**—The clavicles are "prominent" (due to wasting of the overlying tissue); the one over the affected lung appears to be more prominent than the other.

**Scapulae.**—The scapulæ are "winged"—that is, owing to wasting of the muscles and subcutaneous fat, they "stand out."

**Motion.**—On respiration there is restricted motion of the affected side, most noticeable in the infra-clavicular region. It is best detected by standing behind the seated patient and looking down, over the shoulders.

**Precordial Area.**—In tuberculosis of the left apex there may be increased area of impulse in the precordial region, in the second, third and fourth interspaces.

**Skin.**—Late, the skin is pale and anemic; it is thin, without subcutaneous fat; the blue veins show through; in some cases (late) the skin is orange-yellow; brownish-yellow, or dark-brown patches (pityriasis versicolor) appear on the front of the chest, in the axillæ or on the back.

**Palpation.**

**Deficient Expansion.**—Place the hands in the subclav-icular spaces, one on each side; have the patient slowly take a full breath; deficient expansion (if it exists) of one side will be detected. Repeat with the hands on the sides of the chest.

**Fremitus.**—Place the hand over the region affected (usually the apex); let the patient count "nine ninety-nine;" fremitus will be more pronounced if there is consolidation (normal fremitus is more pronounced on the right side). The fremitus is decreased over (a) great pleuritic thickening; (b) pleural effusion. It is increased over a cavity.

**Percussion.**

**Dulness.**—Dulness (higher pitch) appears over areas of consolidation. **Locations:**—Early, (a) just above the clavicle; (b) over the clavicle; (c) just below the clavicle; (d) the supra-spinous space (of the scapula); (e) the interscapular space (beside the spine on a level with the fifth rib); (f) along the inner border of the scapula. **Method:**—Have the patient take a full inspiration and hold the breath, then compare the two sides; repeat on expiration. Also, compare the percussion-note taken at the apex with the note lower down (allow for normal difference).

**Variations.**—The percussion-note may be but slightly altered:—(a) if the consolidated areas are small, with normal lung tissue between; (b) if there are numerous small cavities, with much fibroid tissue, or thickening of the pleura. "Wooden" dulness occurs in old cases, with much fibroid change. Over a **cavity** the pitch changes with the mouth open or closed (Wintrich's sign). Cracked-pot sound is given forth on percussion over large cavities with thin walls.

**Auscultation.**

**Early.**—The **breath-sounds** are usually feeble; some-times scarcely audible (less air enters the affected portion of the lung, owing to swelling, secretion, and narrowing of the smaller bronchi). Compare the two sides:—(a) with quiet breathing; (b) with deep inspiration. **With consolidation:**—Tubular breathing. **Over cavities:**—Cavernous; amphoric. **Over unaffected lung:** —Harsh, or puerile respiratory murmur. Sometimes, early, there is harsh murmur.

**Interrupted Respiration.**—The respiratory sound is interrupted, "jerky," "wavy," "cog-wheel" (due to loss of resilience of the lung tissue). This sign is not peculiar to phthisis.

**Expiration.**—The expiratory act is prolonged; it is of higher pitch,

**Voice-Sounds.**—Bronchophony; voice-whisper; pectoriloquy; ægophony.

**Rales.**—Crepitant; sub-crepitant (due to the accompanying bronchitis). With cavity-formation:—Moist sounds—bubbling, gurgling; metallic tinkle.

**Heart-Sounds.**—The heart-sounds are transmitted when there is a large cavity in the left lung.

**Friction.**—Pleuritic friction-sound may occur very early; in some cases it persists. There is **Pleuro-pericardial friction** if the lappet of lung over the heart is involved in the pleuritic inflammation. This is not peculiar to phthisis.

## COMPLICATIONS.

Owing to the fact that there is no tissue or organ of the body that may not be the seat of tuberculosis, the complications that occur in connection with chronic pulmonary tuberculosis are many and various. An enumeration would include those belonging to the:—I. Respiratory System; II. Circulatory Organs; III. Digestive System; IV. Abdominal Organs; V. Glandular System; VI. Meninges and Brain.

**I. Respiratory System.**—(a) Tuberculosis of the larynx. (b) Bronchiectasis. (c) Pneumothorax. (d) Pulmonary abscess. (e) Gangrene of the lung.

II. **Circulatory Organs.**—(a) Pericarditis. (b) Endocarditis.

III. **Digestive System.**—(a) Tubercular ulceration of the pharynx, esophagus, stomach, and intestines. (b) Perforation of the intestine.

IV. **Abdominal Organs.**—(a) Tubercular peritonitis. (b) Amyloid degeneration of the (1) Liver; (2) Spleen; (3) Kidneys. (c) Miliary tubercle of the (1) Liver; (2) Spleen; (3) Kidneys. (d) The bladder and the generative organs in both male and female are liable to secondary tuberculous infection.

V. **Glandular System.**—Tuberculosis and caseation of the bronchial, mediastinal, cervical, or mesenteric glands.

VI. **Meninges and Brain.**—(a) Tubercular meningitis; (b) Cerebral abscess.

## TREATMENT.

**Hemoptysis.**—When this complication occurs in the course of chronic pulmonary tuberculosis the first measure is absolute rest in bed. The patient should not so much as talk, or raise an arm. He should be told not to try to restrain the flow of blood, but let it come as freely as it will. Have the room quiet, and no commotion or excitement on the part of those present.

**Reassure the Patient.**—Tell him that of itself the symptom is no more serious than an attack of nosebleed, or any other symptom belonging to his condition, and that an untoward result is something unknown.

Give to the patient small bits of ice to hold in the mouth or to swallow.

**Ligation.**—If the hemorrhage is great, ligate the legs and arms, near the body, by means of flannel bands, or handkerchiefs. Bind only tightly enough to obstruct the superficial venous flow, but not enough to affect the arterial pulse. Loosen the bands about every half-hour, or sooner if pressure on a nerve, or if cerebral anemia demand. Place a hot-water bag at the feet while the ligatures are on the legs.

**Salt-Solution.**—In order to restore the volume of the

blood and also to keep up bodily temperature, give colonic injections of hot (105°-120° F.) normal salt-solution.

**After the Attack.**—Still keep the patient quiet; let the meals be light, but more frequent, and of liquid food. Do not permit the patient to remain recumbent too long after the attack of hemorrhage; it favors hypostatic congestion of the lungs. In three days, at the most, he should be up and walk about. Respiratory exercise and deep breathing are helpful.

### Therapeutics of Hemoptysis.

**Aconite.** (3x).—Bright red blood; incessant, hacking cough; warm feeling in the chest; red face; great anxiety; arterial excitement.

**Ipecac.** (3x).—Sensation of bubbling in the chest, followed by copious bleeding; tickling beneath the sternum; spitting of blood after the least effort; nausea.

**Hamamelis.** (3x).—Venous hemorrhage; blood dark, thin, coming into the mouth without effort, like a warm current.

**Millefolium.** (3x)—Profuse flow of thin, bright-red blood; oppression; palpitation; not much cough.

**Veratrum vir.**—Violent congestion, with full, hard, bounding pulse.

**Phosphorus.** (3x).—For the inflammatory symptoms following an attack of hemoptysis. Tight feeling in the chest, with dry, tight cough, followed by hemorrhage.

**Ferrum phos.** (3x).—Hemorrhage of bright, red blood, occurring in the course of phthisis.

**Sulphuric acid.**—Persistent hemorrhage of dark blood; quantity slight; a continuous oozing; in feeble and anemic subjects. **Dose:**—Ten drops of the chemically pure acid in a glass of water; teaspoonful dose every hour.

**Chininum ars.**—For the anemia following excessive loss of blood.

**Cough.**—The irritable, dry cough of the early stage may often be allayed by such simple measures as sipping ice-water, or orange-juice, or by the use of lozenges of slippery-elm bark. It is sometimes a "habit-cough," when it may be controlled by effort of the will, or by holding the breath for a few seconds.

For relief of the hard morning cough, let the patient take a glass of hot water, with lemon-juice, and very little sugar.

Vomiting after coughing is generally due to mechanical disturbance of the stomach induced by the violent effort. In such case let the patient eat but moderate quantity at a time, and rest quietly after eating.

For the almost incessant and distressing cough of the late stage, **Codeine** is the most efficient palliative.

**Insomnia.**—Living in the open-air all day, and free ventilation of the sleeping-room at night, will do much to promote sleep. Other measures which will aid are:— Bathe the patient's feet in hot water, and rub dry with a crash-towel; with the palm of the hand stroke the spinal column from the back of the neck downward; give a glass of buttermilk, or matzoön or koumiss.

**Pityriasis Versicolor.**—For this parasitic condition of the skin, first wash the part with warm water and soap. Then apply a solution of the **hypo-sulphite of soda,** one dram to the ounce.

**Tuberculous Arthritis.**—This condition can occur at any stage of the disease. It is indicated by severe pain in the joint, and sometimes swelling of the overlying tissues. Bier's method of treatment, by ligature of the affected limb with elastic bands, gives most relief. Apply the elastic band on the limb, above the joint. Use a wide band. Do not bind too tightly—only enough to impede the venous circulation. The object is, not to produce anemia of the affected joint, but hyperemia and swelling. If the presence of the band creates intense pain, it must be removed. It should be applied several times a day, and kept, at first, from 10 to 30 minutes, increasing the length of time from day to day. Change the place of ligation on successive days. Give the joint rest.

**Diarrhea.**—Few cases run their course without more or less diarrhea. It is most common in the advanced stage, when it is due to intestinal tuberculosis, with ulceration. The discharges are colliquative in character. Treatment is too often unavailing, for the general condition of the patient at this stage is approaching the critical. The measures for relief include absolute rest in bed, and a supporting treatment.

The diarrhea which is due to enteritis should be treated as it is in other diseased conditions, by careful regulation of the diet and the appropriate remedies. Patients subject to repeated attacks of diarrhea should keep the abdomen well covered.

**Edema of the Ankles.**—The edema of the ankles which appears late in the course of the disease is due to the weak heart, the impaired nutrition, and the state of the blood. There is no special treatment that will affect it.

**Therapeutics.**

**Arsenicum iod.** (3x).—The most important remedy in incipient phthisis, especially when there is rapid loss of weight. Fever; cough; dyspnea; muco-purulent expectoration; prostration; diarrhea.

**Phosphorus.** (3x).—Especially in phthisis following pneumonia. Adapted to tall, thin, "hollow-chested" subjects. **Symptoms:**—Dry cough; soreness in the larynx and trachea; long-continued hoarseness; pain in the stomach after meals; diarrhea, especially after meals; palpitation; blood-streaked sputum; sweats; loss of strength; emaciation; pale skin.

**Kali carb.** (6x).—Sharp, stitching pains in the chest; cough dry, or with scanty expectoration; or, in advanced cases, profuse expectoration, with sharp stitching pains.

**Iodine.** (1x).—Tuberculosis in those of previously "scrofulous" habit; enlarged lymph-nodes; fair skin; persistent, short, hacking cough; night-sweats; morbid appetite; fever.

**Iodide of Antimony.** (3x).—It may with advantage be substituted for Iodine.

**Ferrum phos.** (3x).—Of use only in the early stages. Exacerbation of the pulmonary condition from exposure; congestion of the lungs, with blood-stained expectoration.

**Nux vomica.** (3x).—For the digestive disturbances, sometimes a prominent symptom in phthisis; morning headache; sour or bitter taste; vomiting, or violent retching; gastralgia; constipation, with ineffectual urging.

**Strychnin.** (3x).—With the symptoms of indigestion, as for **Nux vom., Strychnin** often has prompt action.

**Baptisia.** (1x).—As an intercurrent remedy, late in the disease, when there is fever; morning chills, followed by fever and perspiration; anorexia.

**Stannum.** (6x).—Cough attended by profuse, greenish or muco-purulent expectoration; hectic and emaciation; coarse râles; soreness in the chest after coughing; sense of weakness in the chest; talking causes fatigue; expectoration sweetish in taste.

**Calcarea carb.** (6x).—In incipient phthisis, in those of fat and flabby flesh; inability to take fat food; acid eructations; "acid dyspepsia"; free perspiration; rapid emaciation; loose, rattling cough; soreness of the chest, which is painful on pressure; persistent hoarseness; diarrhea; amenorrhea.

**Bryonia.** (1x).—Sharp pleuritic pains, with accompanying fever.

**Silicea.** (6x).—The presence of cavities; profuse expectoration of pus or muco-pus; fever and profuse sweats.

**Arsenicum.** (3x).—In advanced cases, with fever, anxiety and restlessness; diarrhea, due to intestinal ulceration.

**Arseniate of Quinine.** (2x).—In advanced cases, with the condition described under **Arsenicum**, this will have a "tonic" effect, rendering the patient's state more comfortable.

**Cuprum ars.** (3x).—Cramps in the abdomen, with vomiting and diarrhea, following stomach disturbance.

**Agaricin.** (2x).—For the night-sweats of phthisis. **Dose:**—One-grain tablet at bedtime; sometimes necessary to give two or three doses during the latter part of the day and in the evening.

**Phosphoric acid.** (3x).—Feeling of weakness in the chest; cough with feeling of tickling under the sternum; muco-purulent expectoration; night-sweats.

**Pilocarpine.** (2x).—Profuse sweats occurring in the course of acute phthisis.

**Atropine.** (2x).—In extreme cases, to check the exhausting sweats. **Atropine** may be used as a palliative; it is not curative in its action. **Dose:**—One one-hundredth of a grain, by hypodermic injection, given at bedtime.

**Aconite.** (3x).—For slight hemoptysis occurring in the early stages, with fever and excitement of the circulation.

**Antimonium iod.** (3x).—Fever; cough, with profuse muco-purulent expectoration.

**Ferrum ars.** (2x).—In cases with marked anemia; pale skin, and lips; in females, amenorrhea.

**Repertory.**

**Cough.**—Phosphorus; Nitric acid; Stannum; Hyoscyamus; Belladonna.

**Night-Sweats.**—Agaricin; Phosphoric acid; Arsenicum; Cinchona; Silicea; Atropin.

**Fever.**—Arsenic iod.; Baptisia; Ferrum phos.; Chininum ars.; Silicea.

**Digestive Disorders.**—Nux vomica; Strychnin; Arsenicum; Cuprum ars.; Ferrum ars.

**Pain in the Chest.**—Bryonia; Aconite; Kali carb.; Cimicifuga.

**Insomnia.**—Caffein; Digitalis.

**Hemoptysis.**—Millefolium; Phosphorus; Ferrum phos.; Acalypha.

## GENERAL MEASURES.

**Climate.**

No special climate is a specific for pulmonary phthisis. Climate is an adjuvant measure in the treatment of the

case.  In general, the climate that has the greatest number of sunshiny days affords the most favorable conditions for recovery.  But the climate best suited to the
individual case must be prescribed, as are other measures.

**Altitude.**—Recovery is best promoted in a region elevated from 1,000 to 5,000 feet above sea-level.  A rarefied atmosphere causes deep breathing and promotes
chest expansion.  A mean of about 2,000 or 2,500 is suitable to many cases.

**Class of Cases.**—Advanced cases (if permitted to go
from home) may be sent to a warm climate of little elevation—the California coast or Florida.  But it is far
better to keep them at home.

Patients with nasal and bronchial catarrh, with irritable pyrexia, may be sent to Southern Arizona, New Mexico, Western Texas, the highlands of California.

Incipient cases generally, or cases in the second degree with fair chances of recovery, may be sent to Col-
orado, Northern New Mexico, Arizona, the mountains
of North Carolina, Tennessee and Georgia, the Adirondacks.

Cases in which great altitude is contra-indicated:—
(a) Advanced phthisis; (b) complicated with emphysema; (c) with albuminuria; (d) with organic heart-disease;(e) with laryngeal ulceration; (f) with empyema;
(g) rapid progress and constant pyrexia; (h) great emaciation; (i) cases that suffer from insomnia and feel constantly cold at a great altitude.

**Considerations.**—Climate should not be prescribed re-
gardless of other local conditions.  Consideration should
be given to the matter of the patient being able to secure
suitable accommodations, proper food, and the surroundings which will promote contentment and comfort.  The
patient should also be under the constant care of a com-
petent physician.

**Drainage.**—A well-drained and dry soil must be chosen
for the residence of the phthisical.  Dampness of soil is a
potent predisposing factor in this disease.

**Mental Rest.**—Whether at home or in a distant resort, the consumptive patient must enjoy mental composure, and be cheerful and hopeful. A state of anxiety or worry will counteract the effect of other salutary measures. This must be taken into consideration in all treatment, and especially in sending a patient far from home.

**Home Climate.**—Under modern methods in many cases recovery may be brought about in the patient's home climate. Such recoveries are more enduring than those which are made in remote "resorts." If the patient will submit to be "managed" by his family physician, faithfully carrying out all prescribed measures, in incipient cases a favorable prognosis may be given in almost all instances, and some cases in a later stage may recover.

**Camp-Life.**—Of all methods to promote recovery in phthisis, none is superior to that of camp life. It should be adopted in all cases in which it is feasible. Unfortunately, for various reasons, it is not possible for many to take advantage of it. But all should do so who can. It affords in the fullest sense the greatest measure of outdoor life, the constant breathing of pure, fresh air, light and agreeable occupation, and change of scene, all of which induce hearty appetite and increased powers of digestion, thus favoring rapid recovery.

**Class of Cases.**—All curable cases will be benefited by this method. In the incipient stage of the disease there are few cases in which a cure cannot be guaranteed. Many cases in the second stage may make permanent recovery.

**Methods.**—There are two methods of carrying out this plan—by team outfit, traveling by wagon-road from place to place, establishing camp at a new spot each day, or every few days. The other is, with tent and camp outfit to go by rail to the objective point and there establish camp for the season.

**Outfit.**—For the first-named method, there should be a party of three, or two at the least. Secure a good horse and proper covered wagon, with a small "A" tent, and the usual camping outfit, such as hunters use, together with blankets, water-proof clothing, hammocks, and all the usual accessories. For the other method, make up an outfit with all except the wagon and horse, and pack the articles for shipment by rail.

**Season of the Year.**—The start should be made in early spring. Travel to the north. In New England, to the pine woods of Maine; in New York, to the Adirondacks; in Pennsylvania, to the mountain region; in the middle states, to Canada, northern Michigan or northern Wisconsin; in the west, to the mountains.

**Location.**—Seek some appropriate spot, preferably in the pine woods, and if possible near a body of water where there is fishing, but avoiding damp soil. Let there be a good drainage, and protection from high winds.

**Diet.**—In this mode of life the appetite is always such that the patient is not fastidious. Delicate dishes and variety are not demanded. It is always possible to obtain fresh milk, butter, eggs, poultry and vegetables, which with fish, bacon, fresh meat occasionally, and the cereals, especially shredded-wheat biscuit (in order to get all the elements of the whole wheat), make up a diet-list sufficient for all cases, and on which they thrive.

**Period.**—Remain in camp through the summer and into the autumn. On the first approach of cold weather return may be made to the patient's home. But at this time, in almost all cases, it may be said in all incipient cases, recovery, to appearances, will be complete. If the "home treatment" be carried out through the following winter, and the camping trip repeated the next summer, permanent recovery will be established in a greater number of cases than will follow any other method of treatment. Or, what is still better, on the return trip in the autumn continue the journey to the southward, traveling through Kentucky and Tennessee, or Virginia, making the objective point for the winter the pine regions of North Carolina or Georgia.

Recovery from incipient phthisis can be guaranteed in almost all cases if this plan is pursued.

**Regime.**—The patient should sleep as much as possible. Wet weather need not compel confinement, only being particular to protect with suitable underclothing and water-proof boots and outer garments. Through the middle of the day take rest in a hammock. The duties of camp-life, fishing, and walks in exploring the surrounding country will afford variety of occupation and exercise. Moving camp several times will add to the variety.

### Home Treatment.

Since, as has been said, all cannot indulge in this method, it is necessary for those who are deprived of its advantages to make use of the "home treatment."

By this term is meant a method of treatment of phthisis, but recently widely exploited, by means of which the patient receives the benefit of breathing fresh, outside air, instead of the confined air of a closed house. This, together with a carefully regulated diet, adapted to the case, and attention to proper exercise, lung-gymnastics and hydrotherapeutics, and rest when there is fever, make up the modern method of home treatment.

**Method.**—This consists in keeping the patient in the open-air for the entire twenty-four hours, essentially, in all seasons of the year when weather permits; at other seasons in the open-air during the greater part of the day, and with wide-open windows when sleeping inside at night. The details of this method of treatment will differ according to the location of the patient's home, whether in the cramped and closely-built city, or in the country.

**In the Country.**—In small towns and in the country, where there is plenty of space and wide lawn, the entire day must be spent by the patient out-of-doors. For this purpose make use of a "sun-trap."

**Sun-trap.**—This is a small structure about six-by-six feet square, made of light lumber, built on the plan of a lean-to shed. It is inclosed on three sides, in each of which is a window-like aperture, guarded by a canvas curtain. The large side is open, and also hung with a curtain, running on a wire. This sun-trap, which is readily movable, is to be set on the lawn in various positions, according to the direction of the wind and the inclination of the sun's rays. For the day it has placed in it a reclining steamer-chair. It thus becomes the patient's **liege-halle.** During the greater part of the day he reclines upon the chair, properly protected by furs and shawls in cool weather. At meal-time the reclining chair may be removed and in its place a table and chair substituted, for experience shows that the patient eats with better appetite out-of-doors than in the house.

**Sleeping-Room.**—The patient's bed-chamber, preferably on an upper floor, should have a southern exposure. It should be plainly but comfortably furnished, having no upholstery or other dust-gathering articles. The windows should remain open night and day. Only in cold weather should the windows be closed one hour before retiring, and one hour before rising in the morning. At no other time should the windows be closed except during a storm accompanied by wind. After the storm has subsided the windows should be reopened. For protection from cold and to maintain the heat of the body reliance should be placed upon blankets and other bed-clothing. On cold nights the face only need be exposed. "Catching cold" is impossible. In order not to become chilled when preparing for bed the patient may disrobe and put on flannel night-dress or pajamas in a warm room adjoining the bed-chamber.

The method here outlined should be consistently pursued, varied summer and winter in order to adapt it to the season, the object being to have the patient at all times, day and night, breathe pure, fresh air. Do not let there be a foolish dread of "night air." At night what other kind of air is there?

**In the City.**—In a close-built city, where yard and lawn are not available, an attempt must be made to approach so far as possible to suburban conditions. If there is a porch or veranda it must be converted into an out-door apartment for the invalid. The exposure should be to the south. Let the veranda be enclosed with wire netting, to keep out insects, and to give sense of privacy. Inside it should be hung with canvas curtains, which can be rolled up or lowered. These curtains can be let down on the windward side, as occasion requires. The apartment so constructed should be used as the living-room and liege-halle of the invalid, both summer and winter. In it he should sleep and eat and rest and take his exercise. It should be his sleeping-room both summer and winter, except in the stormiest weather, when there should be an inner room to which he can temporarily retire. But cold weather alone should not drive him in. Let him sleep in his improvised apartment even with the thermometer below zero. With sufficient blankets and bedding the cold may be defied. Note what is done by the Klondiker in his sleeping-bag of bear-skin.

Even in a modern city flat the regimen here described may, under necessity, be carried out. Let the flat be the top one of a tall apartment building. If there is a balcony or loggia, use it as the open-air liege-halle and sleeping-room. If there is no loggia, then use a corner room, with open windows. A room in a modern steam-heated flat with open windows on a December day should afford a very comfortable temperature.

In connection with this method of home treatment in the close-built city there should be a nearby park in which the patient may walk, for the sake of the all-important out-door exercise.

A rigorous carrying out of the method of home treatment here described will bring return of health to many cases of incipient phthisis which perish under old methods.

**Rest.**—An essential part of this method of treatment is the "rest-cure." Whenever the patient's temperature is above 100° F., the rest-cure should be made imperative. In phthisis the greatest antipyretic is fresh air.

In carrying it out the patient should, whenever the bodily temperature is at the point indicated (over 100° F.), be kept at rest, in an easy reclining chair by day, well-protected by wraps in cold weather.  The rest should be taken in a sun-trap, on a protected veranda, or other place used as the patient's **liege-halle.**

Winter weather does not contraindicate this treatment. From an hour after sunrise to an hour before sunset it should be pursued.  The patient should not, however, remain upon his back without interruption.  To do so favors hypostasis in the lungs, and also heats the back, making it sensitive to cold on arising.  At intervals of a half-hour or an hour he should take a short walk or very light exercise, and then return to his couch.

When the temperature has permanently fallen to below 100° F., the rest-cure need no longer be insisted upon.

**Diet.**—The feeding of the patient is one of the most important matters connected with the treatment of phthisis.  The patient with well-preserved powers of digestion and active nutrition will in almost all cases recover.  The one with persistently impaired nutrition will not recover.

**Forced Feeding.**—The principle to be carried out is, so far as possible, to "stuff" the patient.  That is, get him to take as large a quantity of nutritious food as the digestive system can dispose of.  Only by means of the open-air treatment, which improves the appetite and increases digestive powers, will this be possible.  Hence, the two must be combined.

**Articles of Diet.**—The diet-list should contain variety enough to tempt the appetite, yet all food should be of the most nutritious quality.  There should be a large proportion of red meats, for the most part rare roast-beef and rare broiled sirloin or porterhouse steak.  The patient should get into the habit of eating portions of the hot suet of the roast or steak.  The way to do this

is with each mouthful of the rare meat to take a small bit
of the suet.

In addition to beef, English mutton-chops should form
part of the meat diet, as well as other easily digestible
meats, and fish, game and oysters.

**Milk,** butter and eggs should be taken in liberal quantities. Milk should be taken in any and every form in
which it is agreeable to the patient, and should form
part of as many dishes as possible. If the stomach becomes sensitive at any time, milk-porridge will give it
rest, and still nourish the patient. Other forms of milk
may be buttermilk, matzoön, and koumiss. Milk disagrees with some persons. In order to render it more
digestible, to each glass of milk add of bicarbonate-of-
soda, six grains; common salt, five grains, dissolved in
two tablespoonfuls of hot water, and then added to the
milk.

**Meat-pulp** is readily taken by some patients. This
consists of scraped beef, raw, seasoned with salt-and-
pepper and spread on bread.

**Eggs** should form an important part of the diet. They
should be taken raw, soft-boiled, poached, as egg-nogg,
and in all possible forms, except fried. In the case of
those who can take them, a diet made up largely of fresh
eggs, taken raw, will have a wonderful effect in restoring
wasted tissues and promoting nutrition. It is possible
to put some patients on an almost exclusive diet of raw
eggs; by gradual increase as many as two dozen daily
have been taken. Such diet is followed by markedly
beneficial results.

**Vegetables,** of a nutritious and easily digestible kind,
should give variety to the diet. Spinach is especially
recommended. Potatoes, mashed with cream or butter.
Fresh vegetables generally, except cabbage and such as
unduly distend the stomach and are not easily digestible.
Fresh, ripe fruit is always allowable, unless there is diarrhea. Grapes are especially useful.

The class of articles to be avoided are pies, pastry of all kinds, rich puddings, cake, or other heavy desserts, and fried meats.

**Time of Meals.**—There should be three principal meals a day, with light lunch or "bites" at other times.

**Morning.**—On first waking in the morning the mouth should be rinsed with lemon-water, and the patient then should take a glass of hot milk, or a small dish of milk-toast.

**Breakfast.**—About eight o'clock breakfast should be taken. It should consist of broiled·steak, rare, or mutton-chops; or eggs, sweet-breads, fresh-fish, or, if it suits the patient's fancy, broiled ham, or other salt or cured meat or fish may be allowed. Such articles sometimes stimulate a lagging appetite. A dish of whole-wheat cereal food, as shredded-wheat biscuit, with cream, is good. As a drink, if not pure milk, then tea or coffee with a large part of hot milk. But strong tea or coffee should never be regularly indulged in.

**Luncheon.**—After breakfast there should not be enough eaten materially to lessen the appetite for dinner, but with many persons there is a faint feeling about eleven o'clock, which may be overcome by taking a "bite." This should consist of no more than a glass of milk with a few buttered crackers and a little fruit.

**Dinner.**—At about one o'clock the heartiest meal of the day should be taken. This should consist of a first course of soup—a small quantity only—followed by rare roast-beef, in liberal quantity, or other fresh meat, with a variety of vegetables, fruit, and, if any dessert, something light, such as cornstarch, snow-pudding, gelatine, or the like.

**Supper.**—This should be lighter than the midday meal, and yet the appetite should be fully gratified. Let there be cold meats, or hot if the patient is "hungry." Corn-meal porridge—mush-and-milk—is a good supper dish.

Make it of white cornmeal. Toasted bread, well buttered, with weak tea containing a large proportion of hot milk; or chocolate or cocoa.

**Bed-time**—At bed-time should again be taken a glass of milk, hot or cold. If so much milk through the day becomes distasteful, substitute koumiss or matzoön.

**Exercise.**

**Occupation.**—When it is possible to do so the phthisical patient should have some light out-door pursuit, which shall occupy mind as well as body. Let this be gardening, or some similar task. Aim to keep the patient's mind agreeably occupied. When this cannot be done, there should be systematic exercise, of two kinds, walking, and lung-gymnastics.

**Walking.**—The walks should be graduated according to the patient's strength. The chief rule to be observed is that the patient should stop short of becoming tired. The ground over which the walk is taken may have a gentle inclination, so as to make but slight demand upon the heart and lungs. At intervals, as he walks, let the patient take a deep inspiration and then hold his breath while he counts ten. This promotes deep breathing. Along the route of the patient's pedestrian trip there should be seats or benches at intervals, where he can pause to rest. On return from his walk if the clinical thermometer shows a rise of bodily temperature, the next day the walk must be shortened, or it may be omitted. But, as recovery progresses and the temperature subsides or remains stationary, the walks should be gradually lengthened. As strength still further returns exercise may take the form of horseback riding, or, if indulged in moderation, the wheel.

**Lung-Gymnastics.**—Systematic exercise, having for its object the expansion of the chest, development of the muscles of respiration and increased inflation of the lungs, should form part of the treatment in all cases. The best method of accomplishing this is by the use of a hand-swing, consisting of two large rings suspended by ropes from hooks in the ceiling of a porch, or from the limb of a tree. The ropes should be so arranged that the rings can be adjusted to two different heights—on a level with the patient's shoulders, and again at the height to which he can reach with arms extended upwards.

With these suspended rings the exercises consist of two motions. First, grasping the high rings with upward-extended arms, the patient closes the mouth, and, inhaling through the nose, gradually and slowly fills the lungs with air, at the same time raising himself from the ground until he stands on his toes. In this position he should maintain himself for several moments, still holding his breath, and while doing so making upward pressure with the diaphragm, thus compressing the retained air within the lungs. This has the effect of forcing the air into the ultimate air-cells in all pervious portions of the lungs. After this has been done, the air is slowly expelled from the lungs as the patient lowers himself to his feet. The other motion is made with the rings suspended on a level with the shoulders. Taking hold of the two rings, one with each hand, the patient places his feet in fixed position, and then, with arms extended, as he slowly inhales through the nose he leans forward and swings the arms around and back as far as they will go. After remaining in this position a few moments, holding the breath, he brings himself back to the upright posture as he slowly exhales. This exercise expands the chest and develops the external muscles of respiration.

To these exercises may be added the use of the Wolf-bottles, the patient, first taking a deep inspiration, blowing the water from one bottle to the other.

**Night-Sweats.**—A good measure, often effective, to prevent night-sweats, is for the patient to take a glass of hot milk and a cracker on retiring. Then, in the night, two hours before the usual time that the sweat comes on, let him be awakened and given a glass of hot milk, or an egg-nog.

**Hydrotherapeutics.**—The application of hydrotherapeutics, especially with reference to the chest, serves a double purpose. It stimulates the capillary circulation of the skin, and, moreover, the application of cold or tepid water to the surface causes reflex dilation of the lungs.

The patient should begin by a cool sponging of the neck and chest every morning, briskly and rapidly applied, to be followed by friction with a coarse bath-towel until there is vigorous reaction and the skin has a warm and healthy glow.

**Massage.**—Any consumptive patient will be benefited by judiciously applied massage of the chest. The muscles should be rubbed and kneaded, and they should be brought into action by the operator. In the case of patients with loss of strength and energy, passive exercise of the arms and chest should be practiced.

**Clothing.**—The underclothing should be woolen—light or heavy according to the season of the year and state of the weather. Heavy chest-protectors should not be used. The shoulders should be well protected. This is a matter to which sufficient attention is not paid. The feet should always be kept warm and dry. The head should not be too much bundled. In winter, fur outer-garments are best. The legs, as well as the body, should be protected. The important point is to wear clothing that cannot be penetrated by the wind.

**Disposal of Sputum.**—The sputum of a patient with tuberculosis must always be destroyed. Cuspidors and spit-cups containing antiseptic solutions should be used. Promiscuous expectoration is to be absolutely prohibited. As a substitute for handkerchiefs, let the patient use soft muslin cloths or rags that can be burned.

**House Infection.**—The dust of rooms inhabited by tuberculous patients is infective. No persons should sleep in a room or dwell in a house previously occupied by a consumptive without thorough cleansing and fumigation.

---

# FIBROID PHTHISIS.

**Synonym.**—Fibroid tuberculosis of the lungs.

**Definition.**—This disease is a chronic form of pulmonary tuberculosis in which there is induration and contraction of the affected portion of the lung, due to hyperplasia of the connective-tissue elements. The fibrous changes may be primary or secondary.

## ETIOLOGY.

This form of phthisis develops in subjects possessing a higher equation of resistance to the tuberculous process than do those who succumb to the ulcerative form of the disease. It occurs often in those of good muscular development, and in those in whom the etiological factor belonging to heredity is absent.

**Primary Form.**—The primary cases are those in which there is first interstitial pneumonia, with subsequent tuberculous infection.

**Secondary Form.**—The secondary cases are those which begin as tubercular infiltration and subsequently assume the fibrous character, involving not only the tubercule but also the lung-tissue.

**Exciting Causes.**—This form of phthisis occurs most frequently in those who inhale irritating particles of dust; hence, in metal-workers, stone-cutters, and those of like occupation, as in fibroid pneumonia. The disease may have as its precedent condition bronchitis, broncho-pneumonia, pleuritis, and lobar pneumonia (the last named is exceedingly rare).

## MORBID ANATOMY.

**Apex.**—The apex is the seat of the disease in a large majority of cases. The process may remain circumscribed, it may extend to the rest of the upper lobe, or to the entire lung.

**Lung.**—The affected portion of lung is deeply pigmented; it is firm and dense, like fibroid tissue or cartilage. The cut section is smooth, and without granulations.

**Heart.**—There is hypertrophy and dilation of the right ventricle.

**Amyloid Degeneration.**—Late in the disease there may be secondary amyloid degeneration of the liver, spleen, kidneys, or intestines.

## PATHOLOGY.

The development of tubercles begins in the finer bronchi, and the process extends toward the peri-bronchial tissue. The tubercular masses instead of undergoing caseation and softening, undergo fibroid degeneration and become changed into firm, rounded, fibrous bodies, which are deeply pigmented. In the lung-tissue these bodies feel like shot. These bodies are found both in the walls of the bronchi and in the peri-bronchial tissue. The bronchial wall is thickened by small-celled infiltration. Many of the indurated bodies may coalesce, and new masses form on their margins, presenting a racemose arrangement ("Carswell's grapes"). The interlobular connective-tissue undergoes fibroid thickening, forming bands in the lung structure. A few small caseous masses may form, but they are generally absent. Cavity-formation is rare, though it does occur. There is contraction and induration of the affected portion of the lung, with some emphysematous areas. The pleura inflames, becomes much thickened, and forms adhesions.

## SYMPTOMS.

**Onset.**—The oncome of the disease is always insidious. In some cases the first symptom may be hemoptysis; in others, the signs will be those of localized bronchitis and pleurisy at the apex of one lung.

**Cough.**—This is an early symptom, and for a long time may not be very severe. It is a slight hacking. It is not paroxysmal in character, as in the ulcerative form. Later, as the disease develops, the cough increases.

**Expectoration.**—For a long period there may be no expectoration; later, the sputum increases in amount and becomes muco-purulent.

**Bacillus Tuberculosis.**—Usually the number of bacilli in the sputum is very small, and often repeated attempts, at intervals, must be made before they are detected.

**Nutrition.**—General nutrition is but little impaired, and emaciation is but slight for a long period.

**Respiration.**—There is some "shortness of breath," but not much dyspnea until emphysema is developed; then there may be dyspnea even to a state of bronchial asthma.

**Fever.**—The disease usually pursues an apyrexial course. For short periods there may be some fever, probably due to retained secretions.

**Pulse.**—The pulse is usually not increased in rapidity.

**Course and Duration.**—In some cases the disease process may undergo early arrest with complete recovery, leaving as the only sign permanent depression of the sub-clavicular region. In other cases, in which the disease continues, its course is usually chronic. It may last for ten, twenty, or even as long as thirty years. Towards the end, to an increased degree, the patient loses flesh and strength, the cough increases, there is increase of dyspnea, loss of appetite, and gradual exhaustion. The terminal event may be due to dropsy from the secondary dilation of the right heart, or to conditions determined by amyloid degeneration of the liver, spleen, kidneys or intestines.

## PHYSICAL SIGNS.

**Inspection.**—Inspection shows early impaired expansion in the supra- and infra-clavicular regions of the affected side; also, retraction in these regions, and emaciation of the overlying tissues. Later, when the lung changes have far progressed and a large portion or a whole of one lung has become indurated, the side of the chest is deeply retracted, and the lung is in a condition of sclorosis, as in pulmonary fibrosis (page 102).

**Palpation.**—This confirms the signs observed on inspection, and reveals vocal fremitus over the indurated lung-tissue.

**Percussion.**—This gives the usual signs of lung induration, modified according to the extent of accompanying emphysema.

**Auscultation.**—All the breath-sounds are weak; expiration is prolonged. There are fine, crackling râles. If there are cavities they are usually small, and revealed by the usual signs. The cavity is usually dry.

## DIAGNOSIS.

The tubercular character of the disease will be masked by signs of bronchitis and of emphysema. The diagnosis must, in the early stage, chiefly be determined by physical examination over the affected apex. The finding of the specific bacilli will, of course, determine diagnosis, but often this requires repeated attempts for a considerable period. Late in the disease the diagnosis is not so obscure.

## PROGNOSIS.

Very early the disease may become arrested; but when fibroid changes have progressed to involve a great extent of lung tissue, recovery rarely occurs, although there may be long periods of marked remission in the symptoms. The prognosis as to time is generally favorable, the patient living for years.

## TREATMENT.

The treatment in this form of phthisis must be on the lines indicated in the other forms of pulmonary tuberculosis, and in that of fibroid pneumonia.

---

# DISEASES OF THE BRONCHIAL GLANDS.

**Number and Location.**—The bronchial glands are twelve to fifteen or more in number. They lie in the mediastinum, chiefly near the bifurcation of the trachea and about the main bronchi. Smaller glands lie in the interlobular connective-tissue accompanying the bronchi in the lungs.

**Enlargement.**—The bronchial glands become enlarged in a variety of diseased conditions, among which are:— (a) The acute infectious diseases; (b) bronchitis, acute and chronic; (c) broncho-pneumonia; (d) lobular pneumonia; (e) pulmonary gangrene; (f) pneumonoconiosis; (g) syphilis; (h) tuberculosis.

## ETIOLOGY.

### Enlarged Tuberculous Glands.

**Source of Infection.**—The infection of the bronchial glands may be from:—(a) **The lungs** (the direction of the lymph-stream is from the lungs towards the bronchial glands); (b) **the tonsils** (bacilli absorbed from the tonsils may pass to the cervical, the tracheal, and thence to the bronchial glands); (c) **General infection.**—Tubercle bacilli may enter through the intestinal mucous membrane conveyed by milk from a cow with tuberculous disease of the udder.

## MORBID ANATOMY.

**Gross Appearance.**—In acute cases the glands are inflamed, swollen, soft, and pinkish. Later, the color is grayish. The gland may be studded with tubercles; many of them show caseation and softening. Glands that have long been affected may show calcareous masses, or thickened fibrous capsule.

## SYMPTOMS.

The symptoms vary in severity according to the degree of enlargement.

**Large Glands.**—The presence of large glands gives rise to:—**Cough.**—The cough may be short, frequent, and hacking; or, paroxysms of spasmodic cough, with dyspnea. Hoarseness and aphonia may exist. The cough may be due to pressure upon the pneumogastric or direct pressure upon the trachea and main bronchi. **Pain.**—Pain is usually present; when it occurs it is along the sternum, or in the back, about the fourth or fifth dorsal vertebra. **Pressure symptoms.**—Pressure on adjacent structures may cause congestion of the superficial veins, and puffiness or edema of the face or neck; dyspnea and stridor; difficulty in swallowing; bradycardia or tachycardia (from pressure on the pneumogastric).

## PHYSICAL SIGNS.

**Auscultation.**—The most distinctive signs are revealed by auscultation. Bronchial breathing and bronchophony may be heard over the inter-scapular region. The breath-sounds may be feeble over one or both lungs. Have the patient throw the head well back, place the stethoscope in the suprasternal notch, and sometimes a purring sound may be heard, due to pressure of the glands on the venous trunks.

**Diagnosis.**—When signs of the presence of enlarged bronchial glands are obscure, keep the condition in mind in the case of children with persistent cough or with difficult breathing that cannot be otherwise accounted for.

**Course.**—Tuberculous inflammation of the bronchial glands may result in:—(a) Miliary tuberculosis. (b) Hemoptysis. (c) Abscess-formation, with rupture and escape of pus into various surrounding parts. (d) Perforation of a bronchus. (e) Gangrene of the lung. (f) Perforation of the trachea with escape of pus and sometimes sudden death.

**Treatment.**—The treatment must be of a general nature, as for the form of tuberculosis found to be present.

# HEMOPTYSIS.

**Synonyms.**—Pulmonary hemorrhage; hemorrhage of the lungs; "spitting of blood."

**Definition.**—Hemoptysis is the expectoration of blood that has escaped into the air-passages.

**Note.**—Hemoptysis is the expectoration of blood having its source in any part of the air-passages, including the nose, throat, trachea, bronchi, or lungs. Hence there may be hemoptysis, that is, the expectoration of blood, without the occurrence of true pulmonary hemorrhage. Also it must be understood that there may be true pulmonary hemorrhage without the expectoration of blood. In order for there to be hemoptysis the part of the lung in which the hemorrhage occurs must communicate with a bronchus. In rare instances a branch of the pulmonary artery may rupture in a closed cavity, in which case there would be pulmonary hemorrhage without hemoptysis. Again, the blood may escape from the surface of the lung into the pleural cavity. But ordinarily, when the term hemoptysis is used it is applied to the **expectora-ation of blood** the source of which is a pulmonary hemorrhage; though the following description will cover all forms of the condition under consideration.

## ETIOLOGY.

**Source of the Blood.—The Lungs.—Hyperemia:**—Active or passive congestion from the bronchial or pulmonary capillaries may cause an escape of blood on the surface of the bronchial mucous membrane, thus giving rise to hemoptysis. Usually, the amount of blood lost in this form is small. The conditions in which this form of hemoptysis occurs are:—

(a) **Tuberculosis:**—Capillary hemorrhage not infrequently occurs in the early stages of tuberculosis; also it may occur from time to time in the course of chronic pulmonary tuberculosis.

**(b) Bronchitis:**—Capillary hemorrhage sometimes occurs in acute bronchitis when the degree of pulmonary congestion is very great. The sputum is blood-streaked. It also may occur in any other inflammatory condition of the lung. Although the amount of blood lost in this form of pulmonary hemorrhage is usually small, in rare instances the hemorrhage has been known to be profuse.

**Phthisis.**—Phthisis is the condition in which hemoptysis is most common. The hemorrhage may be from: —(a) Rupture of an aeurysm on the edge of the pulmonary artery. In many cases the artery is exposed in the cavity; **(b)** in the later stages of the disease the rupture may occur in a blood-vessel weakened by tuberculous ulceration.

**Tumors.**—The presence of tumors of the lungs in hydatids, actinomycosis, and carcinoma is often attended by hemorrhage.

**Bronchiectasis.**—This condition is sometimes attended by hemorrhage.

**Traumatism.**—Wounds of the lung usually give rise to hemorrhage with hemoptysis.

**Gangrene.**—This is sometimes a cause of pulmonary hemorrhage.

**Irritants.**—The inhalation of chlorine gas, of dust, and other irritants may cause hemorrhage by inducing congestion and rupture of bronchial capillaries.

**Exertion.**—Severe exertion, such as straining or lifting may produce hemoptysis.

**Heart.**—Static congestion of the lungs secondary to mitral-valve lesions often leads to the rupture of over-distended capillaries and consequent hemoptysis.

**Blood.**—Diseases due to blood degeneration—as hemophilia, leucocythemia, scurvy and purpura, are often attended by pulmonary hemorrhage and hemoptysis.

**Blood-vessels.**—Degeneration of the walls of the blood-vessels of the lungs in arterio-sclerosis and in emphysema may give rise to rupture and consequent hemorrhage.

**Aneurysm.**—Rupture of an aneurysm of the aorta into the trachea, the bronchi, or the lung, may be followed by profuse and fatal hemoptysis. A small leakage of blood usually precedes the final rupture in these cases.

**Vicarious Hemoptysis.**—In rare instances in suppressed menstruation vicarious hemoptysis occurs.

**Fibrinous Bronchitis.**—This condition often has hemoptysis as one of its symptoms.

**Pulmonary Edema.**—In edema of the lungs the expectoration is often blood-streaked, or the sputum is intimately mixed with blood.

**Altitude.**—With diminished atmospheric pressure, at an altitude of over 10,000 feet, in some persons spitting of blood occurs.

**Hysteria.**—In some hysterical subjects a little blood is sometimes coughed up. It is usually due to local congestion or some unusual exertion.

**Pulmonary Apoplexy.**—Embolism of the pulmonary artery (hemorrhagic infarction) is often followed by hemoptysis or the expectoration of dark, blood-stained mucus.

**Infectious Diseases.**—The acute infectious diseases—such as yellow-fever and typhus—may be accompanied by severe hemoptysis.

**Gout.**—In gouty subjects degeneration of the pulmonary vessels may lead to rupture and consequent "arthritic hemoptysis."

**Syphilis.**—Syphilis of the lung with syphilitic degeneration of the blood-vessels may be accompanied by hemoptysis.

## PATHOLOGY.

In pulmonary hemorrhage the blood may come from— (a) a highly congested mucous membrane with rupture of the underlying capillaries; (b) ulcerated tissues in or about a blood-vessel; (c) rupture of an aeurysmal dilatation of the bronchial or pulmonary vessels; (d) the passage of the blood through the vessel-walls in hemophilia and other forms of blood degeneration.

## MORBID ANATOMY.

**Post-mortem.**—After a fatal attack of hemoptysis the mucous membrane of the air-passages is blood-stained; blood is found in the trachea, bronchi, and the lungs; numerous pinkish patches may be found on the surface of the lungs due to the presence of blood that has been inhaled and drawn to the terminal lobules in the lungs. The blood is found most abundant in the neighborhood of the ruptured vessel.

## SYMPTOMS.

**Onset.**—The attack of hemoptysis is usually sudden. The patient has a saltish taste in the mouth. On expectorating the fluid he finds it to be blood. In some cases the sputum may be slightly blood-streaked before the severe attack of hemoptysis occurs.

**The Blood.**

**Quantity.**—The quantity of blood may vary from a mere streak of blood-stained sputum to a profuse hemorrhage of one or two pints. If the hemoptysis is slight the blood is brought up at intervals by coughing, or there is only frothy, blood-tinged sputum. In a severe attack the blood pours out of the mouth and nose in great quantity.

**Reaction.**—The blood is alkaline in reaction.

**Color.**—Early in the attack the blood is bright-red, but if the quantity is great it may be dark and venous in color. Blood that has remained for some time in the lungs before being expectorated is dark-red, blackish, or brown. Small clots of this character are usually present in the sputum some days after an attack of hemoptysis.

**Form.**—The blood may be frothy, or fluid, or clotted in the form of the mold of the tube in which it has been lying.

**General Symptoms.**

In profuse hemoptysis there is pallor, faintness, great anxiety, feeble pulse, and cold extremities.

**Temperature.**—During the attack the temperature may be sub-normal. After the bleeding ceases and the symptoms of shock have passed, the temperature rises to normal or even above that point. There often is a rise of temperature for several days following the attack; sometimes for a longer period. This feverish action is due to broncho-pneumonia which is caused by particles of blood being drawn into the scattered pulmonary alveoli, carrying with it micro-organisms from the diseased portion of the lung.

**Mental Symptoms.**—There is usually great mental depression and feeling of apprehension on the part of the patient, whether or not it is a primary attack.

**Recurrence.**—In young subjects with previously good health but a single attack may occur, even though the condition be one of incipient phthisis; or, it may be repeated after a long interval. On the other hand, profuse hemoptysis in an advanced stage of phthisis may be repeated at intervals of a day or two, and finally end fatally. Such bleeding doubtless always comes from a ruptured aneurysm of the pulmonary artery leaking through a blood-clot in a cavity.

**Differential Diagnosis.**

**Blood from the Nose.**—Inspect the nares carefully. Pass a pledget on a probe back in each nostril to the posterior nares. This is almost certain to determine whether the hemorrhage is nasal or not.

**Blood from the Pharynx and Larynx.**—Examine these parts with an illuminating mirror or the laryngoscope.

**Hematemesis.**—Blood from the stomach is generally acid in reaction, brown in color, or like coffee-grounds; it is not frothy; it is often mixed with food. It must be kept in mind, however, that blood from the lungs may be swallowed and afterwards vomited.

**Spurious Hemoptysis.**—Anemic young girls with amenorrhea sometimes spit blood, or find the pillow stained in the morning with blood which has drooled from the mouth. In such cases it is found that the patient has

acquired a habit of sucking the gums, which are pale
and spongy. If the blood appears only in the morning,
it is indicative of a case of spurious hemoptysis. There
is also absence of physical signs belonging to pulmonary
hemorrhage.

**Physical Signs.**—While no extended examination of
the chest should be made at the time of the hemorrhage,
yet auscultation with the stethoscope over the upper lobes
of the lungs in some cases will reveal the presence of
moist râles.

## PROGNOSIS.

**Phthisis.**—It is only in rare instances that hemoptysis
is immediately fatal. Such cases, when occurring, are
usually in advanced phthisis when there has already
been great destruction in the lung. In primary cases
of hemoptysis in subjects showing but little impairment
of the general health, the prognosis is almost always
favorable under proper conditions. Profuse and repeated pulmonary hemorrhage in advanced tubercular
disease is always a grave condition.

**Aortic Aneurysm.**—Hemoptysis occurring in the case
of an aneurysm of the thoracic aorta, even though the
quantity of blood at first is but slight, is of fatal import,
for it announces early rupture.

**Heart.**—Hemoptysis due to pulmonary congestion in
mitral disease is sometimes followed by heart-failure.
Hemoptysis secondary to ulcerative endocarditis is cause
for grave prognosis. In cases of mitral stenosis accompanied by hemoptysis, the prognosis is more favorable.
**Therapeutics.**

**Erigeron.**—Bright red blood; the flow is increased by
every motion. **Dose:**—Give three drops of the **Oil-of-
erigeron** on a lump of sugar.

**Aconite** (1x).—Bright red blood; incessant, hacking
cough; warm feeling in the chest; red face; great anxiety; arterial excitement.

**Ipecac** (2x).—Sensation of bubbling in the chest, followed by copious bleeding; tickling beneath the sternum; spitting of blood after the least effort; nausea.

**Hamamelis** (Tr.)—Venous hemorrhage; blood dark, thin, coming into the mouth without effort, like a warm current.

. **Millefolium** (1x).—Profuse flow of thin, bright-red blood; oppression; palpitation; not much cough.

**Cactus** (2x).—Hemoptysis, with over-action of the heart; secondary to heart disease; sensation of constriction.

**Veratrum vir.** (Tr.)—Violent congestion, with full, hard, bounding pulse.

• **Phosphorus** (3x).—Hemoptysis occurring in the course of low fevers; also, inflammatory symptoms following an attack of hemoptysis. Tight feeling in the chest, with dry, tight cough, followed by hemorrhage.

**Ferrum phos.** (2x).—Hemorrhage of bright, red blood, occurring in the course of phthisis.

· **Geranium** (Tr.)—Bright, red blood; persistent, free flow.

**Sulphuric acid.**—Persistent hemorrhage of dark blood; quantity slight; a continuous oozing; in feeble and anemic subjects. **Dose:**—Ten drops of the chemically pure acid in a glass of water; teaspoonful dose every hour.

**Hydrastin hydrochlorate** (2x).—In subjects of old bronchial catarrhs; with friable mucous membrane.

**Digitalis** (Tr.)—Secondary to obstructive heart-lesions; feeble action of the heart. This drug must be used with caution. Its too free use favors separation of thrombi and pulmonary infarct.

**Chininum ars.** (1x).—For the anemia following excessive loss of blood.

## TREATMENT.

**General Measures.**

**Rest.**—This is of importance. Even though the hemorrhage is but slight, place the patient in bed and command absolute rest with quiet surroundings. Let the patient make no exertion whatever. He should not so much as raise an arm or use his voice.

**Position.**—Place the patient in a semi-recumbent position with the shoulders and head elevated.

**Room.**—Let the temperature be moderate; about 65° F.

**Ice.**—The patient may be given small bits of ice in the mouth.

**Salt.**—As a domestic measure, in an emergency, put a small pinch of salt on the tongue.

**Cough.**—If blood gathers in the mouth encourage the patient to expectorate. During the continuance of the hemorrhage moderate effort at cough may be encouraged. After the hemorrhage has ceased, then seek to allay the cough.

**Diet.**—Give no hot food of any kind while the hemorrhage lasts. Give no stimulants whatever. Immediately following the attack milk, meat-essence and bread-and-butter will be the best diet.

**Extremities.**—Apply hot-water bags to the feet and make warm applications to the extremities.

**Back.**—Apply over the cervical spine a hot-water bag (120° F.).

**Applications.**—Do not put cold compresses or other applications to the chest. The hot water to the cervical spine is far preferable.

**Bandaging.**—If the hemorrhage is profuse apply temporarily an Esmarch bandage to the upper thighs.

**Fainting.**—If but little blood has been lost and the patient faints, make no active efforts to revive him, for in such cases fainting is salutary.

**Salt-solution.**—If a great quantity of blood has been lost and the patient is much depleted, a copious rectal injection of normal salt-solution may be given after the attack.

**Caution.**—Give no alcohol, no ergot, or astringent of any kind. They do no good and they may do harm.

**Enjoin quiet.**—Let the patient's surroundings be quiet; keep nervous people out of the room. Encourage and reassure the patient, observing a calm demeanor.

**After-treatment.**—After the attack use inhalations of anti-septic sprays to guard against infection in retained clots.

# SECTION IV.

## PLEURISY.

**Synonym.**—Pleuritis.

**Definition.**—Pleurisy is an inflammation of the costal or visceral pleura; the attack is usually marked by chill, fever, sharp pains in the chest, and exudation or effusion in the pleural cavity.

**History.**—B. C. 400.—Before the time of Hippocrates it was recognized as a "feverish affection of the respiratory organs, accompanied by a stitch in the side."

**A. D. 1802.** Pinel first defined pleurisy as an inflammation of a serous membrane.

**1820.** Laennec first made known its pathological relation and diagnostic signs.

**Frequency.**—Pleurisy is a very common affection; a large percentage of autopsies show old adhesions.

**Season.**—It is most common in winter and spring.

**Age.**—Every age is liable; it occurs even in the fetus. The greatest number of cases occur between the ages of 20 and 50.

**Sex.**—Males are affected to a greater number than females, because of greater exposure.

## VARIETIES.

1. According to sequence of events—**(a)** Primary; **(b)** Secondary.

2. According to duration—**(a)** Acute; **(b)** Subacute; **(c)** Chronic.

3. According to the pathological condition:—
I.    Plastic Pleurisy.
II.   Sero-Fibrinous Pleurisy.
III.  Purulent Pleurisy.

## I. PLASTIC PLEURISY.

**Synonym.**—Fibrinous Pleurisy; Dry Pleurisy; Pleuritis Sicca.

**Definition.**—Plastic pleurisy is inflammation of the pleura characterized by a fibrinous exudation on its surface.

## ETIOLOGY.

It occurs in two forms—(1) Primary; and (2) Secondary.

(1) **Primary.**—Cases of the primary form have for their exciting or predisposing causes:—(a) Tuberculosis; (b) rheumatism; (c) "cold." **Occurrence.**—(a) The tuberculous form of primary plastic pleurisy is the most frequent.  (b) The rheumatic diathesis as a predisposing cause is common.  (c) "Cold," from refrigeration of the body on exposure is an active exciting cause.

(2) **Secondary. By extension:**—By far the greater number of cases of plastic pleurisy occur by extension from adjacent structures, as in:

(a) All forms of pneumonia, abscess, trauma, etc.

(b) **Pulmonary tuberculosis:**—In this diseased condition dry pleurisy is one of the most common complications; there are few cases in which it is absent; sometimes it is the initial lesion.  In only a small number of cases, however, does the pleura contain tubercles.

## BACTERIOLOGY.

**Relation.**—All forms of pleurisy are due to infection by bacteria or their toxins; other causes are only predisposing or exciting.

**Micro-organisms.**

(a) **Bacillus Tuberculosis.**—A large proportion (at least one-third) of primary pleurisies are tuberculous.

**(b) Pneumococcus.**—The **diplococcus lanceolatus** of Fraenkel is the infective agent in the majority of pleurisies (either sero-fibrinous or purulent) accompanying pneumonic fever; but it is also found in primary pleurisies in the absence of pneumonic fever.

**(c) Streptococcus.**—This organism is the agent in typical septic cases; the infection may be through the lung, as in broncho-pneumonia, or from other sources. It is the organism most commonly present in empyema.

**(d) Other Organisms.**—Other organisms that have been found are:—Staphylococcus; colon bacillus; bacillus of Eberth; various saprophytic bacteria.

**General Conclusion.**—Inflammation of the pleura, as of other serous membranes, is due to the direct action of the various pathogenic bacteria or their toxins. In the case of the rheumatic and syphilitic forms no organisms have as yet been demonstrated, but the presence of the specific toxic agent is undoubted.

**Predisposing Causes.**

**General.**—Predisposing causes of pleurisy are the infectious diseases generally, and those in which there is a toxic agent in the blood:—Tuberculosis; pyemia; septicemia; rheumatism; scarlatina; Bright's; syphilis; scurvy; cachexia in general.

**Exciting Causes.**

**Traumatism.**—Fracture of ribs, or trauma of the thoracic muscles, or of the lungs; also, a fall, blow, concussion.

**Exposure.**—"Cold," from a draft, cold rain, etc.

**Local.**—By Extension:—(a) From the lung—pneumonia; phthisis; pulmonary abscess; gangrene; echinococcus; infarct; pneumothorax.

**(b) From the Abdominal Cavity:**—Peritonitis (direct conveyance through the lymphatics of the diaphragm); abscess or hydatids of the liver, spleen, kidneys; perinephritis; psoas abscess; appendicitis; ovarian cyst.

(c) **From the Heart**:—Pericarditis; endocarditis or valvular disease (secondary pulmonary infarct).

(d) **From Other Parts**:—Cancer of the mammary gland; abscess of the esophagus (from lodgment of foreign body); abscess of the cellular tissue of the neck; inflammation of bronchial or axillary glands; perforation of gastric ulcer.

## PATHOLOGY.

The process may be considered under three stages:—

I. **Congestion.**

II. **Exudation.**

III. **Organization (or, Resolution).**

I. **Naked-eye Appearance.**

I. **Stage of Congestion.**—In spots or patches the membrane is rosy-red in color; it becomes dull (due to clouding of the endothelial cells), losing its shining, glistening appearance; the surface is slightly rough, or granular, due to distended blood-vessels, swollen endothelial cells, and minute proliferating connective-tissue cells.

The **duration** of the stage of congestion is several hours.

II. **Stage of Exudation.**—The surface is covered with a layer of soft, plastic lymph; early, this is a thin, delicate film, which can be easily scraped off, revealing the deeply congested surface beneath. But this layer of soft fibrin rapidly increases in thickness, making the surface rough and shaggy, with small prominences, villi and granules. The opposing surfaces of the pleura become agglutinated, and bands of fibrin pass from one to the other. In thickness the layer of lymph varies, but in some cases it may become enormous, from a half-inch even to an inch. Usually it is about one-quarter inch.

III. **Stage of Organization.**—When adhesion takes place the opposing surfaces of the pleura are united by a dense tissue, of variable thickness, composed of fibrous tissue. The fibrino-plastic lymph itself does not organize; during the process of organization it only acts as a

supporting medium to be penetrated by the newly-proliferated connective-tissue cells.   When the process is
completed the lymph has all undergone degeneration
and been re-absorbed.

**Stage of Resolution.**—When the inflammation has
been mild in degree and of but short duration, with slight
amount of exudate, the latter can be re-absorbed and
the pleura regain almost, but not entirely, its normal
condition.   The affected area will remain opaque, with
slight thickening.   This is due to a slight hyperplasia
of connective-tissue that remains, forming a thin, fibrous
induration.

## Microscopic Changes.

### I.   Stage of Congestion.

(a) **The blood-vessels.**—Both the capillaries, arterioles
and venules are distended with blood, for the most part
with red blood-corpuscles, but with a large proportion of
leucocytes.   Large numbers of leucocytes are massed
in the cellular tissues, outside the venules, which position
they have gained by diapedesis, or migration through the
vessel-walls.

(b) **The endothelial cells** undergo rapid proliferation;
the old ones are clouded; they are cast off from the basement membrane by the force of effusion beneath; this
leaves the membrane in spots denuded of its endothelial
covering.   Some of the cells are multi-nuclear; others
are undergoing fatty degeneration.

(c) **The fixed cells.**—The connective-tissue cells undergo rapid proliferation.

### II.   Stage of Exudation.

**Changes in the Pleura.**—In the pleura the changes
are the same as in the stage of congestion, viz., distended
blood-vessels; edematous fibrous tissue; proliferated endothelial and connective-tissue cells; exuded leucocytes.
The lung tissue immediately underlying the pleura is
also always congested.   Covering the pleural surface,
**early** there is seen a thin, delicate, almost transparent

film of fibrin (coagulable lymph) with a few leucocytes
scattered through it. **Later,** the layer of fibrin becomes
thicker. It is now composed of a soft mass, containing
a network of delicate fibrillæ, running in all directions.
In the meshes of this network are entangled some red
blood-corpuscles, wandering cells (leucocytes), and a
few detached endothelial eells. The underlying lung may
suffer from a lymphangitis (by extension) in the lymphatics of the interlobular septa.

### III. Stage of Organization.

(a) **Blood-vessels.**—New capillary vessels are formed
and projected into the reticulated layer of fibrin; the
walls of the new vessels are composed of the young
proliferated connective-tissue cells, flattened and spindle-
shaped. Some of these vessels are in the form of loops;
others run at various angles to the surface and anasto-
mose with vessels from the opposite side, thus establishing a crossed circulation. The source of the newly-
formed vessels is from the blood-vessels in the subserous
layer.

(b) **Connective-tissue.**—Running through the mass are
many newly-proliferated connective-tissue cells, which
gradually replace the fibrin. In shape these cells are
variously round, elongated, spindle-shaped, or in definite
lines. They interlace with cells from the opposite side,
thus completing the process of adhesion.

(c) **Granulation-tissue.**—At this stage of the pathological process the structure is essentially the same as
granulation-tissue. The proliferated leucocytes and
young fixed cells constitute a small, round-celled mass,
or embryonic tissue; when this structure becomes vas-
cularized, it is granulation-tissue. Later, this becomes
organized into fibrous-tissue.

(d) **Fibrin.**—Small masses of fibrin (plastic lymph)
are scattered in the meshes of the connective-tissue
stroma; finally the last particle disappears (by fatty de-

generation and absorption). A thin layer persists longest on the free surface, in the shape of a granular mass, entangling many leucocytes.

**(e) The Lung.**—The hyperplasia of connective tissue invades the lung structure, and the inter-alveolar walls near the pleural surface participate in the sclerosis, producing a condition of pleurogenic fibrosis.

## SYMPTOMS.

**Degrees of Intensity.**—The symptoms vary from mild to severe. In some instances they are so mild as to be unnoticed, for in autopsies adhesions are found in many cases which gave no history of pleurisy during life.

**Onset.**—Usually there are no premonitory symptoms.

**Pain.**—Usually the first sign is sharp pain in the side of the chest.

**Character.**—The pain is sharp, stitching lancinating; it is usually bearable, but sometimes excruciating.

**Location.**—The pain is oftenest referred to the mammary region; also it is felt in the axillary or the scapular regions. Rarely, it is distant from the seat of inflammation—on the opposite side; or, even in the umbilical region.

**Aggravation.**—The pain is greatly increased by motion; either the motion attending the respiratory act, or voluntary motion.

**Duration.**—After the first two or three days the pain usually gradually subsides.

**Posture.**—For relief of pain the patient fixes the muscles of the chest, leaning toward the affected side.

**Cough.**—It is almost always dry; there is slight expectoration only in case there is an accompanying bronchitis.

**Character.**—The cough is restrained, to avoid the accompanying distressing pain.

**Respiration.**—The respiratory act is short, hurried, and shallow, until the pain subsides.

**Dyspnea.**—There is some dyspnea, determined by the shallow respirations.

**Constitutional Symptoms.**

**Primary Form.—Chill.—**In dry pleurisy a preliminary chill is of rare occurrence. In the severest cases there may be a distinct chill.

**Fever.—**The temperature range is usually moderate, seldom higher than 103°, often below 101° F., lasting for two or three days. In severe cases, 104° F.

**Pulse.—**The characteristic pulse of pleurisy is small and tense, though it may be soft; rate, 90 to 120.

**Absence of Symptoms.—**Many cases of dry pleurisy occur without appreciable disturbance, or any symptoms pointing to its existence. On the post-mortem table adhesions, some very extensive, are found in subjects who in life had no history of an attack of pleurisy. Eighty per cent. of subjects, on autopsy, show old adhesions.

**Secondary Form.—**Secondary dry pleurisies are not, as a rule, attended by marked symptoms. The pleurisy occurs merely as an incident in the primary disease— pneumonia or phthisis, or the various local inflammations, which, by extension, excite the pleuritis.

**Note.—**There are various conditions, marked by the presence of fluid of different kinds in the pleural cavity, and also marked by unusual location of the contained secretions, which have been classified as "pleurisies," and which it is convenient to describe in this connection. They are:—

**Subvarieties.—(1)** Hemorrhagic Pleurisy; **(2)** Chylous Pleurisy; **(3)** Pulsating Pleurisy; **(4)** Encapsulated Pleurisy; **(5)** Diaphragmatic Pleurisy; **(6)** Interlobar Pleurisy; **(7)** Mediastinal Pleurisy; **(8)** Double Pleurisy.

**(1) Hemorrhagic Pleurisy.**

**Definition.—**When the effusion contains a considerable quantity of blood.

**Source of the Blood.—**Cancer; tuberculosis ( pleural); hemorrhagic diathesis.

**Quantity of Blood.**—Rarely more than ten per cent. of the effusion.

#### (2) Chylous Pleurisy.

**Definition.**—The effusion has a milky appearance.

**Forms.**—(a) Chyle from direct lesion of the thoracic duct; (b) a milk-like appearance due to the presence of fat from fatty degeneration of the formed elements.

**Diagnosis.**—Exploratory puncture only.

#### (3) Pulsating Pleurisy.

**Definition.**—Pulsation synchronous with the heart-beat in (a) the intercostal spaces; or (b) in one or more tumors. In almost all cases the effusion is purulent, and always on the left side. Pneumothorax sometimes accompanies.

**Condition.**—Unusual tension of the fluid, together with lessened resistance of the chest wall.

#### (4) Encapsulated Pleurisy.

**Definition.**—The effusion (serous or purulent) is limited by old adhesions.

**Forms.**—(a) Unilocular; (b) multilocular; (c) areolar.

**Diagnosis.**—The physical signs are many and varied, and must always be confirmed by exploratory puncture.

#### (5) Diaphragmatic Pleurisy.

**Definition.**—The pleuritis is limited to the diaphragm.

**Diagnosis.**—Early the diagnosis is difficult, the symptoms rather pointing to abdominal disease.

**Symptoms.**—Onset, acute, with chill, fever, severe pain (in the epigastrium; hypochondrium; iliac region); hiccough; bent posture; legs drawn up; rapid pulse; embarrassed respiration. **Later,** the acute symptoms subside and friction-sounds or signs of effusion appear.

#### (6) Interlobar Pleurisy.

**Definition.**—The inflammation (which is always purulent) is in the fissures between the lobes.

**Symptoms.**—Diagnosis is difficult, the symptoms being very obscure. A dull area corresponding to a pulmonary fissure would be suggestive.

### (7) Mediastinal Pleurisy.

This rare form is very difficult of diagnosis. It is attended by pain, dyspnea, and a dull area beneath the sternum.

### (8) Double Pleurisy.

This is very rare. When it occurs it is usually tuberculous. In children double empyema sometimes occurs.

---

## II. SERO-FIBRINOUS PLEURISY.

**Synonym.**—Pleurisy with effusion.

**Definition.**—Inflammation of the pleura, with fibrinous exudation on the costal and visceral surfaces, accompanied by effusion of serum into the pleural cavity.

## ETIOLOGY.

The causes of sero-fibrinous pleurisy are the same as those which have been enumerated as producing plastic pleurisy. The difference in the pathological process— that is, the addition of serous effusion—is due to greater intensity of the inflammation. This is determined by greater activity of the specific virus, or by lessened power of resistance of the tissues in the subject.

### Causative Factors.

(1) **Tuberculosis.**—Fully thirty-five per cent. of cases are of tuberculous origin. A large number of cases of sero-fibrinous pleurisy eventually develop some form of tuberculosis.

(2) **Rheumatism.**—As a causative factor of sero-fibrinous pleurisy rheumatism is next in order of frequency to tuberculosis.

(3) **Pneumonia.**—Sero-fibrinous pleurisy secondary to pneumonia is due to the action of the **diplococcus lanceo-**

**latus** of Fraenkel. In some cases of the primary form the diplococcus is also found. (Many cases of this class become purulent.)

**(4) Syphilis.**—In either the primary or secondary stages of syphilis sero-fibrinous pleurisy sometimes occurs.

**(5) Acute Infectious Diseases.**—Cases of sero-fibrinous pleurisy may be due to the action of the specific virus of typhoid (bacillus of Eberth); scarlet fever; rheumatism; influenza. Non-purulent cases have been found due to infection by the pyogenic cocci, but most of these cases become purulent.

**(6) Cardiac.**—Sero-fibrinous pleurisy accompanying endocarditis is generally due to secondary pulmonary infarction.

**(7) Renal.**—Sero-fibrinous pleurisy secondary to Bright's disease is invited by the greater susceptibility due to the general cachexia.

(For a more detailed account of the etiology of pleurisy see pp. 178 and 179.)

## PATHOLOGY.

**The Fibrin.**

**Early Changes.**—The same as those occurring in plastic pleurisy. (See p. 180.)

**Area.**—The deposit of fibrin may be in circumscribed areas, or it may be general.

**Color.**—This may be white, yellow, gray or brown.

**Thickness.**—The deposit varies from a thin membrane, to a thickness of a half-inch, or even more.

**Surface.**—The surface is rough and shaggy; filaments and bridles extend out from it.

**Consistence.**—Early it is soft; when old, tough and elastic.

**The Serous Effusion.**

**Quantity.**—This varies greatly; it may be a few ounces, or as much as a gallon or more.

**Color.**—Usually amber, or straw-color; it may be greenish-yellow; or, when blood is present, reddish or dark-brown. Usually the fluid is clear and translucent; it may be turbid from the presence of flocculi of fibrinous exudate, or from leucocytes or fat granules.

### Formed Elements.

**Fibrin.**—Masses of coagulated fibrin of various size, small and large, will float free in the serum, forming a sediment. Other formed elements in the fluid are:— Leucocytes; red blood-corpuscles; micro-organisms; Charcot-Leyden crystals (rare); fat—in old effusions— is sometimes in considerable quantity, giving it a milky appearance.

**Composition.**—The fluid is almost the same as blood-serum, but with a larger proportion of water. Specific gravity, 1012 to 1022.

**Organic Constituents.**—A total of 5 to 6 per cent. They consist of urea; uric acid; fat; cholesterin; fibrin (about 0.1 per cent.); albumin; sometimes biliverdin, or glycogen.

### Disposition of the Fluid.

**Absorption.**—In most cases the fluid is disposed of by being absorbed by the lymphatics, which communicate with the pleural sac by stomata which open at the angles of the endothelial cells. Most of the fibrinous exudate may at the same time be absorbed, but almost always some thickening of the pleura remains, together with many adhesions.

**Encapsulation.**—When the fibrous membrane is very extensive and very thick a pocket of serous fluid may become confined and remain unabsorbed for years.

**Caseation.**—In some cases, after absorption of the fluid, masses of the fibrinous exudate undergo cheesy degeneration.

**Calcification.**—In some cases the masses of fibrin undergo calcareous degeneration, producing **"pleuroliths."**

**Fibroid Degeneration of the Lung.**—After absorption of the fluid there may be abundant proliferation of the connective-tissue cells; this process invades the lung structure along the lymphatics of the inter-lobular septa; there results contraction of the lung, with consequent deformity of the chest-wall (pleurogenic fibrosis).

**Encapsulation.**—If there are old adhesions the fluid becomes encapsulated in various locations and shapes; it may be diaphragmatic, interlobar, mediastinal, costo-pulmonary. The encapsulated portion may be multi-locular. It may be in the meshes of a false membrane—areolar.

**Position of the Fluid.**—When unconfined by adhesions, the fluid gravitates to the bottom of the pleural sac, and, when moderate in amount, to the lower, inner and posterior corner. When large in amount it rises, compressing the lung. The upper surface is never horizontal. The line is lowest next the spine and highest in the axillary region, forming a line somewhat the shape of the letter ∽ —*Demoiseau's curve.*

## SYMPTOMS.

**Early.**—The early symptoms may not differ from those of plastic pleurisy.

**Chill.**—Slight chilly sensations; sometimes for several days.

**Pain.**

**Intensity.**—The pain varies greatly in severity. It may be only a feeling of soreness, later becoming acute. Or, from the onset it may be sharp and lancinating.

**Location.**—Usually the pain is referred to a spot outside the mammillary-line, in the fifth or sixth interspace. It may occur in other regions—beneath the sternum, under the clavicle, in the spinous fossa, or in the abdomen.

**Cause.**—The pain is probably due in great part to involvement of the intercostal nerves. There is often friction of the pleural surfaces with absence of pain.

**Excitants.**—The pain is excited by pressure, motion, cough, deep breathing.

**Duration.**—Usually the pain is not of long continuance; generally it has a period of two or three days.

**Dyspnea.**—This is a constant symptom. Its causes are **(a)** pain; **(b)** fever; **(c)** retraction of the lung; **(d)** pressure on the heart and great vessels. Sometimes the dyspnea induces orthopnea.

**Cyanosis.**—With intense dyspnea cyanosis may appear.

**Cough.**—Usually the cough is short and dry; the effort excites pain. During absorption cough is again excited by the irritation accompanying expansion of the lung.

**Expectoration.**—It is slight or absent. Rarely what appears may be blood-streaked.

**Fever.**—Usually the temperature-range is moderate—a continued fever of 102° to 103°; in some cases, 104°. **Duration:**—Seven to ten days, gradually falling to normal. There are many variations from the usual range.

**Pulse.**—It is rapid; in quantity it is usually small and compressible; due to pressure on the great vessels. Sometimes it is tense.

**Urine.**—Scanty and high-colored; when absorption begins, there is a great increase in quantity, with excess of chlorides.

**Gastro-Intestinal.**—Anorexia; coated tongue; constipation. Rarely, nausea and vomiting.

## PHYSICAL SIGNS.

**Early Stage.**—In the early stage the signs are the same as already given under **Plastic Pleurisy.**

**Stage of Effusion.**

**Time of Beginning.**—The effusion usually begins within several hours of the initial symptoms of the disease.

**Quantity that can be Detected.**—The quantity of fluid must be 300 to 500 cc. before it can be detected by aid of physical signs.

**Inspection.**

**Small Quantity of Effusion.**—When the effusion is small in quantity it creates no changes. At this time there may be restricted motion of the affected side due to the pain.

**Moderate Quantity of Effusion.**—With a moderate quantity of effusion—the pleural sac being about half filled—there is immobility of the lower half of the chest; only slight motion of the upper part.

**Large Quantity of Effusion.**—With a large quantity there is complete immobility of the affected side; separation of the intercostal spaces; if the chest walls are very thin, prominence of the intercostal spaces. There is bulging of the entire side of the chest, especially in the lower and middle third.

**Dislocation of the Liver.**—Another sign is prominence in the right hypochondrium from the downward dislocation of the liver and sagging of the diaphragm, in pleurisy of the right side.

**Traube's Semilunar Space.**—With large quantity of effusion on the left side there is obliteration of Traube's semilunar space.

**Displacement of the Heart.**—The apex-beat is seen to be displaced. In right-sided effusion it may be to the left of the mammillary line (5th or 6th interspace); in left-sided, it may be under the sternum, or to the right of the right mammillary line (4th or 5th interspace).

**Palpation.**

**By Palpation are Detected:**—Chest-immobility; obliteration of the depressions corresponding to the intercostal spaces; rarely, edema of the tissues of the chest-wall.

**Vocal Fremitus.**—It is diminished if the effusion is moderate; absent if the effusion is great. If there are adhesions, fremitus may be present.

**Displaced Organs.**—Displacement of the heart, spleen and liver may be detected if the amount of effusion is great.

**Percussion.**

**Small Quantity of Effusion.**—The earliest change in the percussion-note is at the base of the chest, posteriorly; there is flatness to a height of two or three inches. The line curves from the spine outwards to about the mid-axillary line.

**Moderate Quantity of Effusion.**—When the pleural sac is about half-filled, the line marking the upper limit of flatness starts at the spine, extends outward, then curves upward to the region of the axilla, and then downward to about the fifth or sixth rib. This line is called the "letter ᴗ curve," or *Demoiseau's curve.*

**Large Quantity of Effusion.**—When the pleural sac is completely filled with effusion the line of dulness marking its upper limit begins posteriorly at the fifth or sixth dorsal vertebra, extends outward and upward over the shoulder, and downward and inward in the front of the chest to the cartilage of the second or third rib.

**Skoda's Sign.**—When the upper limit of the fluid is at the third rib, in the infraclavicular space there is a tympanitic, or vesiculo-tympanitic note, called Skoda's sign. It is from the compressed lung. It can be elicited behind, but is most evident in front.

**Williams' Tracheal Tone.**—Just below the inner end of the clavicle strong percussion elicits a high-pitched tympanitic note, which changes with opening and closing the mouth. It is from the trachea and large bronchi, the vibrations being transmitted through the compressed lung.

**Diaphragm.**—The diaphragm is depressed if the quantity of effusion is great. Its convexity may be reversed. The liver and spleen are also depressed.

**Lung.**—The retracted lung becomes airless and col-lapsed. It retracts upward and inward toward the spine.

**Auscultation.**

**Early**—The signs are the same as in plastic pleurisy.

**Moderate Quantity of Effusion.**—With a moderate quantity of effusion interposed between the two layers of the pleura, the respiratory murmur is still heard, but it is diminished in intensity, and "distant" in quality.

**Effusion in Sufficient Quantity to Compress the Lung.**—When the lung is compressed the quality of the sound becomes broncho-vesicular, and finally bronchial. In some cases there is total absence of sound.

**Voice-Sounds.**—There is a "distant" sound to the voice when heard over a moderate thickness of fluid. Bronchophony is heard over compressed lung.

**Pectoriloquy.**—There is great distinctness of the whis-, pered voice, transmitted through the fluid. This is not peculiar to pleurisy.

**The Unaffected Lung.**—Over the unaffected lung there is exaggerated respiratory murmur.

**Re-absorption.**—The signs which characterized the early stage reappear in reverse order. Friction-sounds return when the surfaces of the pleura are again in con-tact. The progress of re-absorption is best followed by determining the change in the upper line of flatness be-hind.

## PROGNOSIS.

**Dry Pleurisy.**—This form is usually of short duration, two to five days; adhesions may remain. Rarely, con-nective-tissue proliferation may follow, resulting in con-traction and induration of the lung, with deformity of the chest-wall.

**Mortality.**—In primary sero-fibrinous pleurisy the prognosis as regards life is almost always favorable (four deaths in 180 recorded cases). If the pleurisy is secondary to a serious diseased condition, the prognosis must be modified accordingly.

**Duration.**—Acute stage, one to two weeks; the effusion is usually reabsorbed in four to six weeks. In some cases the effusion persists, and lasts for months (a small amount of effusion has been known to remain for ten or twenty years).

## TREATMENT.

**Therapeutics.**

**Aconite.** (1x).—To be of service **Aconite** must be given early. Its place is in the treatment of acute, uncomplicated pleurisy. **Indications:**—Acute pleurisy; coming on with chill, followed by fever; thirst; quick and rapid pulse; skin hot and dry; rapid respiration; great nervous restlessness; stitching pains in the chest; dry cough.

**Bryonia.** (1x).—This is the leading remedy for plastic pleurisy; it is no longer of use after serous effusion has begun. **Indications:**—Plastic pleurisy, with acute, stitching pains, greatly aggravated by breathing, or the slightest motion; respirations short and rapid. Also, for the "dry" pleurisies accompanying pneumonia and phthisis.

**Cantharis** (3x).—This is the most efficient remedy, following Bryonia, when there is serous effusion or serofibrinous exudation. Sensation of heat and burning in the chest; the characteristic urinary symptoms.

**Apis** (3x).—For the stage of effusion, to promote reabsorption, especially when the effusion is of recent origin; also, in pleurisy following scarlatina. Absence of thirst; dark and scanty urine; edema of the chestwall; severe, burning pain in a circumscribed spot.

**Colchicine** (3x).—Acute, general pleurisy, in rheumatic or gouty subjects. A peculiarity of the condition calling for this medicine is often, aversion to the smell of food, which causes nausea and loathing.

**Arsenic** (3x).—In the later period of the stage of effusion, which has failed to yield to other remedies. There is great dyspnea, with but little pain; much prostration, the patient being weak and cachectic; cyanosis; restless anxiety.

**Hepar sulph.** (2x).—Persistent plastic pleurisy. Great sensitiveness to the open air; moist skin; the patient easily perspires.

**Rhus tox.** (3x).—Acute attack coming on after exposure to cold and damp; after a wetting while heated and perspiring. Muscular pains in various parts; pains in the extremities; disposition to change the position of the parts, which is followed by relief.

**Sulphur.** (6x).—Plastic exudation, slow to disappear. Also, in cases of serous effusion, coming on insidiously, and lingering. Great need of fresh air; feet and head hot; hands and feet burn; palpitation; atonic dyspepsia.

**Kali carb.** (3x).—Dry pleurisy complicating phthisis.

**Mercurius corr.** (3x).—Pleurisy complicating Bright's.

**Phosphorus** (3x).—Pleuro-pneumonia.

**Iodine** (2x).—In "scrofulous" subjects it replaces **Bryonia.**

### General Measures.

**Room.**—Dry, well-ventilated; about 70° F.

**The Patient.**—However mild the attack, insist upon the patient's remaining in bed. Absolute rest promotes recovery. Let the patient seek the most comfortable position, but remain quiet. Give attention to the state of the bowels.

**Immobility.**—Immobility of the affected side may be secured by bandages, as for fractured rib.

**Pain.**—For relief of pain, hot compresses—as hot as the patient can bear, frequently changed. Poultices are an abomination. Cold applications should not be used.

**Thoracentesis.**—This is called for under certain conditions.

**Indications:**—(1) **Moderate amount** of effusion:—If after the acute stage has subsided it remains stationary for ten days, aspiration may be performed. (2) **Large amount** of effusion:—When the fluid rises as high as the third rib in front; aspiration should be performed. (3) **Large amount of effusion:**—If respiration is embarrassed or an attack of syncope occurs, aspirate at once.

**Method.—Asepsis:**—Sterilize the surface of the skin, and use all antiseptic precautions in the care of the operator's hands and the instruments.

**Instrument.**—Use the aspirator, with the vacuum jar.

**Needle.**—Use a small-sized needle (No. 2).

**Location of the Puncture.**—The fifth or sixth interspace, in the axillary line.

**Position of the Patient.**—Semi-recumbent, and partially rotated towards the sound side.

**Introducing the Needle.**—Enter the needle midway between the ribs; thrust steadily and forcibly inwards (do not use a rotating or boring motion).

**Anesthesia.**—Do not use a general anesthetic; local anesthesia by **Cocain** or **Ethyl-chloride.**

**Amount to Withdraw.**—The rule is:—Slow withdrawal of a moderate quantity. The sudden withdrawal of a large quantity is liable to cause edema of the lung, or syncope from heart-failure. No accident has been known to attend slow withdrawal of a small quantity.

**Quantity.**—Withdraw little more than two pints (three at the most) at one time. It is not necessary to empty the pleural cavity completely.

**Precautions.**—At any time in the course of withdrawal of the fluid, **stop** if any one of the following symptoms appears:—Pain in the chest; sense of suffocation; faintness; uncontrollable paroxysms of cough.

**Time.**—Ten minutes should be consumed in the withdrawal of one pint.

**The Site of the Puncture.**—Place over the site of puncture a small pad of sterile absorbent cotton and secure it in place with collodion.

**Possible Accidents.**—In introducing the needle accidents to be avoided are puncture of the lung, liver or spleen.

**After-treatment.**—Following the withdrawal of the fluid the patient should spend the first twenty-four hours

in bed. Then he may go about. Re-expansion of the
affected lung should be brought about by systematic
lung-gymnastics

**Repetition.**—After a single withdrawal absorption
sometimes continues until all the fluid is removed. If,
on the contrary, it remains stationary, or increases, repeat the operation.

# PURULENT PLEURISY.

**Synonym.**—Empyema.

**Definition.**—Pus in the pleural cavity.

## ETIOLOGY.

**Specific Cause.**—Empyema is always due to invasion
of the pleural sac by pyogenic bacteria.

**Bacteriology.**—The streptococcus is the most common
form, being the micro-organism present in about 40 per
cent. of cases. Others are:—Staphylococcus; pneumococcus; bacillus tuberculosis. Putrid empyema is due to
the saprogenic bacteria.

**Source of Infection.**—In a great majority of cases the
empyema is secondary. The primary conditions are:—

(a) **Lung.**—Pneumonia; broncho-pneumonia; bronchiectasis; tuberculosis; gangrene; cancer.

(b) **Mediastinum.**—Pericarditis; abscess; cancer of the
esophagus.

(c) **Abdomen.**—Peritonitis; subphrenic abscess.

(d) **Infectious Diseases.**—Scarlet fever; diphtheria;
erysipelas; pyemia.

## PATHOLOGY.

**Pleural Walls.**—The walls of the pleura are covered
with a fibrinous deposit; color, yellow or grayish-white;
or green or brown (in putrid empyema). A suppurative
lymphangitis sometimes accompanies. In old cases there
is a granulating surface. In the tubercular form, the

pleura is much thickened, the surface uneven; in the depressions are grayish or yellowish spots consisting of caseous matter.

**The Pus.—Consistency:**—The pus varies from a thin fluid (an opaque serum) to a thick, creamy mass. On standing the upper layer may be thin and watery, the lower thick.

**Color.**—Yellow; gray; light green; reddish (from the presence of blood); dirty-brown (putrid form).

**Odor.**—Sweetish; or, very offensive (in putrid cases).

**Composition.**—Serum; leucocytes; red blood-corpuscles; endothelium; cholesterin crystals; free fat globules; Charcot-Leyden crystals.

**The Ribs.**—In chronic cases the ribs sink in as the lung retracts.

**The Pleura.**—The pleura becomes greatly thickened.

**Discharge of the Pus.**—When not artificially evacuated the pus may discharge through:—(a) the chest-wall (empyema necessitatis); (b) the lung; (c) the pericardium; (d) the diaphragm; (e) the retroperitoneal tissues; (f) the mediastinum; (g) the esophagus.

## SYMPTOMS.

**Forms.**—According to the severity and duration of the disease, three forms may be recognized:—(a) **Pleuritis Acutissima;** (b) **Subacute Empyema;** (c) **Chronic Empyema.**

(a) **Pleuritis Acutissima.**—This form is acute and violent. It may be puruient from the first, or the primary affection may have passed unrecognized. **Onset.**—It usually sets in with a distinct and sometimes a severe chill; cough; dyspnea; pain in the side; fever. The cases vary in severity. In some a typhoid-like condition supervenes, with repeated rigors. The prognosis is unfavorable.

(b) **Subacute Empyema.**—This form develops gradually from the sero-fibrinous form. **Onset.**—Pain, dyspnea, cough, as in other forms. **Fever:**—Early, moderate;

later (seven to ten days) it persists, and rises; hectic follows, with repeated chills. **Symptoms:**—Night-sweats; emaciation; anorexia; prostration; dyspnea; rapid pulse; edema of the ankles; clubbed fingers. **Course:**—If surgical interference is not resorted to, evacuation may take place spontaneously, through the lungs (most common), chest-wall, or other structures.

(c) **Chronic Empyema.**—The chronic and latent form is generally tubercular. It may persist for years. The accompanying fever is generally slight. **Positive Diagnosis:**—The diagnosis can always be confirmed by use of the exploring-needle, which will show the presence of pus in the pleural cavity. **Caution:**—Do not draw from the upper surface of a contained fluid; the pus-cells may all be in the sediment.

## PHYSICAL SIGNS.

**Auscultation and Percussion.**—The signs are similar to those which characterize sero-fibrinous pleurisy (page 190).

**Baccelli's Sign.**—On auscultation the whispered voice as conveyed to the ear is not so distinct as in sero-fibrinous pleurisy. This sign is not constant.

**Other Signs.**—Inflammatory edema of the chest-wall (general or local) is a significant sign.

**Empyema Necessitatis.**—This term is applied to the condition when the surface of the costal pleura becomes necrosed and the pus burrows outward, making its way under the skin of the side. When this occurs it causes peripheral inflammation, swelling, redness, heat, edema of the skin, pain on the slightest pressure, and there is fluctuation. When the skin is perforated there is discharge of the pus, with sinus communicating with the pleural cavity.

**Pulsating Pleurisy.**—**Synonyms:**—Pulsating empyema; empyema pulsans. Pulsating empyema is a condition in which pulsations of the heart are communicated to the tumor of empyema necessitatis. Pulsations in the tumor may be felt by palpation, the pulsations corresponding in rhythm to the heart-beats.

**Differential Diagnosis.**—Pulsating empyema must be differentiated from aneurysm of the thoracic aorta. In making the diagnosis note the following:—

(1) **Aortic aneurysm.**—(a) Aortic aneurysm bears a definite relation to the central vertical line of the chest; (b) Aortic aneurysm is circumscribed; (c) The aneurysm is the seat of murmurs or other sounds synchronous with the rhythm of the heart.

(2) **Pulsating empyema.**—(a) Pulsating empyema is almost always on the left side; (b) It is usually at some distance from the median line; (c) The percussion dulness is at the base of the chest, and is quite extensive; (d) Arterial murmurs are not present; (e) The pulsation is influenced by pressure and by respiratory movements.

## TREATMENT.

**Medicinal.**—Hepar sulph., Silicea, Arsenic, Mercurius, Calcarea, Phosphorus—and other remedies related to the suppurative process, as well as to the constitutional condition.

## SURGICAL MEASURES.

**Indications.**—Pus in the pleural sac is essentially an abscess, and should be promptly treated as such. In children, in whom the tendency is often to recovery, the demand is not so urgent; thoracentesis may be tried. But in adults, unless there is some special contrary reason, operation should be resorted to without delay.

**Methods.**—I. Thoracentesis; II. Simple incision; III. Resection of rib; IV. Siphon-drainage; V. Thoracoplasty.

## I. THORACENTESIS.

**Indications.**—This method has but limited use; in the great majority of cases the radical operation is demanded and is necessary to a cure. It may be resorted to:—

(1) In Mild Cases; (2) In Urgent Cases.

(1) **In Mild Cases.**—Indications:—Thoracentesis may be resorted to in mild cases when there is no apparent danger from delay in the more radical operation.

**Limitations.**—Unless prompt improvement follows, only one or two aspirations should be made; if at the end of one week the temperature is not reduced to normal, adopt radical measures.

**Note.**—In children, if the fluid obtained by exploratory puncture shows pneumococci only; or, in adults, if it shows the bacillus tuberculosis only, treatment by thoracentesis may be followed.

(2) **In Urgent Cases.**—Indications:—Thoracentesis may also be resorted to in urgent cases when immediate relief of dangerous symptoms is demanded.

**Conditions.**—Edema of the lungs, marked dyspnea, extreme weakness, or threatened syncope are indications for prompt aspiration. But this should be followed by operation in a few hours.

**Instrument.**—The aspirator, including the needle and tubing, should be boiled and then immersed in an antiseptic solution.

**Skin.**—The skin in the field of operation and in the axilla should be rendered thoroughly aseptic by being washed, scrubbed, and disinfected with **Mercuric bichloride solution** (1:2,000). The hands of the operator should be similarly treated.

**Position of the Patient.**—Let the patient be supported by pillows in a semi-recumbent position, with the arm raised over the head; the patient should be lowered as the fluid is gradually withdrawn.

**Precautions.**—Give alcoholic stimulants before and during operation, to anticipate cardiac weakness. Watch the pulse and respiration; if the pulse becomes feeble, stop the withdrawal of the fluid, promptly push stimulants and lower the patient to the supine position.

**Anesthetics.**—Never use general anesthesia. At the point of puncture anesthetize the skin by a spray of

**Ether,** or preferably, **Chloride-of-ethyl.** A drop of **Carbolic acid** will accomplish the purpose.

**Point of Puncture.**—If there is any doubt, determine this by previous puncture with the exploring-needle. Usually it will be where the dulness on percussion is most marked; or, there will sometimes be a point of bulging in the intercostal space. When the fluid is not circumscribed make puncture in the mid-axillary line, just in front of the border of the latissimus dorsi muscle, in the fifth intercostal space on the right side, the sixth on the left, and just above the upper border of the lowermost rib of the selected space.

**Introducing the Needle.**—In the entire process be careful to admit no air. Draw the skin up, make a slight preliminary incision, and then introduce the needle. This method provides a valve-like opening at the point of puncture when the needle has been withdrawn. **Caution.**—Do not injure the liver, lung or other viscera.

**Removal of the Fluid.**—Withdraw slowly. If there is sudden stoppage of the flow, which may be due to a plug of fibrin or caseous pus, remove it by introducing a stylet, previously rendered aseptic. Or, under precautions to prevent the entrance of air, a small quantity of an antiseptic fluid may be slowly injected, to remove the obstruction.

**Amount to be Withdrawn.**—This depends upon the amount present, and the condition of the patient. If there is a large quantity, withdraw only one-half. As soon as the patient begins to cough, or becomes faint, or the pulse becomes feeble, stop.

**After-Treatment.**—Seal the wound by cleansing the surface again, placing over it a thin layer of sterile cotton and painting with **Collodion.** Keep the patient perfectly quiet.

**Irrigation of the Pleural Cavity.**—This is never to be adopted unless the contents are fetid. In the ordinary

case treatment by irrigation prolongs the disease process, and, moreover, it is sometimes attended by fatal
accident.

**Method of Irrigation.**—The best method is to place
the patient in a warm bath of sterilized water, keeping
the chest submerged. With the expiratory and inspiratory acts the water will enter the pleural cavity, and
return pus-laden. Continue until the water returns clear.

## II.—INCISION.

**Indications.**—Incision is the preferable operation in
**children**; also, in **adults** when general anesthesia cannot
be used.

**Location.**—In the axillary line, 4th, 5th or 6th interspace; or, just below the angle of the scapula (in this
location the diaphragm is liable to rise and interfere
with drainage).

**Patient.**—Have the patient in the lateral semi-recumbent posture, with the arm raised above the head.

**Incision.**—Render the skin aseptic. Anesthetize the
surface with **Ethyl-chloride.** Cut near the upper border
of the lower rib of the two. The knife may be thrust
through all the tissues, and then the opening enlarged by
means of a sinus-dilator. When the incision is complete, insert one or two fingers into the opening to prevent the too rapid escape of the pus. Evacuate slowly.

**Drainage.**—Insert a drain, and apply dressings as described on p. 204.

## III.—RESECTION.

**Indications.**—Resection is to be used in adults, when
general anesthesia is admissible. It is still called for
even after spontaneous evacuation has occurred, whether
through the lung or through the chest-wall. The percentage of recoveries by this method is greater than
by any other.

**Anesthetic.**—**Chloroform** is to be preferred. Do not
turn the patient after he is unconscious.

**The Incision.**—Prepare the patient as for other methods. Over the middle line of the chosen rib make a single cut, three inches long, exposing the rib. Hold the wound open by retractors. Crowd the periosteum to each side, for a length of two inches, extending the process to the edges and inner surface of the rib. At the lower edge carefully separate the intercostal artery with the periosteum. The pleura is still intact. Grasp the bared rib with strong forceps, and cut out a piece 1½ inches long with bone-forceps or a rib-cutter.

**Evacuation.**—Now open the pleura by a small incision, insert the finger and sweep it about in all directions to clear away pockets or clumps. Let the pus escape slowly. When the patient has partially recovered, change his position in order to favor evacuation.

**The Wound.**—After thorough evacuation, insert a rubber drainage-tube the size of the finger; dust it with Iodoform; secure it with safety-pins. Close the external wound on each side by two or three deep stitches.

**Dressing.**—Put iodoform-gauze between the safety pins and the skin. Cover all with iodoform-gauze, sterilized gauze, and a large pad of sterilized cotton, reaching from the axilla to the crest of the ilium. Secure in position with bandages.

**After-Treatment.**—The dressings may remain until their removal is demanded by (a) rise of temperature; or, (b), saturation with pus. Generally this is in one or two days (in rare instances, a week). The second dressing can usually remain longer than the first. Only in exceptional cases is it necessary to dress daily.

**Drainage.**—By Posture:—Place the patient on the affected side, in the lateral posture; raise the hips and lower the shoulders; then reverse this motion; do this several times. Repeat the process four times daily in the first week; later, two or three times a day.

**The Tube.**—At each successive dressing, shorten it. Its final removal is determined by the amount of discharge, and by careful probing of the fistula with a soft catheter.

### IV. SIPHON DRAINAGE.

**Method.**—Under local anesthesia, puncture the chest with a large trocar (6 to 13 mm.). Withdraw most of the pus, slowly. Then insert a soft-rubber catheter, through the canula, withdrawing the canula over the catheter. Attach a long rubber tube to the end of the catheter, letting the other end of the tube pass into a large bottle, partly filled with an antiseptic solution.

**Indications.**—This method is especially applicable to chronic tuberculous empyema, and to the pneumococcus variety in adults. Good results have been obtained by this method.

**Special Conditions.**—If there is already an existing perforation, operate without regard to it, selecting the usual location. In encapsulated empyema make the incision over the seat of the pocket. In double empyema, operate on one side, and on the other side five to ten days later.

**Re-expansion of the Lungs.**—Use Wolff's bottles; light chest-gymnastics; hill-climbing.

### V.—THORACOPLASTY.

**Indications.**—In old cases that resist the usual methods; the fistula continues to discharge for months. It is a serious operation, and should be resorted to only to save life. It consists in the resection of several ribs. Reference must be made to works on surgery.

---

## CHRONIC PLEURISY.

**Varieties.**—There are two forms:—**(a)** Dry pleurisy; **(b)** Pleurisy with effusion.

**Chronic Dry Pleuritis.**—On the post-mortem table it is the rare exception to find a pair of lungs in which there is not some pleuritic adhesion. The amount of adhesion varies greatly. Slight adhesions may form during life unattended by obvious symptoms.

**Pleurogenic Cirrhosis.**—This term is applied to the

non-tuberculous dry pleurisy, with great thickening of
the pleura, the thickened membrane extending into the
lung along the interlobular septum, producing fibroid
changes.

**Chronic Pleurisy with Effusion.**—This is of two forms :
—(a) Latent; (b) Secondary.

**(a) Latent.**—The latent form begins without marked
symptoms. The patient is so little disturbed that he
does not seek medical advice. The fluid gradually accumulates. The case may come under observation only
when there is sufficient fluid to produce dyspnea. Some
of these cases are probably tubercular.

**(b) Secondary.**—In some cases the chronic form of
pleurisy with effusion follows the acute. Paracentesis
is performed, but the fluid .re-accumulates as often as
withdrawn. Such cases may continue for years, the
pleural cavity constantly occupied by a quantity of
serous fluid.

**Treatment.**—In chronic pleurisy with effusion paracentesis should be performed whenever there is sufficient fluid to produce dyspnea. Draw off only a part
of the fluid at a time. Deep breathing and other lung
gymnastics should be systematically performed. For
medicinal treatment, see the remedies recommended in
acute and subacute pleurisy.

---

# TUBERCULOUS PLEURISY.

**Frequency.**—A large proportion of cases of primary
pleurisy are tuberculous. By different authorities the
number is put at from one-third to two-thirds of all
such cases.

**Bacteriological Demonstration.**—The demonstration
of the presence of the bacillus tuberculosis must be
made by inoculation of the lower animals. In order to
do so, as much as 15 cc. of the effusion must be used ;
a smaller quantity may not give results.

**Varieties.**—Tuberculous pleurisy may pursue an (1) Acute; or, a (2) Chronic course.

**Acute.**—The acute cases present three forms:—(a) Acute tuberculous pleurisy with subsequent chronic course; (b) Secondary and terminal forms of acute pleurisy; (c) Acute tuberculous suppurative pleurisy.

**Chronic.**—The chronic cases are those with **sero-fibrous effusion,** and those with **chronic adhesion.**

**Etiology.**—The source of infection in tuberculous pleurisy is usually through the subpleural lymphatics, or from the bronchial or tracheal lymph-glands. The bacilli may reach the pleura from the peritoneum through the lymphatics of the diaphragm, secondary to tuberculous peritonitis. Secondary tuberculous pleurisy accompanying pulmonary tuberculosis is of common occurrence.

**Symptoms.**—The symptoms of tuberculous pleurisy do not differ essentially from those of the other forms. The onset is marked by pain in the side, chill, pyrexia, cough, and the other characteristic symptoms.

**Treatment.**—Recovery is possible in many cases. The treatment is such as is indicated for pleurisy, and for pulmonary tuberculosis. There should be fresh-air treatment, lung-exercise, and attention to diet and nutrition.

---

# PNEUMOTHORAX.

**Definition.**—Pneumothorax is the presence of air in the pleural cavity.

## ETIOLOGY.

Air may gain access to the pleural cavity:—(a) From lesions within the chest; (b) From lesions in the chest-wall.

**Lesions Within the Chest.**

**Pulmonary Tuberculosis.**—In about 90 per cent. of cases pneumothorax is secondary to pulmonary tuberculosis. It occurs in not more than 5 per cent. of cases of phthisis. **Process.**—The air gains access through the softening and rupture of a superficial tubercular nodule. In the case of large cavities previous adhesive pleurisy occurs and thus prevents perforation.

**Empyema.**—Next in order of frequency, **empyema is** the primary condition. **The lesion.**—The form of lesion is necrosis of the spot on the visceral pleura, thus creating communication between a bronchus and the pleural cavity.

**Other Causes.**—Other conditions which may lead to pneumothorax are:—(a) Pulmonary gangrene; **(b)** Bronchiectasis; **(c)** Pulmonary abscess; **(d)** Cancer; **(e)** Hydatid cyst; **(f)** Cancer of the esophagus; **(g)** Various abdominal conditions attended by abscess and perforation of the diaphragm, creating communication between the gastro-intestinal canal and the cavity of the pleura; or **(h)** In ulcer of the stomach.

### Lesions of the Chest-Wall.

These may consist of:—(a) Traumatic perforation; **(b)** Abscess of the chest-wall, opening both externally and internally.

**Decomposition.**—It is still an open question whether the putrid contents of the pleura can decompose, producing gases.

**Accidental Pneumothorax.**—Pneumothorax, in rare instances, occurs in those who are apparently in perfect health. All literature affords a record of but 37 cases. Although the subject appears to be in perfect health, yet it is supposed that the air is admitted to the pleura through a small rupture in the lung due to an atypical emphysema, or to the rupture of a rapidly-developing tubercular nodule.

## MORBID ANATOMY.

In pneumothorax the lung is compressed to about one-eighth of its normal size. It is like a fleshy mass, bluish or reddish-brown. In most cases the perforation is in the upper lobe. Sometimes the pleural surface is covered by fibrinous exudation. The perforation is usually small, not larger than a pin's-head; it may, however, be a half-inch or more in diameter. The lung is airless and full of blood. The perforation is usually valvular in action. The air in the pleural cavity in open pneumothorax is that of the external atmosphere. In closed pneumothorax it parts with its oxygen and the carbon-dioxide increases. The heart, mediastinum, and the diaphragm are displaced. The heart may be displaced entirely to the right of the median line. The diaphragm may even curve downwards. Pneumothorax is usually complete. A circumscribed pneumothorax may occur when there are old adhesions.

**Re-expansion.**—Re-expansion of the lung takes place when the air is absorbed. In favorable cases the rate of absorption of air may be very rapid.

## SYMPTOMS.

**Onset.**—The onset is usually sudden and violent, and attended by great pain, intense dyspnea, and anguish; there is cold, clammy perspiration; the heart suffers from temporary shock; the face is pale or cyanotic; the voice is reduced to a whisper; there is violent paroxysmal cough; the temperature is usually subnormal; the entire condition is one of threatened collapse. In very rare instances death may follow. If the function of the affected lung has already been much reduced by disease, or if the escape of air is gradual, the initial symptoms are not so violent.

**Course.**—Following the severe onset the early symptoms gradually subside, and in two or three days the pain and dyspnea are considerably relieved. But the destructive process in the diseased lung continues, and the patient usually fails from progressive exhaustion.

## PHYSICAL SIGNS.

**Inspection.**—The affected side is motionless and enlarged. The intercostal spaces are obliterated or bulging. The heart's impulse may be much out of place. There is exaggerated movement of the unaffected side.

**Palpation.**—On the affected side vocal fremitus is diminished or absent. The displaced heart's impulse may be felt when in a right-side pneumothorax the liver is found to be much depressed.

**Percussion.**—The note on percussion is usually tympanitic, but if the air in the pleural cavity is under high tension the pitch may be high and give forth a dull note on percussion. The characteristic note is found to extend far beyond the normal boundaries of the lungs in every direction. There is dulness over the compressed lung if it is in apposition to the chest-wall. The displaced heart may be located by percussion.

**Auscultation.**—There is entire absence of all respiratory and vocal sounds. Transmitted sounds have an amphoric quality. With the stethoscope on the front of the chest and a coin placed at the back, on tapping the coin with another coin it transmits a bell-sound *(bruit d'airain.)*. An amphoric blowing sound is heard with inspiration and expiration if there is open perforation.

**Succussion.**—If there is fluid, the result of effusion, it gives forth a splashing sound on succussion. It is elicited by giving the patient a sudden shake while the ear of the examiner is held to the chest. If the amount of fluid becomes great its presence may be detected by the usual signs on percussion. The upper level will be horizontal and will vary and change with the position of the patient.

## DIAGNOSIS.

In a well-marked case the diagnosis of pneumothorax is not difficult. It has been mistaken for unilateral emphysema. A large pulmonary cavity should not mislead the examiner. With the presence of a cavity in the lung there is retraction of the chest wall instead of expansion. Diaphragmatic hernia should be kept in mind.

## PROGNOSIS.

In cases in which the lung is not much affected, and air only is effused, there is usually absorption of the air, followed by recovery. In traumatic cases the prognosis is determined by the nature of the injury. Double pneumothorax is almost always rapidly fatal. In pneumothorax secondary to empyema a case may do well after external drainage has been established. In pneumothorax occurring in the course of pulmonary tuberculosis the prognosis is always grave.

## TREATMENT.

**Onset.**—If the case is marked by severe initial symptoms, with great pain and intense agony, **Morphine** hypodermically must be given for immediate relief. If the signs of shock are severe, with threatened heart-failure, give repeated injections of **Ether** as a stimulant; at the same time apply warmth to the extremities. The medicinal treatment is essentially the same as indicated in pleurisy and in empyema.

**Accidental Pneumothorax.**—In this class of cases keep the patient absolutely quiet and give remedies to restrain the cough, and often the air is absorbed and recovery follows.

Surgical Treatment.

**Relief of Tension.**—If at the time of perforation air continues to accumulate in the pleural sac, owing to the valve-like action of the rupture, the high tension of the contained air may cause pressure which will produce intense dyspnea and threaten life. In such case the air must be evacuated. For this purpose, under strict aseptic precautions, introduce through an intercostal space a trocar and canula. The canula must remain until it is known that the air will not re-accumulate. The canula should be fixed in position and kept covered by clean surgical dressing.

**Removal of Serum.**—If serum is present in small amount it may be neglected. If in great amount it should be withdrawn by aspiration, removing but a small quantity at a time.

**Removal of Pus.**—In pneumopyothorax, secondary to empyema, the indications are to make the radical operation by incision in the chest-wall and drainage, as in empyema.

**Tuberculous Pneumopyothorax.**—In pneumopyothorax, secondary to pulmonary tuberculosis, operation should be deferred as long as possible. Such cases usually do not do well after operation. Each case must be considered on its own merits. Some recover by the climatic cure. If the amount of fluid becomes large and increasing, producing dyspnea, try aspiration for relief. If this fails, remove the pus from the chest and replace it by warm **boric acid** solution by means of two needles; one inserted into the anterior chest-wall, the other into the posterior. With an India-rubber tube attached slowly inject the solution through one tube and let the pus escape from the other, having the end of the lower tube during the process under water in a basin set on the floor. Continue to introduce the solution until the pus is removed and the solution becomes clear.

# HYDROTHORAX.

**Synonym.**—Dropsy of the pleura.

**Definition.**—It is a non-inflammatory accumulation of serous fluid in the pleural cavity.

## ETIOLOGY.

Hydrothorax is almost always associated with general anasarca, though it may be due to local conditions.

**General Conditions.**—The general conditions which produce hydrothorax are disease of the heart, of the kidneys, of the liver, and conditions of profound anemia.

**Local Conditions.**—The local conditions which in most cases produce hydrothorax are:—mediastinal tumor and aneurysm. In these conditions the dropsy is due to pressure upon the azygos veins. Thrombosis of the azygos has also been known to produce hydrothorax. Hydrothorax also sometimes accompanies the late stages of cirrhosis of the liver.

**Side Affected.**—The dropsy is bilateral when from general causes. When from pressure on the azygos it is unilateral. Exceptionally, in heart-disease it is unilateral; the reason for this is not clear.

**Effusion.**—The amount of fluid varies from a few ounces to many pints. The quantity on the two sides may differ within wide limits. In character the effusion resembles blood-serum. It contains no fibrin or cellular elements. The serous effusion of the pleura contains more albumin than effusion found in any other serous sac.

## MORBID ANATOMY.

In old effusions the pleural wall is swollen and boggy. It is of a grayish-white color, due to a fibrinous film which forms on the surface. This exudation can be peeled off. The lung is collapsed, from compression by the fluid.

## SYMPTOMS.

Hydrothorax, as a symptom accompanying anasarca, is often overlooked owing to failure to make critical examination of the chest. The symptoms are those of lung-compression, with sense of oppression, dyspnea, and cyanosis.

**Physical Signs.**—Vocal fremitus is absent. There is dulness on percussion. Baccelli's sign is often present. The intercostal spaces are not so much obliterated as in the effusion of pleuritis.

## DIAGNOSIS.

From pleuritis with effusion hydrothorax is differentiated by the absence of pain, of fever, and by the general history. It must be kept in mind that hydrothorax is sometimes unilateral.

**Course.**—In hydrothorax, secondary to heart disease, the course is usually rapid; when from disease of the kidney there may be moderate pleural effusion for a long period preceding death.

## TREATMENT.

**Local.**—If the fluid is of a quantity to embarrass respiration it should be withdrawn by aspiration, and the operation repeated as necessary. The general treatment will be directed to the primary condition.

# HEMOTHORAX.

**Definition.**—Blood in the pleural cavity.

**Etiology.**—Hemothorax may be due to traumatism, the injury being to the chest-wall; to rupture of intra-thoracic aneurysm; rupture of an intra-thoracic vein; rupture of pulmonary infarction; as an accompanying condition in scurvy and purpura.

**Symptoms.**—The symptoms are those of hemorrhage generally :—syncope, pallor, cold extremities, etc. The physical signs are those of pleural effusion.

**Course.**—The blood usually quickly coagulates. In cases pursuing a favorable course the serum and the clot will be slowly absorbed. If there is infection, empyema results.

**Treatment.**—The treatment must be expectant, and governed by the nature of the cause.

# CHYLOTHORAX.

**Synonym.**—Chylous pleurisy.

**Etiology.**—Chylothorax is caused by occlusion or by

rupture of the thoracic duct, or of the receptaculum chyli.

**The Fluid.**—The fluid in chylothorax is milky in character, with a large quantity of fat in emulsion.

**Symptoms.**—The symptoms are those of lung compression, and such as would be caused by the primary disease. The physical signs are such as are found in pleural effusion.

**Prognosis.**—The prognosis is always unfavorable.

**Diagnosis.**—Diagnosis will probably never be made except by paracentesis, or use of the needle.

**Treatment.**—The treatment is to be symptomatic and expectant. A small quantity of the fluid should be withdrawn by aspiration only when it accumulates in sufficient quantity to embarrass respiration.

# SECTION V.

## EMBOLISM OF THE PULMONARY ARTERY.

**Definition.**—Embolism of the pulmonary artery consists in the lodgment in the artery of an embolus, a particle of solid matter, conveyed by the blood-stream from some distant part.

## ETIOLOGY.

**Characters of Emboli.**—(a) **Detached thrombus.**—A thrombus may become detached in a systemic vein. In the puerperal state the thrombus may have formed in the uterine, ovarian, or pelvic veins; other sources are the femoral and the saphenous veins; the lateral sinuses, and the jugular vein, in middle-ear disease. Venous thrombus may form in marasmic conditions, in typhoid, pleurisy, and in, various septic conditions. **Cardiac thrombus.**—Thrombus may form in the right auricle or right ventricle. In asystolism of the right ventricle clots may form about the columnæ carneæ and become detached. In vegetative endocarditis emboli may become detached from the valves. **Pulmonary thrombus.**—In various lung affections parietal thrombus may form in the pulmonary artery, become detached and carried to the smaller branches. **Fat embolism.**—In bone-fracture, in rupture of the liver, extensive injury to the subcutaneous tissue, fat emboli may be carried to the pulmonary artery. **New-growths.**—New growths may perforate a systemic vein and minute particles become detached, forming emboli. **Hydatids.**—

The ova may be carried to the lungs by the blood-stream. **Phlebolith.**—A phlebolith may pass into the circulation, becoming an embolus.

## PATHOLOGY.

The lung change depends upon the size of the vessel obstructed and the **septic** or **aseptic** character of the embolus.

**Aseptic.**—A small **aseptic** embolus produces transitory collateral hyperemia; occlusion of large branches is generally accompanied by edema.

**Septic.**—A septic embolus becomes the focus of a suppurative process, with necrosis of lung-tissue and abscess-formation. Gangrene may follow.

**Hemorrhagic Infarction** (pulmonary apoplexy).—**Definition.**—Hemorrhagic infarction is a condition in which the portion of lung beyond the point of obstruction of the pulmonary artery by an embolus becomes solidified by being surcharged with blood.

**Shape.**—The infarction is wedge-shaped, with the apex at the point of obstruction and the base at the pleura. It is solid, and sharply-defined.

**Color.**—It is deep purple-red in color; when old the color becomes brownish-red.

**Size.**—Infarctions vary in size from that of a pea to the size of a lemon, or it may involve an entire lobe.

**Pleura.**—The pleura overlying the affected area is usually inflamed, and may be covered with fibrinous exudation.

**Microscopic appearance.**—The bronchioles, alveoli, and capillaries are distended with red blood-corpuscles.

**Time.**—It requires two or three days for the process of formation to be completed.

**After-history.**—When old the tissue may contract, leaving a pigmented fibrous area.

**Method of formation.**—The method by which the blood reaches the affected area is not known. The view is advanced that it is by reflux from the veins and capillaries.

## SYMPTOMS.

The symptoms of **pulmonary embolism** vary in severity according to the size of the vessel that is blocked. If there are many emboli, or the blocked vessel is of large size, the symptoms are sudden and severe. There is sudden embarrassment of respiration and great **dyspnea.** There is severe **pain** in the chest. The **face** becomes deadly **pale.** There is clammy **sweat.** The superficial veins are distended; the lips are blue; the **pulse** is feeble, rapid, and irregular. There is great **agony,** and fear of impending death. Death may follow in a few minutes, in several hours, or in several days; the time varying according to the size of the obstructed vessel and the area of affected lung. The immediate cause of death may be **asphyxia** with convulsions, or **syncope** due to cardiac paralysis.

**Course.**—Sometimes recovery occurs in seemingly hopeless cases; the urgent symptoms gradually subside; or, there may be temporary subsidence of the symptoms, and a few days fresh embolism, resulting fatally.

If a small vessel is blocked the symptoms are less severe. If the emboli are infective, pneumonia or abscess follows, with rigors, hectic fever, profuse sweat, great prostration, diarrhea, and other symptoms of pyemia. If there is destruction of lung tissue the sputum may be chocolate-colored; the pleura may become perforated, with consequent pneumothorax.

**Physical Signs.**—If infarction is on the surface of the lung there will be dulness on percussion, crepitation, tubular breathing, and often pleural friction.

**Diagnosis.**—The diagnosis of pulmonary embolism may be made when there is very sudden onset of severe dyspnea, pain in the chest, accompanied by intense agony, in any condition in which venous thrombosis is known to exist.

**Prognosis.**—The prognosis in almost all cases must be grave. In the case of septic embolism a fatal result from pneumonia, from pulmonary abscess, or from pneumothorax, may be looked for. Extensive fat embolism of the capillaries is almost always fatal.

## TREATMENT.

**Prophylaxis.**—In all cases in which there is possibility that emboli may find their way into the circulation, keep the patient at absolute rest. In thrombosis of the veins of an extremity do not let the limb be moved for a long time after edema has entirely disappeared.

**The Attack.**—In embolism of the pulmonary artery death sometimes occurs before any treatment can be administered. When death is not immediate, support the action of the heart by cardiac stimulants. To overcome the effects of the intense mental agony that always accompanies, the senses may be obtunded by the use of **Morphine**. If recovery occurs, keep the patient at absolute rest for a long period.

# THROMBUSIS OF THE PULMONARY ARTERY.

**Definition.**—The formation of thrombus in the pulmonary artery.

**Pathology.**—The thrombus consists of a clot, either of nearly pure fibrin, or of nearly all the solid elements of the blood. It adheres to the wall of a vessel. The clot undergoes gradual contraction and conversion into firm fibrous tissue, occluding the vessel. Should the clot be septic there is necrosis and abscess-formation.

## ETIOLOGY.

Thrombus may form in the pulmonary artery:—**(a)** In the slow blood-current during the process of dying; **(b)** In various pulmonary diseases (pneumonia, tuberculosis, cirrhosis); **(c)** There may be secondary thrombosis in embolism of the pulmonary artery on the cardiac side of the obstruction, if life be sufficiently prolonged; (d) It may occur in connection with atheroma of the artery.

## SYMPTOMS.

The formation of the thrombus is accompanied by embarrassed respiration and severe dyspnea, but the symptoms are indefinite and there is nothing pathognomonic. In conditions in which it might occur, increasing dyspnea and rapid heart's-action will be suggestive. It is an unsettled question whether thrombosis is attended by the sudden and severe symptoms marking the occurrence of pulmonary embolism, as already described.

**Treatment.**—This will be on similar lines to those recommended in embolism.

# SECTION VI.

## HYPEREMIA OF THE LUNGS.

**Synonym.**—Pulmonary congestion.

**Varieties.**—(a) Active Hyperemia. (b) Passive Hyperemia.

**Active Pulmonary Hyperemia.**—Congestion of the lungs occurs as the first stage of pneumonia, but there may be pulmonary hyperemia which does not go on to pneumonitis.

**Etiology.**—Active congestion of the lungs may result from exposure to cold, or it may have for its exciting cause the breathing of very cold air, or very hot air; inhalation of irritating gases; also, inhalation of illuminating-gas in poison-cases; rarefied air, as at great altitudes; alterations of atmospheric pressure, as in miners and in caisson-workers. It may occur as the result of violent exertion or exercise, as in athletic sports, running, bicycle-riding, etc. It may result from cold drinks, or from cold bathing when the body is warm.

### PATHOLOGY.

In active congestion of the lungs the arterioles are dilated, there is swelling of the mucous membrane and of the lung-tissue, and the interchange of gases is interfered with.

### MORBID ANATOMY.

The lung is bluish, purple, livid, or blackish in color. The area affected may be local or general. On section, a quantity of blood may be pressed out, escaping from the cut surface; the interstitial connective-tissue is more or less distended with serum; the capillaries are swollen so as to compress the alveoli; minute points of extravasation from rupture of small capillaries appear.

## SYMPTOMS.

**Dyspnea.**—There is rapid breathing and dyspnea, varying in severity according to the degree of congestion.

**Pain.**—There is feeling of fullness and tightness across the chest, but no actual pain.

**Cough.**—Cough is a constant accompaniment, varying in severity.

**Expectoration.**—There is usually expectoration, which may be clear mucus, or blood-tinged. If there is much accompanying edema the expectoration is watery.

**Hemoptysis.**—Congestion may be so intense as to produce hemoptysis.

**Face.**—It is flushed, or may be cyanotic. The eyes are injected.

**Head.**—There is usually severe headache, and throbbing of the carotids.

**Fever.**—There is usually little if any rise of temperature. There is absence of chill.

**Pulse.**—The pulse is full and strong at first, but later it is small, thready and intermittent.

**Edema.**—When there is intense congestion there is usually much accompanying pulmonary edema.

**Late Symptoms.**—If the condition persists and becomes extreme there is cyanosis; severe headache; small pulse; cold, clammy sweat; extreme restlessness; shallow breathing; rapid respiration (40, 50, or 60 per minute). In cases that end fatally this condition is followed by subsidence of the cough, inability to expel the secretions, increasing difficulty in breathing, and finally edema, stupor, coma, and death.

### Physical Signs.

**Inspection.**—There is increased respiratory action, and either redness, or lividity and cyanosis of the skin.

**Percussion.**—At first the note is clear, or even tympanitic, but later there is localized or general dulness.

**Auscultation.**—The respiratory sounds are weak and harsh. Late, with accumulated secretions, or edema, there are various moist râles, fine or coarse.

## DIAGNOSIS.

If the exciting cause be taken into consideration the diagnosis of active congestion of the lungs can usually be made. In the condition in which there is rapid breathing, dyspnea, with absence of vesicular murmur over the chest, not preceded by chill, and not accompanied by fever, active congestion of the lungs is the probable condition.

## PROGNOSIS.

The prognosis in active pulmonary congestion, depending upon the etiological factors which have been enumerated, is almost always favorable. The prognosis in passive hyperemia, which is considered elsewhere, presents a graver problem.

## TREATMENT.

**General Measures.**

**Baths.**—A hot bath (105° to 110° F.) is beneficial. Immerse the patient in it for from five to ten minutes. Take him out and wrap him in blankets and there will be free perspiration.

**Local.**—If for any reason the general bath cannot be given, apply a hot compress over the chest for ten minutes. Take it off and re-apply at intervals until perspiration is induced. An ice-bag applied the length of the spine will sometimes act promptly and give great relief.

**Bowels.**—The bowels must be kept clear. Give free · enemata.

**Therapeutics.**

**Aconite.** (1x).—When due to inhaling cold air, to chilling of the body, or to violent exercise. **Indications:** —Violent heart's action; pulse quick and hard; burning, pressing pains in the chest; anxiety and restlessness, especially in plethoric subjects.

**Belladonna.** (2x).—Intense congestion; rapid breathing; flushed face; skin red; throbbing carotids; voice hoarse; dry cough; blood-tinged expectoration.

**Veratrum vir.** (Tr.).—Pulse full and hard; heart's beat loud and strong; great arterial excitement; faint feeling at the stomach; nausea.

**Cactus.** (2x).—Hyperemia of the lungs secondary to heart-disease; respiration much oppressed; acute pains; feeling of constriction.

**Phosphorus.** (3x).—In cachectic subjects; anxious panting; great oppression under the sternum; threatened edema.

## PASSIVE HYPEREMIA OF THE LUNGS.

**Synonyms.**—Passive pulmonary congestion; hypostatic congestion.

**Passive Congestion.**—It is of two forms:—**(a)** Mechanical; and, **(b)** Hypostatic. The mechanical form is that which results in **Brown Induration of the Lungs,** for which see page 108.

**Hypostatic Congestion.—Etiology.**—It is due to the effect of gravity in patients who are long confined in a recumbent posture, with degeneration of tissue and weak heart's action as the result of disease. It occurs in typhoid, prolonged coma, paralysis, and other debilitated conditions. **Morbid anatomy.**—The posterior parts of the lungs are most affected. The lung is engorged with blood and serum, it is dark in color, and contains no air. On section the lung drips blood and serum. **Symptoms.**—The condition does not announce itself. In all diseases where it might occur it should be searched for. At the back and at the bases of the lungs there will be dulness, feeble respiration, and moist râles. **Treatment.**—The treatment is that belonging to the primary disease from which the patient is suffering. The patient should be changed from side to side, and not permitted to remain long in one posture.

# EDEMA OF THE LUNGS.

**Definition.**—Edema of the lungs is a condition in which there is escape of serous fluid into the pulmonary areolar tissue and into the air-cells.

**Etiology.**—The causes of edema are of two kinds:— (a) Disturbance of circulation; (b) Morbid conditions of the blood.

(a) Pulmonary edema due to disturbance of circulation:—

**Inflammatory Edema.**—In inflammation of the lung the active congestion may be attended by transudation of serum, producing a condition of edema. The exciting causes of active congestion may be the inhalation of very hot or very cold air; sudden changes of temperature; inhalation of irritating gases and vapors; ingestion of cold drinks when the body is warm; sudden chilling of the surface; over-straining of the vocal organs.

**Edema from Venous Stasis.**—Any condition which retards the pulmonary circulation may be attended by transudation of serum and consequent edema. The most common diseased conditions which lead to this are:—mitral stenosis; mitral regurgitation; feebleness of the heart; congenital heart affections; pericarditis; emphysema.

**Collateral Edema.**—When the function of one lung is much impaired the other lung may suffer from collateral edema. This usually occurs in extensive pneumonitis, or in pleuritis of one side, with disability of the lung.

**Hypostatic Congestion.**—In hypostatic congestion of the lungs, as in low fevers, the congested area may be surrounded by edema.

**Edema Due to Hydremia.**—Pulmonary edema may occur in any condition in which there is a hydremic state of the blood, poverty of red blood-corpuscles, and poorly nourished blood-vessels and tissues. The diseases in which this most commonly occurs are:—nephritis, leukemia; the various forms of primary anemia; and, more remotely, the secondary anemia attending scurvy, purpura, carcinoma, etc. In these latter conditions the pulmonary edema does not usually occur until there is also cardiac debility.

**Acute Angioneurotic Edema.**—This form of edema may occur locally in any part of the body. It consists of a sudden transudation of serum into the cellular tissue of the part. It is believed to be due to irritation caused by some toxic agent in the blood. In its pathology it is thought to be related to urticaria and erythema. It may occur in any mucous membrane. When the pulmonary mucous membrane is the point of attack it suddenly produces a condition of edema, with the usual attending alarming symptoms. The attack is sometimes rapidly fatal.

## MORBID ANATOMY.

The lungs in edema are large, heavy, wet, and pit on pressure; on section a large quantity of serous fluid mixed with air-bubbles may be squeezed out. The edema is most marked at the most dependent parts. There is serous infiltration into the interstitial connective-tissue and into the alveoli. The pleural cavity usually contains an unusual amount of serum.

## SYMPTOMS.

The patient suffers from great dyspnea, labored breathing, and feeling of tightness and oppression in the chest. There is cyanosis. The position is one of orthopnea, and the effort of breathing is labored. There is cough with frothy, liquid expectoration, sometimes bloody. Except in inflammatory edema, there is no rise of temperature, or the temperature is often subnormal.

Physical Signs.—Inspection.—There is labored breathing; anxious countenance; cyanosis; violent action of the heart. Percussion.—There is dulness, most marked in the back and over the lower lobes. Auscultation.— The respiratory murmur is feeble or absent. There are abundant moist râles, varying according to the amount of serous transudation from crepitant and subcrepitant, to coarse mucous, or, when the condition is extreme, rattling or bubbling. The chief characteristic of the râles is that they are uniformly distributed over the lungs.

## DIAGNOSIS.

The onset is without chill, fever, or pain. Both lungs are jointly involved. There are abundant moist râles and serous expectoration. Diagnosis is usually not difficult.

## PROGNOSIS.

The prognosis must always be grave. When pulmonary edema supervenes in bronchitis or pneumonia it is generally fatal, being due to heart-failure. Edema of the lungs is often the terminal event in chronic Bright's disease and in cardiac dropsy, and announces the fatal termination. Old people with feeble heart and emphysematous lungs may have a slight edema persisting for years. Finally, when the heart fails, the edema rapidly increases and marks the end.

## TREATMENT.

The treatment of each case will depend upon the nature of the primary disease, and whether it be of the heart, the liver, the kidneys, or of the blood. In almost all forms, however, the heart feels the burden of the attack, and cardiac stimulation is necessary in order to re-establish the circulation of the lungs. The indications, also, are to promote the action of the skin, kidneys, and bowels.

General Measures.—Change the patient frequently from side to side. If the patient is weak and has difficulty in raising the accumulated fluid from the lungs, raise the hips and lower the shoulders, thus favoring its removal by gravity. Apply warmth to the extremities. Apply hot compresses over the region of the heart. Give hot drinks and hot enemata. Nourish with hot broths.

**Cardiac Stimulants.**—When there is weak heart give cardiac stimulants, as in other similar conditions. For quick action give **Digitalin** hypodermically, 1-100 to 1-50 grain; or, aromatic spirits of **Ammonia,** 30 minims; or, tincture of **Musk,** 1 dram. Strong black coffee by enema is a good heart stimulant.

**Diaphoresis.**—In edema of the lungs occurring in acute Bright's disease, when the condition is threatening, in order to induce free diaphoresis, give **Pilocarpine,** hypodermically, dose one-tenth grain; or, **Jaborandi,** dose one-half dram.

**Catharsis.**—In order to induce watery evacuation give **Magnesium Sulphate** in ½ dram doses every hour until the effect is obtained. Also give heart-stimulants.

**Adrenal Chlorid.**—For acute **angioneurotic edema** of the upper air-passages use with atomizer a spray of **Adrenal chlorid** solution, full strength. This is the most efficient treatment for this condition.

**Therapeutics.**

**Belladonna.** (3x).—In inflammatory edema, or active congestion of the lungs with edema.

**Tartar emet.** (2x).—Useful in acute edema, as well as in the secondary form. Loud, coarse râles; intense dyspnea; the bronchial tubes contain a large quantity of serous fluid; imminent suffocation.

**Phosphorus.** (3x).—The use of this remedy is limited to the treatment of collateral edema occurring as a complication in congestion of the lungs or in pneumonia. Indications:—Great oppression of the chest; violent, strangling cough; expectoration blood-tinged.

**Ammonium carb.**—Feeble heart's action; cyanosis; drowsiness; great accumulation of serous fluid in the lungs, which the patient is too feeble to expectorate.

This marks an extreme condition; reaction in some instances may be brought about by **Ammonium carb.,** which acts as a respiratory and cardiac stimulant. **Dose**:—Each dose should consist of 2 grains of fresh **Ammonium carb.**, dissolved in one ounce of water; repeat at 30-minute intervals.

## ABSCESS OF THE LUNGS.

**Definition.**—A circumscribed collection of pus within the lung.

**Etiology.**—The abscess may be single or multiple. **Single abscess** is generally met with in pneumonia, or as the result of injury, such as fracture of the rib, or a penetrating wound of the chest-wall and lung. **Multiple abscesses** are usually of pyemic origin, due to the softening of infarctions, or to broncho-pneumonia. Suppuration, with a more or less circumscribed collection of pus, may occur in connection with many lung conditions; e. g., tuberculosis (secondary infection); bronchiectasis; hydatid cysts; pulmonary embolism; suppurating bronchial glands (by extension); empyema (rupture into the lung); mediastinal abscess or subphrenic abscess. No attempt should be made to check the cough.

### SYMPTOMS.

The symptoms attending the formation of abscess vary according to the nature of the primary condition, as indicated by the etiology. In some cases the diagnosis will not be positive until there is sudden expectoration of a large quantity of pus, but the formation of abscess can be suspected when in the course of the disease in which it may occur as a complication, there is rise in temperature, with a high range, **fever** of the **hectic** type, and repeated **chills.**

**Fever.**—The temperature reaches a high point, 104°,

105°, or even 106° F., plus. It is of the continued type, but marked by remissions and exacerbations.

**Chill.**—There are repeated chills, which are accompanied by profuse sweat and great prostration.

**Expectoration.**—With the rupture of the abscess into the bronchus there is expectoration of a large quantity of pus. At first the pus may be free from odor, but later it becomes fetid when drainage of the cavity is not free.

**Micro-organisms.**—Any of the bacteria of suppuration may be present; generally it is either the pneumococcus or the streptococcus.

**Perforation.**—Instead of rupturing into the bronchus the abscess may perforate the pericardium, the pleura, or, when there is pleural adhesion it has been known to perforate the intercostal muscles, giving rise to subcutaneous emphysema, or even to perforate the skin and discharge externally.

**Physical Signs.**—If the abscess is circumscribed and of sufficient size, there is dulness on percussion and absence of breath-sounds. After the discharge of pus there are signs of a cavity. In small multiple abscess the physical signs vary greatly.

**Prognosis.**—The prognosis is always grave, though the condition is not necessarily fatal.

**Course.**—The course is often protracted, and death occurs from asthenia, with heart-failure, or from the results of septic broncho-pneumonia.

## TREATMENT.

**General.**—In general the treatment must be to sustain the patient. This demands plenty of nourishing food and placing the patient under the most favorable hygienic conditions. Alcoholic stimulation is in many cases a necessity.

**Drainage.**—As well as may be done, drainage of the abscess-cavity, or of the suppurating portion of the lung, must be attempted. This may be sought to be accomplished by posture, turning the patient from side-to-side, and at intervals placing him in the "down-hill" position. No attempt should be made to check the cough.

**Surgical Interference.**—In some cases surgical interference offers the only encouragement. Its adoption must be determined by consideration of the ·patient's general condition, of the primary disease, of the site of the abscess, the possibility of drainage, and the condition of the overlying pleura.

**Inhalations.**—If the sputum is fetid, antiseptic vapors and sprays should be given by inhalation.

**Medicinal.**—The range of remedies will be those which act in suppuration, such as:—**Silicea** (6x); **Hepar sulph.** (6x); **Arsenicum iodid.** (6x); **Iodine** (1x); **Calcarea iod.** (3x); **Mercurius sol.** (3x).

## GANGRENE OF THE LUNGS.

**Definition.**—It consists of necrosis and putrefaction of portions of the lung tissue.

**Varieties.**—(a) Circumscribed gangrene; (b) Diffuse gangrene. The presence of a limited zone of inflammation cannot always be demonstrated, but yet its division into diffuse and circumscribed has been generally adopted by all authorities.

### ETIOLOGY.

**Micro-organisms.**—The gangrenous process is due to the action of the bacteria of putrefaction. The process is probably due to the combined action of various saprophytic organisms.

**Primary Conditions.**—There must first be necrosis of the part before the gangrenous process sets in. The primary conditions are many and various; they may be:—(a) Putrid bronchitis; (b) Septic broncho-pneumonia; (c) Bronchiectasis; (d) Fibrinous pneumonia; (e) Aspiration-pneumonia; (f) Fecal vomiting; (g) Carcinoma of the tongue, mouth, or esophagus; (h)

'Acute miliary tuberculosis; (i) Suppuration of all forms; (j) Septic pulmonary embolism; (k) Wounds of the lung.

## PATHOLOGY.

**Area Involved.**—The gangrenous area, in most cases, is circumscribed. In size it may vary from that of an olive to that of an orange, or, in some cases, an entire lobe, or even the entire lung, may be involved.

**Location.**—The lower lobes and the superficial parts are oftenest affected.

**The Affected Tissue.**—The affected portion of the lung becomes moist, soft, pulpy, with a greenish-black color, with broken-down foul lung tissue surrounding.

**Evacuation.**—The decomposed lung tissue may escape through a bronchus, leaving a sloughing cavity; or, it may discharge into the pleural cavity.

**Circumscribed Gangrene.**—In circumscribed gangrene the putrefactive micro-organisms enter the lungs through the bronchi by means of air, particles of food, etc.

**Embolic Gangrene.**—In embolic pulmonary gangrene the putrefactive matter enters the lungs through the circulation, producing multiple gangrene. It occurs in extensive gangrenous bed-sores, puerperal conditions, suppurative caries of bones, and pyemic processes.

## SYMPTOMS.

**Onset.**—The onset is usually marked by severe rigor, which may be repeated.

**Fever.**—The temperature often rises to a high point following the initial chill. The fever, however, soon subsides and the temperature becomes subnormal.

**Cough.**—Cough is always present.

**Expectoration.**—The sputum is foul, frothy, dirty-looking, partly liquid, partly muco-purulent. The sputum contains greenish or brownish particles of gangrenous lung tissue; also pus corpuscles, elastic tissue, fatty acids, the staphylococcus pyogenes aureus, and the micro-organisms of putrefaction. The amount ex-

pectorated in 24 hours often reaches 10 or 20 ounces.
In color it may be green, brown, chocolate, yellow, or
blood-stained. On standing it separates into three layers.

**General Condition.**—There is soon marked prostration, the patient sinking into a low, adynamic condition.

**Pain.**—Severe pain indicates involvement of the
pleura.

**Hemoptysis.**—There is liability to hemoptysis, which
may be very profuse.

**Odor.**—The matter expectorated and the patient's
breath have an extremely foul, fetid odor.

**Intestines.**—There may be intestinal irritation, with
diarrhea, due to infection by gangrenous matter being
swallowed.

**Embolism.**—Emboli may be carried to the brain, liver,
spleen, kidneys, there forming infective foci.

**Pleura.**—Purulent pleuritis may occur, communicated
by embolic gangrene near the surface.

**Pneumothorax.**—A gangrenous cavity may open
through the pleura, producing septic pneumothorax.

**Physical Signs.**—There are no distinctive physical
signs; the signs vary with the area affected, and whether
the process is in the stage of consolidation softening,
or already excavated.

## DIAGNOSIS.

The diagnosis is usually not difficult. It will depend
upon the presence of dyspnea, cough, occasional hemoptysis, the fetid breath, and the expectoration containing
broken-down lung tissue and elastic-fibres.

**Differential Diagnosis.**—The conditions which resemble gangrene of the lung are bronchiectasis, putrid bronchitis, and pulmonary abscess when accompanied by
great fetor. It must be differentiated from empyema
with perforation of the lung. The latter condition will
give a history of pleurisy followed by sudden expectora-

tion of a quantity of purulent and sometimes fetid sputa, but the true gangrenous odor is wanting, and there are no elastic-fibres to be found in the sputum.

## PROGNOSIS.

The condition is always grave, and always fatal in the diffuse form. In circumscribed gangrene recovery sometimes, though rarely, occurs. If the gangrene is diffuse or multiple it is always fatal.

**Course and Duration.**—In most cases it runs a short course. Rarely, it is chronic, and still more rarely followed by recovery after the separation of slough and the formation of a cavity.

**Cause of Death.**—Death may be due to asthenia or to complications, such as hemoptysis, purulent pleurisy, pneumothorax, infective emboli in the brain, liver or other organs.

## TREATMENT.

**Indications.**—(a) Support the patient. (b) Drain the cavity. (c) Disinfect the gangrenous area and diminish the fetor of the breath.

**General Measures.**—Give an abundance of rich and nourishing food to conserve the patient's strength. Use alcoholic stimulation freely. **Drainage.**—By every possible means clear the lungs of the gangrenous matter by favoring expectoration and by postural treatment of the patient. **Antisepsis.**—For local antisepsis give inhalations of **Iodine, Bromine, Oil-of-eucalyptol, Boric acid, Guaiacol**, and the like. If deglutition is difficult, the patient should be fed by means of the esophageal tube.

# SECTION VII.

## HYDATIDS OF THE LUNGS.

**Definition.**—It is the formation of cysts due to the introduction into the lung of the ovum of the tænia echinococcus.

### ETIOLOGY.

The disease is most common where human beings are closely associated with infected dogs, as in Iceland and Australia. The ova are conveyed by water. Next in order to the liver, the organs most frequently affected are the lungs.

### MORBID ANATOMY.

**Number and Location.**—One or both lungs may be affected; the right oftener than the left, and in most cases the lower lobes. There may be but a single cyst, or the cyst may be multilocular.

**Mode of Entrance.**—The ovum is first taken into the stomach. The envelope is there dissolved. It then, when liberated, bores through the coat of the stomach or the intestine and finds its way to the blood-stream. In most cases it is arrested in the liver; in others it enters a systemic vein and reaches the lungs through the pulmonary artery.

**Development.**—When lodged in the lung it loses its external hooks and gradually develops into a cyst, with two walls, the **ectocyst** and the **endocyst**. Daughter-cysts may form, or the cyst may be sterile.

**The Fluid.**—The fluid is clear, transparent, colorless, and neutral. Specific gravity, 1005 to 1015. It contains sodium-chloride, and traces of sugar. There is no albumin so long as the cyst is living. After death of the hydatid the fluid becomes turbid and albuminous.

**Changes in the Lung.**—There is usually some inflammatory action in the surrounding lung tissue. If the irritation is prolonged there may be induration of the lung and the formation of a fibrous capsule, but usually this is absent and there is no lining capsule to the cavity occupied by the cyst.

**Rupture.**—The cyst may rupture into a bronchus, and so discharge its contents, giving rise to cavity-formation. The cavity may remain and afterwards discharge pus. The cyst may rupture into the pleura, producing pneumothorax. It may rupture into the pericardium, causing sudden death.

**Pneumonia.**—The inflammation of the surrounding tissue may go on to pneumonia and fibroid induration of the lung.

### SYMPTOMS.

When the cyst is small there may be few or no symptoms. As it increases in size there is cough, dry and hacking. There may be some mucous expectoration. Hemoptysis occurs in some cases. Early, but a small quantity of blood, but profuse hemorrhage occurs before rupture of the cyst. Dyspnea is not urgent. Pain is absent, or only present when the pleura is involved. There is no feverish action and the patient's general health is but little affected prior to rupture of the cyst.

**Rupture.**—At the time of rupture there is usually violent cough, severe pain, urgent dyspnea, and the attack may prove suddenly fatal. If it does not, there is expectoration of watery fluid containing hooklets, and sometimes small daughter-cysts and pieces of hydatid membrane. There may be at this time severe hemoptysis.

**After Rupture.**—There are frequent paroxysms of severe and violent cough, with repeated expectoration of daughter-cysts and fragments of membrane. The expectoration becomes purulent and fetid. Hectic fever sets in, with chills, emaciation, night-sweats, and exhaustion. In other cases the general health may not be so seriously affected, but there will be repeated expectoration of daughter-cysts.

**Physical Signs.**—The physical signs vary according to the size of the cyst and its location in the lung. The signs are those characteristic of a solid body of the size of the cyst in the special case. If the cyst reaches the surface of the lung, coming into contact with the pleura, its further enlargement causes the formation of a globular tumor on the surface of the chest, projecting through an interspace. This is an important diagnostic sign of the disease. On percussion a thrill—the "hydatid thrill"—is felt. After rupture there may be signs of a cavity. If rupture is into the pleural cavity there is sudden, severe pain, urgent dyspnea, and, generally, collapse.

### DIAGNOSIS.

Early, take into consideration the patient's association with dogs, the physical signs of a solid body in the lung, and the presence of hydatids elsewhere in the body. After rupture, the presence of hooklets and fragments of membrane in the sputa renders the diagnosis positive. Never insert an aspirator-needle to draw off any of the fluid; it is dangerous to do so.

### PROGNOSIS.

Recovery after operation takes place in a large proportion of cases. In cases that go on to spontaneous rupture, if death does not occur at the time, ultimate recovery takes place in about one-half the number. Repeated hemoptysis is an unfavorable sign. Fetid abscess following rupture is unfavorable.

## TREATMENT.

Medicinal treatment is useless. Surgical interference by incision and drainage is the only possible method.

## HYDATIDS OF THE PLEURA.

Primary hydatid of the pleura is exceedingly rare. When it occurs it is usually single. Pain is a common symptom. Usually the pain is constant and severe. Cough may be absent, and hemoptysis is rare. There may be a localized globular swelling, or a general bulging of the side. Hydatid of the pleura offers a favorable case for operation, removal and recovery.

**Surgical Treatment.**—In hydatid of the lung or of the pleura the surgical methods are essentially the same as those in opening an abscess of the lung. As a preliminary step the lung must be fixed to the costal surface of the pleura, and the operation is pursued according to surgical principles and practice. The chief mischance to be anticipated is the rupture of the cyst into a bronchus, and sudden asphyxiation of the patient by the escape of a large quantity of fluid into the lungs.

## ACTINOMYCOSIS.

**Definition**—Actinomycosis is the presence of a fungous growth, the **actinomyces bovis** or "ray-fungus." The ray-fungus is a small, yellowish, spherical, granular body about 1-40 to 1-10 in. in diameter.

**Etiology.**—The ray-fungus, when affecting man, is accidentally acquired from the bovine species. It gains entrance to the lungs by way of the mouth.

## PATHOLOGY.

At the initial point of lodgment of the fungus in the lung inflammation is set up. The area of inflammation slowly enlarges, forming a tumor, in the center of which is the radiating fungus. The tumor may become two or three inches in diameter. The mass of the tumor contains pus and radiating threads of the fungus. Its periphery consists of fibrous tissue. The surrounding lung tissue is congested and inflamed. The fungous mass may break down, and degenerated tissue be expectorated, forming cavities. The disease process may extend to the chest-wall, which perforates, discharging pus, broken-down tissue, and ray-fungus.

## SYMPTOMS.

The symptoms are not characteristic, and a positive diagnosis cannot be made until specimens of the ray-fungus are found in expectorated matter or other discharge.

**Onset.**—The onset is gradual. The patient complains of weakness and loss of strength. There is cough, with or without expectoration, and sometimes pleurisy.

**Course.**—The disease is steadily progressive. The patient becomes pale and anemic, with emaciation and increasing cough, with expectoration finally containing yellow granules, which may be identified as ray-fungus. There is fever of a hectic type. The physical signs are those of circumscribed lung-consolidation.

**The Chest-wall.**—The next step is marked by involvement of the chest-wall. The intercostal spaces over the diseased area become obliterated and a swelling appears, gradually increasing in size and becoming brawny and edematous. At one or more spots the skin becomes red, softens, and ruptures, discharging pus, but a smaller quantity than the amount of swelling would lead one to expect. The disease process may cause penetration of the diaphragm as well as of the chest-wall. In the matter discharged, or on the granulations at the mouth of the sinus, may be detected the small, yellow, roundish granules of the ray-fungus. In appearance they somewhat resemble crystals of iodoform.

**The Fungus.**—To identify the fungus pick one off with a needle-point, place it in a drop of water on a glass slide, flatten it out by pressure with a needle on a cover-glass, and by a low power a body, the **mycelium,** consisting of radiating club-shaped bodies, will be recognized.

**Late Symptoms.**—New sinuses form and the old ones do not heal. There is progressive emaciation, night-sweats, hectic fever, loss of appetite, rapid, feeble pulse, and gradual exhaustion.

**Course.**—The disease is slowly progressive, extending over months and sometimes years. Death is from asthenia, or from embolic pyemia.

### DIAGNOSIS.

The diagnosis is only rendered certain by finding the characteristic fungus in the expectoration or the discharge.

### TREATMENT.

There is no specific treatment for the condition. Complete surgical removal of the fungus is the only thing that would prevent its progressive growth, and when it is in the lungs such removal is impossible. No treatment by drugs has ever been discovered that has the slightest effect. Some impression has been thought to be made upon the disease by the use of large doses of **Iodide-of-potassium;** doses of 30 to 40 grains three times a day. Other agents that have been tried are **Argentum nitricum, Tincture of Iodine, Carbolic Acid, Mercurius corr.;** but with indifferent results.

---

## PULMONARY MYCOSIS.

**Synonyms.**—Pneumomycosis; "pseudo-tuberculosis."

**Definition.**—It is the growth of fungi which have found access to the lungs.

**Fungus.**—The fungus which causes this disease is the **aspergillus fumigatus.**

**Etiology.**—It is most commonly found in those who handle grain, flour or meal infected with the spores of the aspergillus, as in millers and seedsmen.

**Symptoms.**—The symptoms resemble those of pulmonary tuberculosis. There will be hemoptysis; loss of strength; emaciation; dyspepsia; loss of appetite; cough; frothy, greenish and purulent blood-streaked expectoration. There is fever and night-sweat. The disease has been called "pseudo-tuberculosis."

**Physical Signs.**—The early signs are those of bronchitis, with, later, evidences of consolidation—usually at the apex of one lung.

**Course.**—The course is variable; there are periods of improvement. The disease sometimes lasts six or eight years, or more. Tuberculosis often supervenes.

**Diagnosis.**—The disease can only be recognized by the discovery of the mycelium in the sputum. These consist of small, rounded, white or yellowish-white bodies.

**Treatment.**—There is no specific treatment that will affect the fungous growth. The resisting power of the patient should be developed by abundant food, and, in general, the line of treatment should be as indicated in pulmonary tuberculosis.

# CLUBBING OF THE FINGERS.

In various chronic diseases of the lungs the fingers, and sometimes the toes, undergo a characteristic change, called "clubbing."

**Deformity.**—In clubbing of the fingers the ungual phalanx is alone affected. The digital pulp is enlarged and thickened, and the nail becomes curved towards the palm. In this way the ends of all the fingers of the hands become enlarged, resembling in appearance the large end of a club. The deformity in some cases develops slowly; in others very rapidly, the rapid development being accompanied by pain. The ends of the fingers are cyanotic. The skin over the root of the nail is shiny and tense. In lung-diseases the affection is bilateral and symmetrical. In disease of the circulatory apparatus it may be unilateral. It is most marked in cases of bronchiectasis; next, in chronic pulmonary tuberculosis with excavation. It occurs also in emphysema, chronic bronchitis, asthma, and empyema.

**Pathology.**—Its exact character has not been determined. It has been attributed to fibrous thickening of the rete mucosum, and to venous congestion.

# PULMONARY OSTEO-ARTHROPATHY.

**Definition.**—A peculiar affection of the bones and joints associated in some cases with chronic diseases of the lungs, usually of a suppurative nature.

**Associated Conditions.**—The lung diseases with which osteo-arthropathy is most commonly associated are empyema, bronchiectasis, tuberculosis, and abscess of the lung.

## SYMPTOMS.

The fingers, including the joints, are much swollen. The bones are in some cases enlarged, while in others the enlargement is confined to thickening of the soft parts. There is similar affection of the bones of the legs and forearms, and of the wrist and ankle-joints. The changes are sometimes present, but less marked, in the elbows, knees and hips. There is impaired movement of the affected joints. The hands and feet are cold and clammy, and there is often excessive perspiration. There is clubbing of the fingers, but this is probably the ordinary clubbing of the fingers found in pulmonary affections, associated with the osteo-arthropathy. There is not much accompanying pain.

**Pathology.**—The enlargement of the bones is due to a more or less extensive sub-periosteal deposit of bone. In the joints the changes seem to be of the nature of an osteo-arthritis.

**Diagnosis.**—The condition somewhat resembles acromegaly, osteitis deformans, and osteo-arthritis.

**Treatment.**—There is no specific treatment. In those cases in which the enlargement is confined to the soft parts, recovery follows if the primary lung disease is cured.

# GLOSSARY

# GLOSSARY

**Acromegaly.**—A disease characterized by enlargement of the bones and other tissues of the face, hands and feet.

**Actinomyces Bovis.** — The ray-fungus, the cause of actinomycosis.

**Actinomycosis.**—An infectious disease of cattle and man due to invasion of the tissues by the ray-fungus; marked by the formation of tumors, usually of the jaw, but sometimes in the lungs.

**Adynamia.** — Deficiency or loss of vital power.

**Adventitious Sounds.**— Abnormal sounds heard on auscultation.

**Amyloid Degeneration.** —A form of proteid metamorphosis resulting in the production of a waxy-appearing material; long-continued suppuration is the most common condition giving rise to it.

**Anasarca.** — G e n e r a l dropsy; dropsy of the cellular tissue of the entire body.

**Aneurism.**—A sac-like tumor containing blood, composed of the dilated walls of an artery.

**Angioneurotic Edema.**— An acute condition due to a sudden transudation of serum into the cellular tissue of a part; believed to be excited by irritation produced by some toxic agent in the blood.

**Anthracosis.**—Deposit of black pigment in tissues, as the fine particles of coal-dust deposited in the lungs in miner's phthisis.

**Aplasia.**—Defective development in a tissue; applied to an airless condition of the lung in deformity of the thorax.

**Apneumatosis.**—Collapse of the air-cells of the lung due to blocking of the bronchial tubes.

**Arteriosclerosis.** — A form of degeneration of the walls of the arteries in which there is connective-tissue overgrowth of the intima and the adventitia. Later, the new tissue undergoes various forms of degeneration.

**Aspergillus Fumigatus.** —The genus of fungi which, when gaining access to the lung, causes pulmonary mycosis.

**Asphyxia.** — Suspended animation from interruption of the respiration, the effect of an excess of carbon-dioxide ($CO_2$) in the blood.

**Asthenia.** — Debility; want of strength; adynamia.

**Atelectasis.** — Imperfect expansion of the lungs in a new-born child.

**Atheroma.**—Changes in the wall of an artery due to a degenerative process following a low form of inflammation. The arterial wall is thickened, and the new mass is firm, hard, and in many cases calcareous and gritty, cutting almost like cartilage or fibrous tissue.

**Baccelli's Sign.** — The whispered voice is transmitted readily and distinctly through a pleural effusion if the fluid is serous; if the effusion is purulent, thus being denser, the whispered voice is not transmitted. A sign used in differential diagnosis between simple serous pleurisy and empyema.

**Bradycardia.**—Abnormal slowness of the pulse.

**Brawny.**—Fleshy; muscular; feeling of the consistency of muscular tissue, on palpation.

**Bronchiolitis.** — Inflammation of the smallest bronchial tubes, which are destitute of cartilage.

**Brown Induration.**—Induration of the lung due to static congestion secondary to obstructive lesions of the heart.

**Cachexia.**—A morbid or depraved condition of the system, the result of previous disease.

**Calcification.**—The abnormal deposition in the tissues of earthy salts, chiefly the phosphates and carbonates of calcium; the oxalates and the magnesium salts may be present.

**Carswell's Grapes.** — A term applied to masses of tubercles (in the lungs) which have become indurated, with later formation of new masses on their margins, thus presenting a racemose arrangement.

**Caseation.**—A name applied to the complex process whose product has a cheese-like appearance. Coagulation-necrosis is always the precedent condition.

**Chalicosis.**—Fibrosis of the lung in which the irritant agent is stone-dust.

**Charcot-Leyden Crystals.** — Colorless, sharp-pointed, octahedral or rhomboidal crystals, supposed to be phosphate of ethylenimine, found in the sputum chiefly in asthma, but also in some other lung conditions.

**Cholesterin.**—A crystalline fat found in blood, nerve-tissue, and bile.

**Cirrhosis.**—Induration of an organ due to hyperplasia of the connective-tissue.

**Coagulation-Necrosis.**—A form of death of tissues which are rich in proteids; the change is similar to a coagulation. The process is allied to hyalin degeneration. It may be due to the action of toxins of bacteria, or to agents derived from the necrobiosis of cells in the affected area, or conveyed to it from other parts by the lymphatics.

**Collateral Edema.**—Collateral pulmonary edema is edema of a part of the lung when, owing to disease of another part, there is deficient functional activity.

**Compensatory Emphysema.**—Local emphysema due to over-action of a part of the lung, when another part is restricted in its functional activity.

**Corpulence.**—A term used to express the relation of the individual's weight to his height.

**Crepitatio Indux.**—Crepitant râles heard in the initial stage of pneumonic fever.

**Crepitatio Redux.**—Crepitant râles heard in the stage of resolution in pneumonic fever.

**Curschmann's Spirals.**—Small bodies composed of mucin, consisting of a minute thread running through a tubular contorted body, formed in oblique spiral lines. They appear as sago-like pellets in the sputum of asthma.

**Damoiseau's Curve.**—The curved line representing the upper border of the fluid in the pleural cavity in pleurisy with effusion.

**Daughter-cysts.**—A hydatid cyst developed within another cyst.

**Defervescence.**—The period of an attack of febrile disease in which the temperature declines.

**Diaphoresis.**—A state of perspiration.

**Diathesis.**—A special state of the body; a constitutional predisposition to disease of a special character.

**Dittrich's Plugs.**—Small, dirty-white or yellowish colored masses consisting of fatty detritus, micro-organisms, and crystals of margarin, found in the sputum of putrid bronchitis and in gangrene of the lung.

**Dry Bronchitis.**—A form of chronic bronchitis with scanty, viscid expectoration.

**Dry Pleurisy.**—Pleuritis with fibrinous exudation.

**Ectocyst.**—The external envelope of a hydatid cyst.

**Embolism.**—The obstruction of a vessel, generally by a blood-clot or embolus, brought from another part by the blood-current.

**Embolus.**—A clot formed in one place and transported by the blood-current to another locality.

**Empyema.**—A collection of pus in the pleural cavity.

**Empyema Necessitatis.**—A condition in which the pus in empyema has burrowed outward, forming a tumor under the skin of the side.

**Encapsulation.**—The surrounding of a body with a fibrous capsule.

**Endocyst.**—The inner envelope of a hydatid cyst.

**Endothelium.**—The cells of the lining membrane of a serous or other closed cavity.

**Epithelioid Cells.**—Cells found in tubercles, so called because they have in their structure a large amount of protoplasm.

**Estlander's Operation.**—See Thoracoplasty.

**Fibrinous Pleurisy.**—Pleuritis with fibrinous exudation.

**Frank Pneumonia.**—Idiopathic pneumonia in a previously healthy subject.

**Fremitus.**—Vibration of the chest-wall detected by palpation.

**Fusiform.**—Spindle-shaped.

**Giant-Cells.**—Large, irregularly-shaped cells with numerous nuclei, found in tubercles; they are enlarged epithelioid cells, or epithelioid cells "run together."

**Gumma.**—Name given to tumors containing gum-like contents; found in many tissues; produced by the virus of syphilis.

**Hebetude.**—Dulness of the senses and of the mental faculties.

**Hemophilia.**—The congenital and often hereditary disposition to hemorrhage, either internally or externally, from the slightest causes.

**Hemoptysis.**—The discharge of blood by the mouth, having its source in any part of the air-passages.

**Hydremia.**—A watery state of the blood.

**Hyperpyrexia.**—Excessively high bodily temperature; 106° F. or higher.

**Hypostatic Congestion.**—Congestion of a dependent part owing to the sluggish venous circulation.

**Infarction.**—A wedge-shaped patch of extravasated blood found in the tissues of the lungs in cases of embolism.

**Kyphoscoliosis.**—Kyphosis combined with scoliosis.

**Kyphosis.**—Humpbacked deformity.

**Leucocythemia.**—A disease characterized by a permanent increase of the white corpuscles of the blood, accompanied by enlargement of the spleen and the lymphatics, and disease of the medullary substance of the bones.

**Leucocytosis.** — Morbid increase in the number of white corpuscles in the blood.

**Liege-halle.**—An apartment, hall or corridor used by phthisical patients for purposes of rest.

**Lymphangitis.** — Inflammation of lymphatic vessels.

**Lymphoid Tubercle.**—A tubercle in which the lymphoid cells greatly preponderate in number over the epithelioid cells.

**Lysis.**—The gradual decline of a disease, especially a fever.

**Mania-a-potu.** — Mania from drink, or excessive indulgence in drinking; delirium tremens.

**Matzoon.**—A beverage made of fermented milk, similar to kumyss.

**Metabolism.**—Tissue-changes taking place in cells.

**Micromillimetre.** — The unit of microscopic measurement; the one-millionth part of a meter.

**Migratory Pneumonia.**—Pneumonic fever in which there is gradual extension of the diseased prócess to new areas of lung-tissue, or in which parts distant from the primary infection become successively invaded.

**Moist Bronchitis.**—Chronic bronchitis attended by abundant mucous or muco-purulent secretion.

**Mycosis.** — Pulmonary mycosis is a diseased condition due to the growth of a fungus in the lungs, the aspergillus fumigatus.

**Obtund.**—To blunt or dull.

**Opisthotonos.** — Tetanic spasm with bending of the head, trunk and feet backward.

**Orthopnea.**—Quick and labored breathing, in which the person has to maintain an upright posture of the body.

**Paracentesis.**—The operation of tapping, or making an opening into the thorax, abdomen, or other cavities, for discharge of fluid in hydrothorax, ascites, etc.

**Phagocyte.**—A name given to leucocytes that destroy microbes by enclosing them.

**Phlebolith.** — Calcareous concretion formed in a vein.

**Pityriasis Versicolor.**—A skin disease in which patches of small thin scales repeatedly form; herpes furfuraceus; branny tetter; tinea versicolor.

**Plastic Lymph.**—A fibrinous exudation occurring in croupous inflammation.

**Pleuritis Acutissima.**—Purulent pleurisy of acute and violent onset.

**Pleuritis Sicca.** — Dry pleurisy; pleuritis without serous effusion.

**Pleurogenic Cirrhosis.**—Induration of the lung secondary to pleuritis.

**Pleurolith.**—A concretion resulting from calcareous degeneration of products of inflammation of the pleura.

**Pleuro - Pneumonia.** — Pleurisy with effusion, secondary to pneumonic fever.

**Pneumonoconiosis.**— An occupation-disease of the lungs, progressive in character, with fibrosis and pigmentation due to the inhalation of dust and foreign particles of various kinds.

**Pneumopyothorax.**— Air and pus in the pleural cavity.

**Pneumothorax.**—Air in the pleural cavity.

**Poikilocytes.**—Red blood corpuscles of abnormal size and shape.

**Poikilocytosis.**—A condition consisting of the presence of poikilocytes in the blood.

**Prodromata.**—Slight and ill-defined symptoms which precede the outbreak of an attack of disease.

**Pseudo-Crisis.**—An early crisis in pneumonic fever followed by recurrence of all symptoms and a second crisis accompanying final resolution.

**Pseudo - Tuberculosis.** — An arbitrary term applied to cases of pulmonary mycosis.

**Pulmonary Osteo-Arthropathy.**—A peculiar affection of the bones and joints associated in some cases with chronic diseases of the lungs, usually of a suppurative nature.

**Purpura.**—A disease characterized by the appearance of purple patches in the skin, due to extravasation of blood.

**Ray-Fungus.**— Actinomyces bovis; a fungus producing actinomycosis.

**Saprogenic Bacteria.**—Bacteria of putrefaction.

**Sarcina.**—A genus of schizomycetes.

**Sarcina Ventriculi.**—A variety of sarcinæ found in the stomach of man and animals.

**Saprophytes.** — Bacteria which live upon decaying animal and vegetable matter.

**Schizomycetes.**—A group of plant micro-organisms

to which the bacteria belong.

' **Scoliosis.**—Lateral curvature of the spinal column.

**Scrofula.**—A condition characterized by chronic tubercular adenitis, in which there is enlargement of the lymph-nodes.

**Siderosis.**—The pigmented condition of the lymphatic glands, liver and kidneys; so-called because the pigment contains iron.

**Skoda's Sign.**—In pleurisy with effusion when the upper border of the fluid is at the third rib, there is a tympanitic or vesiculo-tympanitic note on percussion in the infra-clavicular space. It is from the compressed lung.

**Skoda's Veiled Puff.**—A sound heard on auscultation, occurring at the end of inspiration, giving the impression that a puff of air has suddenly entered a small cavity situated just beneath the stethoscope. It occurs most commonly in bronchiectasis.

**Steno's Duct.**—The duct of the parotid gland.

**Stroma.**—The t i s s u e which forms the framework of an organ.

**Struma.**—A synonym for scrofula.

**Strumous.** — Affected with struma; scrofulous.

**Subphrenic Abscess.**— Abscess beneath the diaphragm, between the diaphragm and the upper surface of the liver.

**Suffocative Catarrh.**—A term applied to capillary bronchitis, or bronchopneumonia in the aged.

**Syncope.**—A suspension of respiration and the heart's action, complete or partial; swooning; fainting.

**Tachycardia.**—Excessive rapidity of the heart's action.

**Thoracentesis.** — Puncturing the chest-wall; done for the purpose of removing collections of fluid from the pleural cavity.

**Thoracoplasty.** — Excision of ribs to permit contraction of the chest in order to obliterate the cavity of an old empyema; Estlander's operation.

**Thrombosis.**—The formation or progress of thrombus.

**Thrombus.**—A clot of blood formed on the spot, as distinguished from an embolus, which is brought by the circulation.

**Toxin.**—An amorphous, nitrogenous poison formed by bacteria in both living tissues and dead substances.

**Traube's S e m i l u n a r Space.**—The space in the left hypochondrium extending from the sixth to the eighth ribs, bounded above and laterally by the contiguous borders of the liver, lungs and spleen. Normally on percussion it gives forth a highly tympanitic note from the underlying stomach. With pleuritis of the left side the effusion gravitates into the pleural sulcus, producing dulness or flatness in the semilunar space.

**Tubercular.**—Relating to the structures called **tubercles**

**Tuberculous.** — Relating to the process of **tuberculosis.**

**Venules.**—Small veins.

**Veiled Puff.**—See Skoda.

**Vicarious Hemoptysis.**— The escape of blood from the lungs taking the place of the escape of blood from some other part, as the menstrual flow.

**White Pneumonia.**—A state of the lung in which the organ is solid, dry, and grayish-white in color; occurring in infants, the subjects of congenital syphilis.

**Williams' Tracheal Tone.** —In pleurisy with effusion strong percussion elicits a high-pitched, tympanitic note just below the inner end of the clavicle, the pitch of the note changing with opening and closing the mouth. It is from the trachea and large bronchi. The vibrations are transmitted through the compressed lung.

**Wintrich's Sign.**—Change of pitch of the percussion note when the mouth is open and when it is closed, indicative of a cavity in the lung.

# INDEX

Abscess of the Lungs....... 231
   Etiology... .............. 231
   Symptoms... ........:... 231
   Treatment..... .......... 232
Accidental Pneumothorax.208-211
Actinomyces Bovis.......... 240
Actinomycosis..... ....... 240
   Diagnosis....... ......... 242
   Pathology .....,....... 240
   Symptoms ............... 241
   Treatment....... ....... 242
Acute Pneumonic Tubercu-
   losis..... ............. 121
Acute Vesicular Emphysema · 53
Angioneurotic Edema....... 228
Apneumatosis.... ......110-112
Apoplexy, Pulmonary....... 218
Arthritic Hemoptysis....... 171
Aspergillus Fumigatus...... 242
Aspiration Pneumonia...... 33
Asthma..... ............. 41
   Diagnosis ................ 47
   Etiology..... .......... 43
   Morbid Anatomy.....,... 42
   Pathology..... ....... 42
   Physical Signs........... 46
   Prognosis..,........ ..... 48
   Symptoms...... ........ 45
   Treatment............... 49
   Varieties........... ...... 43
      Bronchial Asthma...... 43
      Cardiac Asthma........ 43
      Hay-Asthma.......... 43
      Renal Asthma.......... 43
      Spasmodic Asthma..... 43
Atelectasis... ...........110-112

Baccelli's Sign............. 199
Bilious Pneumonia.......... 68
Blood in Phthisis........... 136
Blood in Pneumonia........ 78
Bronchi, Dilation of........ 61

Bronchial Glands, Tubercu-
   losis of................. 167
   Etiology..... .......... 167
   Morbid Anatomy......... 167
   Physical Signs........... 168
   Symptoms... ...........,.... 168
Bronchitis..... .......... 9
Bronchitis, Capillary........ 18
Bronchitis, Dry............. 28
Bronchitis, Moist........... 28
Bronchitis, Putrid.......... 28
Bronchitis of the Larger
   Tubes..... .......... 9
   Diagnosis..... ......... 13
   Etiology............. ....... 9
   Morbid Anatomy......... 11
   Pathology ............... 10
   Physical Signs........... 12
   Prognosis..... ......... 14
   Symptoms..... ......... 11
   Treatment............... 14
Bronchitis of the Smaller
   Tubes..... ........... 18
   Course..... ........... 21
   Diagnosis..... ......... 22
   Morbid Anatomy.........: 18
   Physical Signs........... 20
   Prognosis..... .......... 22
   Symptoms..... ........ 19
   Treatment.... ......... 23
Bronchiectasis.... ........ 61
   Complications..... ..... 66
   Diagnosis............... ..... 65
   Differential Diagnosis..... 65
   Etiology..... .......... 61
   Morbid Anatomy......... 61
   Pathological Anatomy.... 62
   Physical Signs........... 64
   Prognosis..... ......... 65
   Symptoms... ............. 63
   Treatment...... ......... 66
   Varieties..... ......... 61
      Cylindrical.... ........ 61
      Fusiform ...,......... 61
      Saccular......... ..... 62

Bronchiolitis................ 18
Broncho-Pneumonia... .... 33
   Etiology... .. ............ 33
   Pathology ............... 33
   Symptoms...... ......... 35
   Varieties... ............ 33
Broncho-Pneumonia in the
   Adult...... .......... 38
   Complications..... .... 38
   Physical Diagnosis....... 38
   Treatment...... ....... 39
Broncho-Pneumonia in Chil-
   dren......... ........ 36
   Prognosis...... ......... 37
Brown Induration of the
   Lungs ................. 108
   Etiology...... ........... 108
   Morbid Anatomy......... 108
   Symptoms..... ......... 109

Capillary Bronchitis.......18-33
Cardiac Paralysis in Pneu-
   monia...... ..........77-98
Catarrhal Pneumonia....... 33
Central Pneumonia......... 73
Charcot-Leyden Crystals.... 46
Chronic Bronchitis......... 27
   Diagnosis...... ........ 31
   Etiology...... .......... 27
   Complications....... .... 29
   Morbid Anatomy......... 27
   Physical Signs........... 30
   Prognosis....... ....... 31
   Symptoms..... ......... 28
   Treatment... ........... 31
   Varieties...... ......... 28
      Dry Bronchitis......... 28
      Moist Bronchitis....... 28
      Putrid Bronchitis...... 28
Chronic Pleurisy........... 205
Chronic Pulmonary Tuber-
   culosis......... ........ 127
Chylothorax......... ........ 214
Chylous Pleurisy......... 185
Cirrhosis of the Lung....... 68
Clubbing of the Fingers..... 243
Collapse of the Lungs...... 110
   Etiology.. .............. 110
   Morbid Anatomy......... 111
   Physical Signs........... 112
   Prognosis...... ......... 112
   Symptoms ............... 111
   Treatment..... ......... 112
Collateral Edema........... 227

Congestion, Active......... 223
Congestion, Hypostatic..... 226
Congestion, Passive........ 226
Complications in Pneumonia 80
   Circulatory ............. 81
   Respiratory ............. 80
Compensatory Emphysema.. 53
Corpulence...... ......... 134
Crepitatio Indux............ 75
Crepitatio Redux.......... 76
Croupous Pneumonia....... 67
Curschmann's Spirals....... 45

Demoiseau's Curve......189-192
Diaphragmatic Pleurisy..... 185
Dilation of the Bronchi..... 61
Disseminated Pneumonia.... 33
Dittrich's Plugs............ 29
Double Pleurisy............ 185
Dry Pleurisy............... 178
   Angioneurotic ........... 228
   Collateral ............. 227
   Diagnosis ............... 229
   Edema of the Lungs...... 227
   Etiology...... ......... 227
   Morbid Anatomy......... 228
   Prognosis...... ......... 229
   Symptoms..... ......... 228
   Treatment.......... ..... 229

Embolic Pneumonia........ 33
Embolism of the Pulmonary
   Artery....... ......... 217
   Etiology...... ......... 217
   Pathology......... ..... 218
   Symptoms.... ......... 219
   Treatment....... ....... 220
Emphysema ............... 53
   Compensatory ........... 53
   Hypertrophic ............ 54
   Interlobular ............. 60
   Interstitial ...............53-60
   Large-lunged....  .......53-54
   Pulmonary .............. 53
Empyema, Chronic......... 199
   Surgical Measures....... 200
      Incision ............... 203
      Resection .............. 203
      Siphon Drainage........ 205
      Thoracentesis ......... 200
      Thoracoplasty ......... 205
Empyema Necessitatis...... 199
Empyema, Pulsating........ 200

Emphysema, Hypertrophic.. 54
    Diagnosis. ............... 58
    Differential Diagnosis.... 59
    Etiology. ................ 54
    Morbid Anatomy......... 55
    Pathology ............... 55
    Physical Signs........... 58
    Prognosis. .............. 59
    Symptoms............... 56
    Treatment............... 59
Empyema, Subacute........ 198
Encapsulated Pleurisy...... 185

Fibrinous Pleurisy.......... 178
Fibrinous Pneumonia........ 67
Fibroid Phthisis........... 163
    Diagnosis ............... 166
    Etiology ................ 163
    Morbid Anatomy......... 163
    Pathology ............... 164
    Physical Signs........... 166
    Prognosis ............... 166
    Symptoms ............... 164
    Treatment .............. 167
Fibrosis, Pulmonary........ 68
Frank Pneumonia.......... 67

Gangrene of the Lungs..... 233
    Diagnosis ............... 235
    Etiology ................ 233
    Pathology ............... 234
    Symptoms ............... 234
    Treatment .............. 236
Giant Cells................ 129
Glossary ................. 245
Gray Hepatization.......... 70
Gumma ................... 116

Hemoptysis ............... 169
    Differential Diagnosis.... 173
    Etiology ................ 169
    Morbid Anatomy......... 172
    Pathology ............... 171
    Prognosis ............... 174
    Symptoms ............... 172
    Therapeutics ............ 174
    Treatment .............. 175
Hemorrhagic Infarction.... 218
Hemorrhagic Pleurisy...... 184
Hemothorax .............. 214
Hepatization, Red.......... 71
Hydatids of the Lungs..... 237
    Diagnosis ............... 239
    Etiology ................ 237
    Morbid Anatomy......... 237
    Prognosis ............... 239

Symptoms ............... 238
    Treatment ............. 240
Hydatids of the Pleura..... 240
Hydrothorax .............. 212
    Diagnosis ............... 213
    Etiology ................ 212
    Morbid Anatomy......... 213
    Symptoms............... 213
    Treatment............... 214
    Active................. 223
Hyperemia of the Lungs,
    Diagnosis ............... 225
    Etiology. ............... 223
    Morbid Anatomy......... 223
    Physical Signs........... 224
    Prognosis ............... 225
    Symptoms............... 224
    Treatment............... 225
Hyperemia of the Lungs,
    Passive................. 226
Hypertrophic Emphysema.. 54
Hypostatic Congestion...... 226

Idiopathic Emphysema...... 54
Infarction, Hemorrhagic.... 218
Inflammatory Edema....... 227
Interlobar Pleurisy........ 185
Interlobular Emphysema.... 60
Interstitial Emphysema..... 53
Interstitial Emphysema..... 60

Large-lunged Emphysema... 53
Lobular Pneumonia........ 33

Mediastinal Pleurisy........ 185
Migratory Pneumonia...... 73

Phthisis, Florida.......... 121
Plastic Bronchitis.......... 24
    Diagnosis ............... 26
    Morbid Anatomy......... 24
    Physical Signs........... 26
    Symptoms............... 25
    Treatment............... 26
Pleurisy ................. 177
    Plastic Pleurisy.......... 178
        Bacteriology .......... 178
        Etiology .............. 178
        Pathology ............. 180
        Symptoms............. 183
    Varieties ................ 177
    Chylous ................ 185
    Diaphragmatic........... 185
    Double ................. 185
    Dry .................... 178
    Encapsulated ........... 185

Fibrinous ............... 178
Hemorrhagic ............ 184
Interlobar.... .......... 185
Mediastinal ............ 185
Pulsating ...........185-199
Pleuritis Acutissima....... 198
Sicca.................... 178
Pleurogenic Cirrhosis...... 205
Pleurolith ............... 188
Pleuro-Pneumonia......... 68
Pneumomycosis ........... 242
Pneumonic Fever.......... 67
Bacteriology. ........... 68
Bilious ................. 68
Broncho- ..............67-68
Cardiac Paralysis in...... 77
Central ................ 73
Complications in......... 80
Arthritis ............. 82
Circulatory ........... 81
Parotiditis ........... 82
Respiratory ........... 80
Disseminated ........... 33
Embolic................ 33-34
Etiology ............... 68
Fibrinous ..............67-68
History................. 68
Interstitial .............. 68
Migratory ............... 73
Morbid Anatomy......... 73
Pathology. ............. 70
Engorgement. ......... 70
Red Hepatization...... 71
Resolution. ........... 71
Physical Signs............ 74
Pleuro- ................ 68
Primary ................ 67
Prognosis .............. 83
Pulse .................. 78
Secondary .............. 67
Sputum ................ 79
Treatment............... 88
Typhoid ............... 68
Urine .................. 80
Varieties ............... 68
Bilious Pneumonia..... 68
Broncho-Pneumonia ...67-68
Fibrinous Pneumonia..67-68
Interstitial Pneumonia.. 68
Pleuro-Pneumonia ..... 68
Typhoid Pneumonia.... 68
Pneumonic Fever in the
Aged ................ 87
Pneumonic Fever in Chil-
dren. ................ 85
Pneumonic Phthisis....... 121

Pneumonic Tuberculosis.... 121
Pneumonoconiosis. ........ 113
Etiology ............... 113
Morbid Anatomy........ 114
Pathology .............. 113
Prognosis .............. 115
Symptoms.............. 115
Treatment.............. 116
Pneumopyothorax ........ 212
Pneumothorax ........... 207
Diagnosis .............. 210
Etiology ............... 207
Morbid Anatomy........ 208
Physical Signs........... 209
Prognosis .............. 210
Symptoms.............. 209
Treatment.............. 211
Pneumothorax, Accidental..
.................... 208-211
Primary Pneumonia....... 67
Pseudo-Tuberculosis ...... 242
Pulmonary Apoplexy....... 218
Embolism .............. 217
Emphysema ............ 53
Varieties .............. 53
Pulmonary Fibrosis.......68-102
Differential Diagnosis.... 107
Etiology ............... 102
Morbid Anatomy........ 104
Pathology .............. 104
Physical Signs........... 106
Prognosis .............. 107
Symptoms.............. 105
Treatment............... 108
Pulmonary Mycosis........ 242
Pulmonary Osteo-Arthrop-
athy. ................. 243
Pulmonary Syphilis........ 116
Diagnosis .............. 118
Prognosis .............. 118
Treatment.............. 118
Pulmonary Thrombosis..... 220
Pulmonary Tuberculosis.... 121
Pulmonary Tuberculosis,
Chronic .............. 127
Blood Changes.......... 136
Climate ................ 150
Complications ........... 144
Corpulence ............. 134
Diet. .................. 157
Early Diagnosis.......... 131
Etiology. .............. 127
Exercise. ............... 160
Home Treatment......... 154
Hydrotherapeutics........ 162

Pathology. .............. 128
Physical Signs........... 142
Symptoms............... 138
Therapeutics ............ 148
Treatment............... 145
Tuberculin Test.......... 137
X-Ray Examination...... 136
Pulsating Empyema........ 200
Pulsating Pleurisy.......185-199
Purulent Pleurisy.......... 197
Etiology. ............... 197
Pathology .............. 197
Physical Signs........... 199
Symptoms............... 198

Ray-Fungus .............. 240
Red Hepatization.......... 71

Secondary Pneumonia...... 67
Sero-Fibrinous Pleurisy.... 186
Etiology. ............... 186
Pathology. .............. 187
Physical Signs........... 190
Prognosis .............. 193
Symptoms............... 189
Treatment............... 194
Skoda's Sign.............. 192
Small-lunged Emphysema... 53
Spurious Hemoptysis....... 173
Substantive Emphysema.... 54
Suffocative Catarrh........ 18
Syphilis, Pulmonary....... 116
Varieties ............... 116

Tænia Echinococcus........ 237
Thoracentesis ............. 200
Thoracoplasty ............. 205
Thrombosis of the Pulmon-
ary Artery............. 220
Etiology. ............... 220
Symptoms............... 221
Tubercles, Formation of.... 128
Tuberculosis, Acute Pneu-
monic ................. 121
Broncho-Pneumonic Type. 124
Pathology. ............. 124
Physical Signs......... 125
Symptoms............. 125
Treatment............. 126
Pneumonic Type......... 121
Diagnosis ............. 124
Pathology ............. 122
Physical Signs......... 123
Symptoms............. 123
Tuberculosis, Chronic Pul-
monary. ............... 127
Tuberculosis, Pulmonary.... 121
Tumors of the Lungs...... 118
Typhoid Pneumonia........ 68

Vesicular Emphysema...... 53

White Pneumonia.......... 129
Williams' Tracheal Tone... 192
Wintrich's Sign. ........... 143

X-Ray in Diagnosis.......80-136

# POCKET-BOOK

OF

# MEDICAL PRACTICE

INCLUDING

DISEASES OF THE

## KIDNEYS, SKIN, NERVES, EYE, EAR, NOSE AND THROAT,

AND

## OBSTETRICS, GYNECOLOGY, SURGERY

BY

### Ch. Gatchell, M. D.

SPECIAL SUBJECTS BY SPECIAL AUTHORS

DISEASES OF THE

STOMACH—KIDNEYS—MENTAL DISEASES—
NERVOUS SYSTEM—SKIN—EYE—EAR—NOSE,
THROAT AND LARYNX – OBSTETRICS—
GYNECOLOGY - SURGERY—
THE VENEREAL

Gatchell's Pocket Medical Practice is a decided success. Its 400 pages contain more real practical information for the use of students and practitioners than can be found anywhere else in the same space.—*Hahnemannian Monthly.*

CHICAGO
ERA PUBLISHING COMPANY
1902

# Trieste

Trieste Publishing has a massive catalogue of classic book titles. Our aim is to provide readers with the highest quality reproductions of fiction and non-fiction literature that has stood the test of time. The many thousands of books in our collection have been sourced from libraries and private collections around the world.

The titles that Trieste Publishing has chosen to be part of the collection have been scanned to simulate the original. Our readers see the books the same way that their first readers did decades or a hundred or more years ago. Books from that period are often spoiled by imperfections that did not exist in the original. Imperfections could be in the form of blurred text, photographs, or missing pages. It is highly unlikely that this would occur with one of our books. Our extensive quality control ensures that the readers of Trieste Publishing's books will be delighted with their purchase. Our staff has thoroughly reviewed every page of all the books in the collection, repairing, or if necessary, rejecting titles that are not of the highest quality. This process ensures that the reader of one of Trieste Publishing's titles receives a volume that faithfully reproduces the original, and to the maximum degree possible, gives them the experience of owning the original work.

We pride ourselves on not only creating a pathway to an extensive reservoir of books of the finest quality, but also providing value to every one of our readers. Generally, Trieste books are purchased singly - on demand, however they may also be purchased in bulk. Readers interested in bulk purchases are invited to contact us directly to enquire about our tailored bulk rates. Email: customerservice@triestepublishing.com

# You May Also Like

## How to Feed the Sick: Or, Diet in Disease

## Ch. Gatchell

ISBN: 9780649527748
Paperback: 180 pages
Dimensions: 6.14 x 0.38 x 9.21 inches
Language: eng

## Medical era, Vol. XII, July, 1986, No. 7, pp. 223-246

## Ch. Gatchell

ISBN: 9780649194742
Paperback: 36 pages
Dimensions: 6.14 x 0.08 x 9.21 inches
Language: eng

# You May Also Like

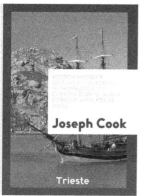

## Boston Monday Lectures: Conscience, with Preludes on Current Events, and a Copious Analytical Index

## Joseph Cook

ISBN: 9780649554966
Paperback: 160 pages
Dimensions: 5.83 x 0.34 x 8.27 inches
Language: eng

## The Whitney and Knox Language Series. Elementary Lessons in English for Home and School Use. Part I.: How to Speak and Write Correctly

## Mrs. N. L. Knox

ISBN: 9780649570492
Paperback: 220 pages
Dimensions: 6.14 x 0.46 x 9.21 inches
Language: eng

www.triestepublishing.com

# You May Also Like

**1807-1907 The One Hundredth Anniversary of the incorporation of the Town of Arlington Massachusetts**

**Various**

ISBN: 9780649420544
Paperback: 108 pages
Dimensions: 6.14 x 0.22 x 9.21 inches
Language: eng

**Biennial report of the Board of State Harbor Commissioners, for the two fiscal years commencing July 1, 1890, and ending June 30, 1892**

**Various**

ISBN: 9780649194292
Paperback: 44 pages
Dimensions: 6.14 x 0.09 x 9.21 inches
Language: eng

# You May Also Like

**Biennial report of the Board of State Harbor Commissioners for the two fisca years. Commeneing July 1, 1884, and Ending June 30, 1886**


# Various

ISBN: 9780649199693
Paperback: 48 pages
Dimensions: 6.14 x 0.10 x 9.21 inches
Language: eng

**Biennial report of the Board of state commissioners, for the two fiscal years, commencing July 1, 1890, and ending June 30, 1892**


# Various

ISBN: 9780649196395
Paperback: 44 pages
Dimensions: 6.14 x 0.09 x 9.21 inches
Language: eng

Find more of our titles on our website. We have a selection of thousands of titles that will interest you. Please visit

www.triestepublishing.com